What is the point of the Ombudsman?

How a group of citizens,

over many years, attempted to hold the

Parliamentary and Health Service Ombudsman

to account for repeatedly failing the public.

Compiled by members of **PHSOtheFACTS**
and edited by Della Reynolds
copyright@phsothefacts

Jonathan Sumption, retired high court judge speaking at the **Reith Lectures** in June 2019 on the nature of democracy:

> *"One thing I will prophecy, we will not recognise the end of democracy when it comes, if it does. Advanced democracies are not overthrown. There are no tanks on the street, no sudden catastrophes, no brash dictators or braying mobs. Instead their institutions are imperceptibly drained of everything which once made them democratic. The labels will still be there, but they will no longer describe the contents. The façade will still stand, but there will be nothing behind it. The rhetoric of democracy will be unchanged, but it will be meaningless. And the fault will be ours."*

Many UK institutions are already nothing more than façades and the rhetoric used by those in authority are just empty words. But this is not our fault. We are the citizens who have dedicated our time to bringing the flaws of our democratic processes out into the public domain. It is the fault of those in authority who have defended the indefensible, failed to listen and failed to act. **You knew, because we told you and you did nothing.**

'**What is the point of the Ombudsman'** is a collection of articles written by citizen campaigners and members of **PHSOtheFACTS**. It is the story of our long fight to hold the Parliamentary and Health Service Ombudsman to account, using the democratic means at our disposal.

The content of this book comes primarily from blog posts first published on the website **phsothetruestory.com** between 2013 and 2020. **Editor's note:** denotes updated information and links the blog posts.

The **Parliamentary and Health Service Ombudsman** (PHSO) sits at the apex of the complaint process. It is the only organisation which handles complaints about government bodies and the NHS on behalf of the public. The popular concept of an Ombudsman is that it is a body which protects the citizen from an abuse of power, by holding those in authority to account.

> *An **ombudsman, ombudsperson, ombud,** or **public***
> ***advocate** is an official who is charged with representing*
> *the interests of the public by investigating and addressing*
> *complaints of maladministration or a violation of*
> *rights.* [generic definition wiki.org]

After 7 years of studying the Ombudsman process we have come to the conclusion that this body is actually 'corrupt by design'. For the purpose of this work the use of the word 'corrupt' is to be defined as endemic, organisational corruption of purpose.

Many of our case stories refer to the NHS. We are all in agreement that the NHS is a wonderful organisation with many hard-working staff saving lives every day. But like the Henry Wadsworth Longfellow's poem about the little girl with the curl right in the middle of her forehead – when the NHS is good, it is very good indeed, but when it is bad it is horrid.

Figure 1. PHSO data table 2016/17 to 2018/19

	2016-17			2017-18			2018-19		
	Data from PHSO Report	% of Total complaints	% Of total assessments	Data from PHSO Report	% Of Total complaints	% Of total assessments	Data from PHSO Report	% Of Total complaints	% Of total assessments
Total Complaints	31,444	100%		32,389	100%		29,841	100%	
Complaints (assessed)	8,119	25.8%	100%	6,739	20.8%	100%	5,658	18.9%	100%
No further action taken	4,251	13.5%	52.3%	4,164	12.8%	61.7%	3,597	12%	63.5%
Put right without formal investigation **Resolution**	101	0.3%	1.2%	146	0.4%	2.1%	444	1.4%	7.8%
Investigations reported on in year	4,239	13.4%	52.2%	2,676	8.2%	39.7%	1,617	5.4%	28.5%
Complaints upheld (fully)	277	0.8%	3.4%	179	0.5%	2.6%	117	0.3%	2%
% of investigations upheld	36.1%	}4.7%	}18.8%	37.5%	}3.0	}14.8%	46%	}2.4%	}13%
Complaints upheld (partially)	1,254	3.9%	15.4%	825	2.5%	12.2%	629	2.1%	11%
Complaints not upheld	2,708	8.6%	33.3%	1,344	4.1%	19.9%	871	2.9%	15.3%
Put right by PHSO in total			20%			16.9%			20.8%

Analysis 2018/19 For the first time the total number of complaints has declined and it would be interesting to know why. Of those who took the time to make a formal complaint access to justice continues to decrease year on year. Having your case assessed and not immediately rejected (in 7 days) has fallen from 25% to 18.9%. An increase in resolutions following assessment has led to fewer investigations. Your chance of resolution rose from 1.2% to 7.8%. Equally your chance of receiving an investigation fell from 52.2% to 28.5 with uphold falling to 13%. Do resolutions without investigations satisfy complainants? Is a report written? Are outcomes monitored?

Figure 2. Parliamentary Complaints 2018/19

Parliamentary Complaints 2018/19	total complaints	investigated	Full/partial uphold
Cabinet Office	5	0	0
Charity Commission	25	0	1
Crown Prosecution Service	32	1	0
Dept for Business, Energy & Ind. Strategy	237	6	3
Dept for Digital, Culture, Media & Sport	194	1	0
Dept. for Education	60	1	1
Dept. for Environment, food & rural affairs	73	11	1
Dept. for Transport	646	15	7
Dept for work and pensions	1553	30	4
Dept of Health and Social Care	79	2	1
Electoral Commission	6	0	0
Food standard agency	6	0	0
Foreign and Commonwealth Office	16	0	0
Forestry Commission	5	0	0
Government Legal Dept.	2	0	0
HM Revenue and Customs	466	11	2
HM Treasury	3	0	0
Home Office	861	21	13
Ministry of defence	28	0	0
Ministry of justice	1027	8	6
Office for standards in education (Ofsted)	18	2	0
Office of Gas and electricity (Ofgem)	91	1	0
Office of qualifications & exam reg (Ofqual)	7	0	0
UK Statistics Authority	2	0	0
Water Services Regulation (Ofwat)	4	0	0
Dept for International Development	2	0	0
Dept for Internation Trade	2	0	0
Unknown	244	0	0
Total	5744 Complaints	110 (1.9%) Investigations	39 (0.6%) Full/partial uphold
NB Just 3 cases fully upheld	NB 35 cases resolved through intervention		

Figure 3. Reviews of PHSO from independent consumer platforms.

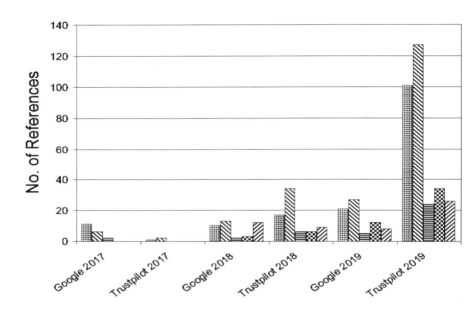

Figure 4. PHSO customer satisfaction data from 2014/15 to 2018/19

PHSO Customer Satisfaction	% satisfied
Fully upheld	
2018/19	86%
2017/18	85 %
2016/17	81 %
2015/16	92 %
2014/15	88 %
Partly upheld	
2018/19	66%
2017/18	67 %
2016/17	73 %
2015/16	69 %
2014/15	71 %
Not upheld	
2018/19	47%
2017/18	49 %
2016/17	51 %
2015//16	41 %
2014/15	49 %

Figure 5. Satisfaction table from 'Sharper Teeth: The Consumer Need for Ombudsman Reform. A 'Money Saving Expert' report p.54

Overall, how would you describe your experience with the ombudsman?			
	Great	OK	Poor
The Motor Ombudsman	30%	4%	67%
The Energy Ombudsman	27%	29%	45%
Ombudsman Services: Communications	23%	26%	50%
Ombudsman Services - any other sector	23%	11%	66%
Financial Ombudsman Service	22%	24%	54%
Consumer Ombudsman	22%	6%	72%
The Property Ombudsman	21%	21%	58%
Legal Ombudsman	18%	9%	73%
Other service known as an 'ombudsman'	17%	22%	61%
Ombudsman Services: Property	17%	4%	79%
The Retail Ombudsman/ RetailADR	14%	23%	64%
The Pensions Ombudsman	12%	8%	80%
The Furniture Ombudsman/ DRO	11%	15%	74%
Non-ombudsman ADR provider	10%	21%	69%
Local Government & Social Care Ombudsman	10%	11%	79%
Parliamentary and Health Service Ombudsman	6%	12%	82%
Housing Ombudsman Service	3%	9%	88%

Percentages are rounded to whole numbers.

(approximately 100 people completed the questionnaire regarding PHSO)

Chapter 1. Dark days at PHSO

Editor's note: In 2013 **PHSOtheFACTS**[1] website started to record the difficulties faced by the public when they made a complaint to the **Parliamentary and Health Service Ombudsman (PHSO).** Prior to this, there was little criticism of the Ombudsman in the public domain. They have a dedicated communications department who control the narrative with apparent collusion from the mainstream media who, when NHS or government scandals break, consistently fail to examine the role of the 'watchdog'. In 2014 this changed and public criticism came from all quarters, leading eventually to the resignation of **Dame Julie Mellor** in July 2016. Some of the most significant and consistent criticism at this time came from the **Patients Association** who provided a summary of the key issues (as reported to them by patients) in their 2018 response to PHSO's new strategic plan.[2] We start with the Patients Association review as it is independent of **PHSOtheFACTS,** substantive, and provides an accurate account of the ways in which PHSO fail the public both then and now.

The Patients Association Reports

Between 2014 and 2017, when **Katherine Murphy** was CEO at the **Patients Association (PA)** three damning reports were issued into

---

[1] phsothetruestory.com
[2] https://phsothetruestory.com/the-patients-association-reports/

the work of the **Parliamentary and Health Service Ombudsman (PHSO).** These reports have since been removed from the PA website but contain important evidence of serious service failure. In 2014 the Patients Association took the radical step of no longer advising complainants to take their case to the PHSO on the basis it would compound their stress rather than alleviate it.

> *The Patients Association says it has lost faith in the service and no longer advises callers who ring its national helpline to go to the PHSO. As one of our recent callers said, 'You may as well ask a poacher to investigate the missing pheasants,' says the charity in its report on the topic. Prolonged investigations, which rely on families to produce all the evidence, can lead to patients or their families having to give up their employment to deal with the demands and inadequacies of the PHSO, it says.[3]*

When, under **Rob Behrens**, the new strategic plan for PHSO was put out to consultation, the **Patients Association** submitted the following response, which provides a good summary of their damning reports:

---

[3] *www.bbc.co.uk/news/health 2014*

Patients Association response to new strategic plan.

This document gives our response to the consultation by PHSO on its new strategic plan. Its contents were submitted to PHSO via their online form.

Introduction

The Patients Association issued three reports from 2014 to 2016 in which we were strongly critical of PHSO's performance in working on behalf of patients: (November 2014); The Peoples Ombudsman – How it failed us, followed in March 2015 with PHSO – Labyrinth of Bureaucracy and a final follow-up report in December 2016, PHSO Follow Up Report.

As well as providing a thematic analysis of what patients were telling us about how they felt PHSO was letting them down, these reports set out in detail the human context for these problems: they occur when patients have suffered harm, and when they and their families are in distress as a result. In the cases we reported, this distress was often compounded by the organisation that was meant to identify what went wrong, and to pave the way to redress.

We found that the reports resonated: after the publication of the first one, we received a substantial volume of new contacts from patients who had been through, or were going through, the PHSO process and wanted to report their concerns and grievances.

We called for substantial changes to PHSO, and we therefore welcome its proposed new strategy as a mechanism for bringing these changes about. Its scope and duration demonstrate a seriousness of purpose about the task, and acknowledgement of its scale, that we are pleased to see.

We summarise below the key themes from our earlier reports, and in our answers to the questions on the proposed strategic plan we will consider its response to the issues we have identified in the past.

Theme 1: PHSO's investigations are not thorough, accurate or timely

Our reports raised multiple concerns about the fundamental quality of PHSO's investigations:

- Many patients reported to us that PHSO's reports on their cases contained serious factual inaccuracies, appeared to ignore evidence that was key to the events under investigation, and rested on unclear or inconsistent reasoning; they expressed doubt that PHSO's investigators possessed the skills necessary to complete their jobs to a high standard

- PHSO's processes were also regularly reported to involve a slow pace and poor communication, with many patients and family members having to chase hard for any update, even after a gap of months

- Some patients also report that the scope of a complaint can be narrowed without any explanation.

Theme 2: PHSO's investigations often appear to display bias in favour of the institution under investigation and against the patient

We also reported a common perception among patients that PHSO exhibited bias in favour of the body it was investigating:

- It often appeared to fall to patients to identify in what respect the Trust's actions had failed to comply with best practice or its own procedures, as PHSO were unwilling to act without this justification, but also unable or unwilling to challenge the Trust and identify the nature of the error themselves

- Some patients reported feeling that they were simply disbelieved by PHSO; in other instances, PHSO insisted on having 'impartial' evidence, and disregarded family members' evidence while accepting that of clinicians on this pretext.

Theme 3: PHSO's processes are not patient-centred

It was strongly evident that PHSO's processes did not make things easy for patients and families indeed, they appeared not to have been designed with much thought for what the experience of a complainant would be. The operation of these processes can often compound this problem.

- PHSO staff were reported as asking questions of patients and family members whose answers were to be found in paperwork that already existed; or, at times, questions that could only be answered with a great deal of effort by the complainant, or not at all

- Processes often rely on patients assembling evidence (although, paradoxically, sometimes this is disbelieved in favour of a Trust's explanation, as noted above), while PHSO reportedly does not make rigorous efforts to uncover evidence itself

- Complainants are refused the chance to meet with the person investigating their case, in order to explain their concerns, agree the remit and terms of reference of the investigation, timelines and communication pathways

- In cases when a re-investigation is necessary owing to faults with the original, families are required to re-submit the same bulk of evidence again

- PHSO shares its draft reports with families, but gives them only a week to respond sometimes to correct very serious errors and issues instructions that the report must be kept confidential, which some families report finding intimidating

- After feedback on the draft report, the final version is agreed within PHSO the process returns into a 'black box' rather than involving any form of consensus-building or co-production (overall this process is often seen as being weighted in favour of the NHS body under investigation)

- A substantial minority of patients reported PHSO staff's attitude to us as dismissive or condescending, and even that they made them feel like a nuisance for complaining.

Theme 4: PHSO's reports and findings are not successful in securing change and improvement within the NHS

- Although this problem extends beyond PHSO, it can be observed that the NHS often appears not to respond and improve as a result of PHSO's reports and findings.

Editor's note: It is unfortunate that the original reports and this response to the PHSO strategy, have since been removed from the Patients Association website, as this detailed criticism should set the baseline for improvement. (They can still be seen in full on the phsothetruestory.com website).

Although the Patients Association refer to the difficulties encountered by NHS complainants, the same is true for those attempting to make complaints about Parliamentary bodies. In fact, the uphold rate for Parliamentary complaints is significantly lower than that for NHS complaints with just 0.6% of all Parliamentary complaints upheld to some extent in 2018/19.[4]

In 2014 there was also criticism in the media about the way in which PHSO handled a complaint made by **James Titcombe** over the avoidable death of his son Joshua, which was initially handled by Ombudsman **Ann Abrahams** and then by **Dame Julie Mellor**.

> Whatever way it's looked at; the Ombudsman's handling of Joshua's case was truly disgraceful. Not only this, but the complaint I made in relation to midwifery supervision (another complaint that was eventually upheld years later), was also rejected by Ann Abraham and only investigated following the threat of Judicial Review. (James Titcombe in response to FOI request on whatdotheyknow.com)[5]

---

[4] See Fig. 2. Parliamentary Complaints 2018/19 on p 7.
[5] /www.whatdotheyknow.com/request/phso_response_to_letter_from_jam

James Titcombe was originally told there would be 'no worthwhile outcome'[6] in the Ombudsman pursuing his complaint, yet many years later an inquiry by **Dr Bill Kirkup** into the **Furness General Hospital,** where his new-born son died, found;

> A "lethal mix" of failings at almost every level led to the unnecessary deaths of one mother and 11 babies in the maternity unit of a Cumbrian hospital[7]

The Ombudsman only investigates a tiny fraction of the complaints it receives. In 2018/19 just over 5% of all the complaints received were resolved via an investigation.[8] Failure to investigate allows unsafe practice to continue and harm is too often repeated. Delay by the Ombudsman into the Titcombe case should be included in the 'lethal mix of failings at every level' as this delay undoubtedly compounded the harm.

In June 2014, the **Health Secretary**, **Jeremy Hunt**, openly criticised **Dame Julie Mellor** over the poor handling of her investigation into the death of **Sam Morrish,** who died of sepsis.

Jeremy Hunt rebukes health watchdog over three-year-old Sam's death

---

[6] ombudsman.org.uk/sites/RadioOmbuds6_transcript_James_Titcombe
[7] https://www.bbc.co.uk/news/health-31699607
[8] See Fig. 1 PHSO data table 2016/17 to 2018/19 on p6

Health ombudsman criticised by Health Secretary Jeremy Hunt over organisation's handling of death of three-year-old Sam Morrish.

The Health Secretary has accused the NHS ombudsman of failing the public and a grieving family in her handling of complaints about the death of a three-year-old boy.

In an unprecedented move by a minister, Jeremy Hunt wrote directly to Dame Julie Mellor, the parliamentary and health service ombudsman (PHSO), severely criticising her organisation's handling of the case of Sam Morrish, who died of blood poisoning after a "catalogue of errors".

Mr Hunt expressed disappointment at how Dame Julie handled complaints by Sam's parents over the way the body conducted its investigation into his death.

He wrote: "I consider you have failed to meet the high standards the public have a right to expect and, most importantly, you have let down Sam's parents in the most serious way."

It took the ombudsman – an independent organisation and the highest authority on NHS complaints – more than two years to investigate and report on the NHS's handling of Sam's case.

During that time it made a series of factual errors, forcing Scott and Susanna Morrish, from Newton Abbot, Devon, to repeatedly correct accounts of what had happened to their son.

In the letter, seen by The Telegraph, Mr Hunt states: "I am concerned that in a complaint of this seriousness and sensitivity there should have been a delay of two years before Sam's parents received your support. I am certain that such a delay must have caused additional untold stress and upset to Sam's parents at an already terrible time for them."

Although Mr Hunt recognises that the ombudsman last week apologised to Mr and Mrs Morrish for taking so long over the complaint, he criticises the organisation for not apologising for the mistakes it made during the investigation.

Telegraph: 28.6.14[9]

Editor's note: We can see a pattern emerging of how the delay in timely investigation puts further lives at risk, plus poor investigation processes often fail to identify the real cause of the harm.

Negative media stories continued to dent public confidence in the Ombudsman service, culminating in a series of critical articles from the **Health Service Journal (HSJ)** following a scandal of cover-up relating to Deputy Ombudsman **Mick Martin**. In March 2016 the HSJ released damning stories of a 'toxic culture' as told to them by PHSO whistleblowers.

> **Hundreds of new investigations carried out by the NHS ombudsman are "relabelled" assessments and being carried out by staff who face "unachievable" targets in a "toxic environment", according to six whistleblowers who have spoken to HSJ.**

---

[9] /www.telegraph.co.uk/news/health/news/10933028/Jeremy-Hunt-rebukes-health-watchdog-over-three-year-old-Sams-death.html

One investigator said "what matters is the number of cases you close". Another investigator said: "I less and less think there is any value in people coming to us."

Another source said they would no longer recommend the PHSO "because I feel the quality of investigations is now so variable. The standard of investigation created by the current leadership is so inadequate it would be better to provide no service at all than to give service users false hope that their concerns will be meaningfully investigated." **HSJ March 2016**[10]

[It is interesting to note that the new service model put in place by Rob Behrens does indeed make final decisions based on 'assessments' and not on 'investigations' but apparently that is now considered to be appropriate.]

Throughout her time in office **Dame Julie Mellor** lurched from one crisis to another as recorded in this PHSOtheFACTS blog from October 2016.

How do you solve a problem like Dame Mellor?

3rd October 2016

With the release of the Sir Alex Allan's independent review into issues concerning PHSO, we now have a greater understanding of why Dame Julie Mellor decided in July 2016 to resign her post following the earlier resignation of her deputy Mr Mick Martin in March. The

[10] https://www.hsj.co.uk/topics/policy-and-regulation/exclusive-whistleblowers-expose-toxic-environment-at-phso/7003384.article

current legislation provides the Ombudsman with omnipotent powers. The Office is independent of government, so beyond the scrutiny of ministers, MPs or civil servants, the Ombudsman handles all complaints about its own service, the wide legal discretion 'to act as she sees fit' prevents uphold at judicial review and the 'secrecy' of the investigation process leaves it shrouded in mystery. The Ombudsman can choose to leave office early, but can only be removed by agreement from both Houses of Parliament. The independence of the Ombudsman allows parliamentarians to walk away from public body scandals with clean hands as they can't interfere with the decisions of the Ombudsman. A neat arrangement until it is clear that someone in parliament needs to take control.

There are two things you need in an Ombudsman. The first is a safe pair of hands, someone who knows the unwritten rules of the establishment. The second is a friendly persona, a smiling face to give confidence to the public that the Ombudsman really cares about them. When **Ann Abraham** stepped down from the Ombudsman hot seat in 2011, following difficult questions over Mid Staffordshire and the failure of PHSO to investigate a single complaint during the time of the Francis review, **Dame Julie Mellor** appeared to be the perfect candidate. She had 30-years experience of public service, had turned around the failing Equal Opportunities Commission (EOC) and in her pre-appointment interview stressed her ability to appeal directly to the public.

I think where the role of the Ombudsman is talked about could be shifted. For example, I used to do lots of breakfast TV, sitting on the sofa, because you reach a much wider audience that way. That is the kind of thing that I think we could do.[11]

And so, the decision was made, **Dame Julie Mellor DBE** stepped in to lead PHSO through a **five-year change programme** in January 2012 and everyone went home happy.

It took until November 2012 for PHSO, under Ms Mellor's leadership, to reveal its new strategic plan – to investigate up to 10x more cases than previously under a scheme entitled **'more investigations for more people'.** The number of cases investigated was to rise from approximately 400 per year to 4,000 per year and all without increasing staff or resources.

The strategy was launched in April 2013 and despite being over a year in the planning there had been little consideration regarding **how** to deliver significantly larger numbers of **quality investigations** with the same resources. Like a factory producing faulty widgets the decision was made to produce 10x more faulty widgets **before** turning attention to improving the quality. Staff

---

[11] Appointment hearing, oral evidence. PACAC Q22

newly reassigned as 'investigators' were given no additional training but told to utilise 'peer support' while senior management benefitted from a significant bolstering of staff and £120,000 kitty for management training. Unsurprisingly, by December 2013 the staff were unhappy. **The PCS Union** submitted a scathing account of the strategy changes to the **Public Administration Select Committee,** (PASC) who had so recently selected Dame Julie to be the new Ombudsman.[12]

> *The strategic shift towards investigating more cases was, therefore, welcomed by our members. But from the outset they questioned how, with a reduced budget, decreasing staff numbers, and the hugely increased work load resulting from the proposed tenfold increase in investigations (4,000 instead of 400)- the Office couldn't possibly cope. It was feared that a massive backlog of cases would build up, and so it has proved.*

> *Short of the Treasury coming up with more funding, or the Ombudsman pruning its well-staffed external facing*

---

[12] written-evidence/public-administration-committee Dec 2013.

departments, or cutting back on other less essential budget heads- including the £430,000 set aside for consultants in 2014/15 and the controversial £120,000 'Board Development Budget' – all of which, at present, seem unlikely, the solution is not immediately obvious.

In 2013/14 the staff turnover rate was 21.3% and despite efforts from Dame Julie to turn this around, by 2014/15 it continued at 21.7%, much higher than expected for a public body.

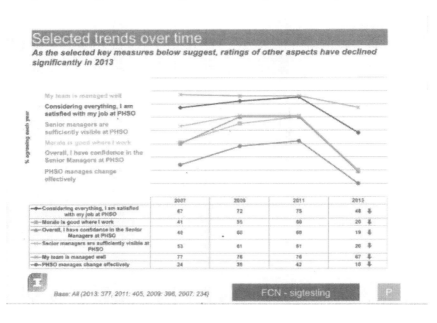

Graph from Staff Survey 2013.

The **staff survey of 2013** reflected the impact of the new Ombudsman since her arrival in January 2012 and on all measures of satisfaction there had been a steep decline.

Only 19% of staff expressed confidence in the leadership of PHSO in 2013 and by 2015 this had fallen to just 11%.

Dame Julie Mellor clearly did not engage the staff with her strategy of setting targets to crank up the number of investigations in a 'never mind the quality, feel the width' manner and by **March 2016,** disheartened by the empty rhetoric coming from the top, they took the unprecedented step of delivering a vote of no confidence in senior staff.

Finance

With 'people skills' well under par let us turn to control of the purse strings. Dame Julie Mellor is the **Accounting Officer** for PHSO with ultimate responsibility for the distribution of a near on £40 million annual budget. In times of austerity it is important that PHSO delivers value for money and if possible, a surplus back to the Treasury. By increasing the number of investigations, the Ombudsman was able to reduce the high headline figure of

£88,000 per investigation, but at the same time there was an increase in other costs such as **external affairs and strategy** which rose by 24%. With a plan to investigate 10x more cases the imperative should have been on bolstering the front-line staff, yet investment was at board and management level during Dame Julie's tenure. We learn from **Sir Alex Allan Report** (p71) that Dame Julie strengthened her immediate office staff by appointing a new principal private secretary supported by an assistant private secretary and a diary secretary while the number of full-time equivalent staff had fallen, leading to a backlog of 1,222 cases for assessment. In September 2014 the **National Audit Office** (NAO) reported on a procurement investigation regarding the employment of **Rosemary Jackson Consulting** to carry out 'Governance Development Coaching' for PHSO on a three-year contract worth over £50,000. Rosemary Jackson was an ex-colleague of Dame Julie's and this close association triggered an investigation by the NAO.[13]

> *The Ombudsman felt it essential to take a strong personal interest in the procurements, drawing on her business experience to identify potential suppliers. Although no conflicts existed, prior relationships gave rise to potential*

---

[13]
ombudsman.org.uk/sites/PHSO_procurement_investigation_September_2014.pdf

conflicts of interest which were not well managed. In the absence of firm procedures, ad-hoc arrangements for managing interests were often made, but these were rarely proportionate to the risk that procurements might be seen to be unduly influenced. As a result, the perception of risk remained; it was only through doing this work that we were able to satisfy ourselves that the risk had not materialised.

Had she been found guilty of arranging lucrative contracts for her friends the integrity of the office would have been severely jeopardised. Steps were immediately put in place to ensure no further oversights occurred. Then in 2014/15 the **accounts were qualified by the NAO** due to a 'lack of management oversight' which resulted in funds being overdrawn by £275,000. Due to a combination of losing all the senior staff in the finance department and flawed information reaching the audit committee and board, PHSO failed to draw down sufficient funds to cover their costs. It is interesting to note that the flawed information was not checked by the Ombudsman personally, although as Accounting Officer she had ultimate responsibility. But once the oversight was highlighted by the NAO Dame Julie Mellor took immediate steps to tighten all financial processes.

The steps that I have taken are that we now have a monthly rolling cash flow, forecast and monitoring, and I have a monthly assurance meeting with the Executive, which now includes updating me on exactly what the cash flow forecast is for that month and to the end of the year. We are putting in place a set of financial management arrangements in terms of process maps, procedure guidance for staff, and the way in which we will audit whether they are being followed. We have put in some new software that will give better information to our finance team so that they have to spend less time on manual spreadsheets and more on what are the implications of the data. Finally, I have asked our executive director of finance, who is new to the organisation, who joined just as we were closing the accounts, what more we can learn from other Departments that have had their accounts qualified for similar reasons about failing to monitor their supply estimates.[14]

With these robust measures in place, it is somewhat surprising to find that in September 2016 the Health Service Journal once again reported that **PHSO failed to follow its own procurement**

---

[14] *phso-annual-review/oral/2016 Q2*

guidance in awarding a £100,000 contract to Baxter Storey to run an on-site cafe for staff.[15] It would appear that Dame Julie is very good at retrospective learning. Very good at describing the plans she will put in place to ensure the same mistakes are never repeated and yet somehow, like Groundhog Day, PHSO has staggered from one crisis to another under her stewardship.

Finally, in February 2016 there came a crisis too many. The Health Service Journal reported that the Deputy Ombudsman, **Mick Martin** had been named in an Employment Tribunal as complicit in a cover-up whilst at Derbyshire Healthcare Foundation Trust.[16] Dame Julie Mellor had been provided with evidence taken directly from the Employment Tribunal report by **Helen Marks** in July 2015. On receipt of this information Dame Julie had an 'off the record', 1 - 1 meeting with Mr Martin where she accepted his account without reading the tribunal documentation. A short letter of acknowledgement was sent to Helen Marks who had questioned whether Mr Martin passed the fit and proper person test.

---

[15] hsj.co.uk/policy-and-regulation/phso-admits-it-failed-to-follow-rules-for-100k-contract/7010271.article

[16] phsothetruestory.com/2016/03/03/deputy-ombudsman-complicit-in-cover-up/

In August 2015 Dame Julie Mellor was again informed of the tribunal findings by **Monitor,** but failed to take any action and failed to inform the board. It was only when the story was released by the **Health Service Journal** in February 2016 that any action was taken. This led to the resignation of Mr Martin and shortly after, the resignation of the Ombudsman herself.

The question this raises is why did the Ombudsman act in such a cavalier manner when provided with correspondence that her Deputy Ombudsman had been found guilty of conspiracy to cover-up a sexual harassment complaint? There is a clue in Sir Allan's report[17] where it is stated that;

> *She explained to me that at the time the letter from Mrs Marks had been received, PHSO had a process for dealing with correspondence alleging cover-up or collusion by staff in relation to casework. Given the nature of PHSO's work, such correspondence was received every week. There was a standard procedure for referring this correspondence for fact-checking and advice, and she had learnt to suspend judgement while the allegations were looked into.*

---

[17].ombudsman.org.uk/sites/default/files/Report_of_a_review_into_issues_concer ning_the_PHSO_0.pdf

Although qualified by the phrase 'given the nature of PHSO's work' this statement reveals a fundamental truth about PHSO which deserves further analysis. Namely, that the Ombudsman **receives correspondence on a weekly basis that PHSO staff have been involved with cover-up or collusion.** If PHSO staff are carrying out independent and unbiased investigations, then why such a high level of correspondence alleging cover-up and collusion? The 'standard procedure' referred to here is not explored further by Sir Allan, but fundamentally it involves taking the allegations of wrong-doing to the accused staff member who denies everything, then sending a short acknowledgement to the complainant or no acknowledgement at all on the basis that 'no further action is required'. No evidence is reviewed and no internal investigation takes place. In this respect, the behaviour of the Ombudsman regarding Mick Martin followed standard procedure to the letter. When you are totally in control of handling complaints about yourself you can devise any system you like. PHSO state in their annual report that they have an error rate of 0.2%; a figure which represents their **accepted error rate** and not the high number of errors reported to them on a weekly basis by complainants.

If Lord Acton is right and 'power tends to corrupt and absolute power corrupts absolutely' then the new **Public Service**

35

Ombudsman must be accountable to parliament and the public. As Dame Julie Mellor herself might say, '... as soon as we realised there was a problem with accountability we took steps to ensure it would never happen again.'

Editor's note: Sir Bernard Jenkin as chair of the renamed, **Public Administration and Constitutional Affairs Committee (PACAC),** solved all the problems by selecting a new Ombudsman. No additional Parliamentary scrutiny was considered necessary. With a twinkle in his eye, Sir Bernard informed us that we would like the new appointment, indicating that all would now be well. He did not inform us that Behrens was known for presiding over a very low uphold rate whilst heading up the **Office of the Independent Adjudicator for Higher Education (OIA).**

> Although the OIA's annual findings are statistically significant in favour of the providers', $p < 0.05$... in the rare event of the OIA finding a complaint to be 'justified' (about 4–6% of complaints annually) or 'partly justified' (about 11%)...[18]

It was suggested by Mr Behrens that under Dame Julie Mellor's leadership, PHSO had 'lost its way' mainly because she was not a 'proper Ombudsman'. It is convenient to hang all the blame on the

---

[18] David Hockey Link.springer.com The Ombudsman Complaint System; a lack of Transparency and Impartiality.

outgoing Ombudsman but that ignores the fundamental flaws in a process which was never designed to deliver justice to the public. Now two years into Rob Behrens 'new strategy' we are to be assured that the Ombudsman service is well on the way to recovery.

In Chapter 2 we review some recent case stories, all of which have been submitted or closed since the arrival of **Rob Behrens** in April 2017.

Chapter 2. Recent case studies:

Editor's note: We have been told that things are improving at PHSO under the new management. At the time of writing (April 2020) we are two years into the three-year programme of improvement. The PHSO staff have all received training in the new investigation methods and the issues reported by the Patients Association and PHSOtheFACTS, should be a thing of the past. All of the cases listed here have been closed or are on-going under the new administration, though some were commenced before the arrival of Mr Behrens. They are cross-referenced with the following hashtags denoting previously identified key failure points. You will see that many of the same problems persist.

#flawed-decisions #misuse-of-evidence
#factual-inaccuracies #delay
#poor-communication #trust
#bias #no-effective-outcome
#poor-case-management #external-advice
#scoping-out-key-issues

Nic Hart:- 2014 – ongoing issues with investigation process

Following the death of our daughter Averil from a treatable eating disorder (Anorexia), who was left to die in her University flat at UEA, Averil's family complained to the NHS trusts that were caring for her. They all said that the care provided had been satisfactory. This was despite the fact that Averil had only been seen by a trainee with no experience of Anorexia and went on holiday leaving Averil to die.

Averil's family complained to the Ombudsman (PHSO) in 2014 about the care Averil received, but it took three and a half years for the Ombudsman to investigate, during which time they failed to investigate thoroughly and produced numerous draft reports containing essential errors: unbelievably, after three years, the PHSO still did not know who the lead NHS clinician looking after Averil was, even though the unit only had eight members.

The quality of the investigation was incredibly poor and relied heavily on the evidence provided by the same clinicians who were looking after Averil and, as the evidence clearly shows, were trying to protect their reputation. Various conflicting evidence was then given to experts who unsurprisingly came up with contradictory conclusions.

As the latest review of the PHSO investigation into Averil's death reveals, this resulted in chaos as numerous investigators at the Ombudsman were assigned for short periods and failed to appreciate the gravity of Averil's case.

The final report into Averil's death, whilst concluding that all of the NHS services failed to care adequately for Averil, was itself three years late and of poor quality, missing many opportunities to identify the failings in Averil's care.

As a consequence of the failure by the Ombudsman's investigation of Averil's death, there are currently five inquests being held in Cambridgeshire alone, looking into the deaths of patients with Eating Disorders who were cared for by Cambridgeshire and Peterborough Foundation Trust. Averil's family feel strongly that if the Ombudsman had done a proper and swift investigation into Averil's tragedy in 2014, that these further unnecessary deaths could and would have been avoided.

Averil's death was totally avoidable and she was failed by all of those who were responsible for her care. Following this her family were failed by the Ombudsman, at great personal cost, and during a time when they should have been allowed to grieve. The family have spent the last seven years fighting to gain the truth from both the NHS and the Ombudsman.

Averil's inquest at Huntingdon is finally scheduled for March 2020, over seven years after she died.

Our hearts go out to those who have been similarly failed both in the NHS and also at the PHSO.

NB: We strongly feel that if the PHSO undertook swift, quality investigations of serious incidents and deaths that many of the major NHS failures such as Mid Staffs, Gosport, Southern Health Care and others could be avoided, saving many thousands of lives.

#flawed-decisions #misuse-of-evidence #factual-inaccuracies #delay #poor-communication #trust #bias #no-effective-outcome #poor-case-management

Jenny Glover:- 2016 – 2020

I submitted my completed forms and supporting documentation to the PHSO London office in **May 2016**. I had exhausted local resolution. Although there had been acceptance of mistakes with many changes implemented to ensure these mistakes were not repeated, many outstanding questions were being ignored. After my husband's sudden and unexpected death it became apparent there had been failings in his care following a diagnosis of terminal lung cancer six weeks previously. The more I questioned those charged with his care, the more I realised I was uncovering a web of intrigue.

I handed over my documents and felt relief, I had every confidence my case would be treated in a fair, independent and professional manner. I initially found my dealings with all staff at PHSO helpful, respectful and supportive.

My first caseworker worked within PHSO Policy Requirements but in December 2016 concluded she would not refer my case for investigation.

May 8th 2017.
I submitted the form and substantial supporting documentation to indicate why I thought the decision PHSO had made about my complaint was wrong.

October 10th. 2017.
Email from PHSO to my advocate explaining lack of progress (zero) was due to shortage of staff.

December 13th 2017.
Email from new caseworker to say she would be in touch shortly, maybe after Christmas, but would try and respond as soon as she could.

July 18th 2018.
My first contact with caseworker, she agreed PHSO had made mistakes and she was seeking medical advice. She was going on annual leave and would be make contact late July early August.

October 11th 2018
Letter of introduction from P. S. senior caseworker RAFT. During telephone call on 12th October she admitted my case had not progressed at all.

February 8th 2019.
Letter from P.S. informing me of their decision and giving reasons for not taking further action. P.S. conclusions contained serious inaccuracies, she glossed over issues she says did not require further investigation and chose to ignore several points outlined in the form I had submitted.

March 19th 2019.
On the advice of my advocate I wrote to Mr Rob Behrens. I enclosed a timeline, timeline summary and documentation to indicate where Policy Requirements had not been adhered to. I asked for explanations regarding questions I had asked of P.S. and of SWHT. I indicated an apology and financial redress to reflect the poor service I had received from the Ombudsman.

April 8th 2019.
P.S. advises a response within 4 weeks. I found it unacceptable not to have a response from R.B. himself. I emailed him to request his office deal with it as my complaint was against P.S.

May 12th 2019.
I ask my MP Nadhim Zahawi to write to R.B.

September 6th 2019.
Update from R.B's office to say how busy he was and therefore could only allocate brief periods of time to casework. During this 5-month period contact had been received from P.S. K. E. Head of RaFT, J. H. an unknown person and R.B.

September 11th 2019.
Letter from R.B. acknowledged timeline issues and made an offer of £400 to redress this failing. He said, greater oversight from head of RaFT is now in place to ensure cases progress as they should.

14th October 2019.
I responded to Mr Behrens - extract below.

Dear Mr. Behrens,

Thank you for your response to the complaint I made in March 2019.There were several apologies for the time it was taking and, in your response, you accounted for it in part, unfortunately you left me second guessing what a full explanation might look like!
Six months to consider a complaint about serious and unnecessary delays without a full explanation is very frustrating.

As a result of my complaint you made assurances that greater oversight from head of RAFT [review and feedback team] is in place to ensure cases are progressing as they should. Could you please explain how this differs from what is already in place and covered by your existing Policy Requirements? Delays on Cases page 65...5.16.

I accept your acknowledgement... I received poor service from you and that your service fell significantly short of the standards you strive to achieve, but I cannot accept your failure to take into consideration the practical difficulty of a third caseworker following a case who was unable to work on an equal level or depth my case would warrant.

I would like to remind you, 14 months after PHSO received my updated case, L.C. made verbal contact with me for the first time. She agreed PHSO had made mistakes and she was seeking medical advice. She told me she was going on annual leave and assured me she would be in touch late July early August. It has never been explained to me what mistakes L.C. had identified or what Medical Advice she had sought, as far as I'm concerned what L.C. told me in July 2018 would stand when P.S. took over as my new Caseworker in October 2018.

Considering some of the most pertinent issues have been missed, together with a number of shortfalls, serious flaws and unacceptable inaccuracies, I find it impossible to have any confidence that the decision P. S. came to was fair and I seriously question her credibility.

Given the scale of evidence I submitted, not to have had anything upheld or any type of remedy included as indicated via Duty of Candour, would clearly suggest my case has not been dealt with according to your Policy Requirements and Service Charter Commitments.

As a consequence of the time lapse while in the hands of L.C. (October 2017/ October 2018) the process of my complaint being investigated in a timely way was compromised and can only be seen as being obstructed by the PHSO.

October 2019
Concerned, I requested all emails and transcripts of phone calls between case workers and R.B's office pertinent to this period. It was shocking to realise the letter I received purporting to come from R.B was actually drafted by P.S. with the support of K. E. and only signed by him. So, P.S. essentially investigated herself.

November 2019.
I wrote to K.E. asking why such a web of intrigue had been formed. Who had revised the initial sum of £200 to £300 with a final offer of £400.

March 17th 2020.
Email from K. E. assuring me R.B would be responding to my MP Nadhim Zahawi within two weeks.

May 1st 2020. A year on!
Promises have been made by K.E with regards to a response, but true to form nothing has come of them. There has been no response from Mr Rob Behrens to my letter from October 2019.
Although my case has been with PHSO for 4 years I have made no progress whatsoever and it is with deep regret I have found myself battling the very organisation I had put so much trust in. I would strongly advise anyone against taking a case to PHSO.

#flawed-decisions #misuse-of-evidence #factual-inaccuracies #delay #clinical-advice

#poor-communication #trust #bias

#no-effective-outcome #poor-case-management

Name withheld:- 2016 – 2020

Background

The PHSO website states:

"We make final decisions on complaints that have not been resolved by the NHS in England and UK government departments and other public organisations. We do this fairly and without taking sides."

This was not our family's devastating experience. Authority bias, victimisation and disability discrimination was rife throughout the NHS/PHSO complaint process even though the only outcomes we sought were apologies and service improvements.

Involving the PHSO made a bad situation far worse. The NHS stabbed us in the back by secretly discrediting us as parents and reporting us to the local Adult Safeguarding Board so they could legally displace us as Nearest Relative if our daughter continued to refuse inpatient treatment and was admitted under the Mental Health Act. No safeguarding investigation took place and we never knew of the false allegations until a DPA SAR revealed them in 2019. But the PHSO really twisted the knife by falsely claiming in the report that our daughter had no medical need for an allergy free diet and by misrepresenting her presentation thereby providing credible documented 'proof' of 'fabrication of illness' and parental 'neglect' where none previously existed. A BBC investigation found such allegations are commonly made in this area: [FII – Fabricated and Induced Illness]

"The BBC has had expert advice to say that it would be expected that a county the size of Gloucestershire would have one case of FII every 2 years – but the programme has heard from over 12 families who claim to have been accused of this (after requesting help / complaining)".

http://www.lukeclements.co.uk/can-you-cope/

Timeline:

- May 2016. NHS complaint submitted: our daughter was admitted to hospital five days later.
- July 2016. Complaint to the PHSO.
- It was suspended on the grounds of prematurity even though the PHSO had a copy of the trust's final response letter (July 2016).
- September 2016. The trust wrote another final letter reiterating the previous one but telling us to raise our concerns with two other trusts about the inpatient treatment it had arranged.
- October 2016. The PHSO closed our complaint, advising us we needed to exhaust the complaint process of the other two trusts before our complaint would be considered.

This was the first PHSO breach of due process we encountered: NHS legislation imposes the duty for trusts to cooperate in complaints as evidenced in the complaint policy of the trust we originally complained about:

17.7 When it is clear that a joint complaint investigation is required, the Trust and the other organisation should seek to agree which organisation should take the lead in coordinating the handling of the complaint and dealing with it under the Protocol agreed

- April 2017. New complaint, involving three trusts, submitted to PHSO.
- October 2017. PHSO investigation began. Just two phone calls took place.
- August 2018. Draft report produced.
  Fault was found with the admission arrangements made by the (first) trust.
  No phone calls took place to discuss the draft or our subsequent comments.
- November 2018. MH Trust minutes revealed Board members were advised that no PHSO recommendations were to be made.
- January 2019. Final report issued, along with new and unseen clinical advice attached.
  The comments we made following issuance of the draft report were dismissed in a separate letter and we found out no recommendations were to be made.
- January 2019. Subject access request (SAR) under the Data Protection Act (DPA) to PHSO.
- March 2019. DPA SAR responded to.
- May 2019. Review request submitted. PHSO agreed to review its decision.
- February 2020. Permission given to Patients Association to raise our case.

- April 2020. Letter from Mr Behrens confirming there was fault in the investigation.
  He was unwilling to quash the report and felt it could be rectified through a new investigation.
- April 2020. Scope for new investigation agreed. Investigation cannot start until COVID-19 NHS restrictions are lifted.

Why we complained to the PHSO

We encountered unethical, unsafe, and unlawful NHS practice. This cannot go unchallenged where vulnerable people are concerned. The scope of the PHSO investigation included:

- Diagnosing an autistic woman with anorexia even though the criteria was unmet
- Failure to take autism and food allergies into account during eating disorder (ED) treatment
- Failing to provide specialist ED therapeutic support during community treatment
- Failure to produce a care or weight restoration plan during community treatment
- Unlawful 'best interest' decision making for a capacitated adult who was not receiving treatment under the Mental Health Act (MHA) and not subject to legal guardianship
- NHS coercion and threat of MHA detainment to force agreement to inpatient treatment
- Failure to advise of a planned admission to a medical ward hospital 10 weeks after the anorexia diagnosis even though weight maintained,

medically stable, and ED inpatient criteria was unmet
- Use of trickery, entrapment, and unlawful use of s5 Mental Health Act at an outpatient appointment to force consent, under duress, to immediate inpatient treatment on a medical ward
- 12-day unlawful deprivation of liberty on a medical ward including medically unnecessary 1:1, 24/7 observation until a bed became available in an out of county hospital
- Failure to undertake ECG's during inpatient treatment
- Failure to accommodate lifelong allergy needs during NHS inpatient treatment
- Inpatient weight loss of 1.6kg on a medical ward causing newfound medical instability
- Imposing sanctions for not eating food items she is allergic to
- Refusal to give permission to have a family holiday

Why we asked for a PHSO review

It was necessary to request a review not just because a valid complaint was not upheld but because the PHSO report demonstrated evidence of administrative unfairness and procedural injustice, evidence of disability discrimination, bias in favour of the NHS and less favourable treatment of the complainant and her family. The PHSO strategically prevented identification of NHS fault: The scope of the complaint included autism, allergies, and mental health yet inexplicably no clinical or

51

professional standards on any of these issues were applied, and no specialist clinical or professional advice was sought either. Clinical standards were applied on eating disorders but were not in existence at the time in question. The PHSO investigation was undertaken by a caseworker and overseen by a manager yet the evidence shows the PHSO's own policy guidance was not followed, NHS Trust policies were disregarded, professional codes of practice were ignored, and the legislative frameworks governing autism, human rights and mental health practice went unheeded. The PHSO muddled the respective responsibilities of the trusts to deflect attention and confuse issues. These PHSO tactics strategically obscured identification of NHS fault. This prevented gap analysis, and vetoed identification and assessment of the personal injustice suffered. The content and presentation of the report, and language therein, demonstrated PHSO spin, deflective argument, and selective reporting. NHS accounts and records were accepted as evidence but submissions by the complainant, including NHS records and extracts from relevant clinical and professional standards were ignored. Key NHS medical evidence was disregarded, including hard evidence which undermined many of the claims in the report. The investigation lacked objectivity, focus, structure, and curiosity. Several misleading and inaccurate statements were made, some with the authority of being informed by clinical advice but the briefest cross reference and examination of clinical records and relevant standards discredited them. Clinical advice was tainted by the PHSO and selectively obtained and used to 'fit' the NHS defence. The PHSO unfairly gaslighted the lived experiences and medical history of the complainant: key evidence was ignored, and the caseworker chose not to use his power to request further evidence. Even where fault was found the PHSO unilaterally decided, without any consideration or discussion of its personal impact, it had been remedied so no recommendations were made. Worse still, evidence exists to reveal the trusts knew two months before we discovered (in the final report) that no recommendations were to be made: i.e. my daughter did not even get an apology. The PHSO report demonstrates unprincipled decision making where coercive, unethical, unlawful, and/or unsafe NHS practice is condoned, and an NHS culture of bullying and victimisation endorsed.

Review outcome

In April 2020 Mr Behrens acknowledged there was fault in the investigation and apologised. However, he refused to quash the report, proposing a new PHSO investigation instead. This only adds to the injustice we have suffered because the PHSO report explicitly states our daughter's dietary needs would have been met if they were medically necessary: This was not an evidence-based statement and the ongoing existence of the January 2019 report will always be used by mental health staff to justify force feeding our daughter allergens if she is ever treated under the Mental Health Act.

Quashing is a sensible, cost effective solution. We cannot help feeling Mr Behrens has a greater need to protect his reputation than to protect our daughter: after all, the investigation and review both took place after his appointment.

We cannot collude with poor, unsafe, or unlawful NHS or PHSO practice. In hindsight we should have bypassed the PHSO and sought legal advice immediately. Four years on we are stuck in the PHSO quagmire with the constant worry of what the future holds for our daughter.

#flawed-decisions #misuse-of-evidence #factual-inaccuracies #delay #poor-communication #trust #bias #no-effective-outcome #poor-case-management #external-advice #scoping-out-key-issues

James Wilkins:- 2018 - 2019

I first went to PHSO in June 2018, I called the organisation and tried to complain about my treatment from a surgeon at Royal Cornwall Hospitals Trust (RCHT). I had several conversations by telephone and was eventually told that the case was premature and wasn't given a further explanation. When I called again, I asked for an explanation and was eventually told I needed formal final written letters from the hospitals that I had been wronged by. I then had to try and get the letters from hospitals after months of waiting and believing that my case was being dealt with by PHSO.

I then had a limited support from a SEAP advocate who helped me with a couple of emails. The advocate told me that she had contacted PHSO on 3rd Dec 2018, they had received the final written letters I had sent.

Since Dec 2018, I have been waiting for an outcome of my complaint, In October 2019, I received a letter to tell me that they couldn't take my complaint any further and there was no outcome. The letter said I had a legal option and I should speak to a solicitor; however, I had informed them I had explored this option and this was not possible.

Throughout the complaints process, the communication has been very poor and they had not accounted for communicating with someone with Asperger Syndrome (which I have a formal diagnosis for) and sent emails to me via Egress secure system. I had told them many times that I did not have the software to use Egress and was happy to accept the email in regular format, however they continued to send the emails through Egress throughout the process and I had to call them each time to tell them I could not access the email.

I had three different case workers and had even spoken to a manager about how long the process was taking, the manager then told me that they would endeavour to support me, however this never happened and I found my final case worker to be rude and ignorant. Documents were sent to PHSO several times and when my wife queried where the original documents had gone when I had initially sent them in June 2018, I was told after 6 months of having my case my documents were deleted. We then had to re-send all of the letters from health care professionals, along with a time line that my wife had created, to explain what had happened and when. PHSO still asked several repetitive questions, where I was required to repeat my story time and time again.

When I initially placed the complaint, I had kept calling to get progress updates, I was told If I continued to call prematurely, my complaint would never be dealt with by PHSO and they would end the enquiry.

I feel very let down by the system and feel I was led on by the PHSO, in the sense that I believed they could help me to gain an apology and some compensation, as that's what their whole purpose is. Now I realise, they are a service that is purely there to take the side of the NHS and offer no real resolution to anyone's complaint.

#misuse-of-evidence #delay
#poor-communication #trust #bias
#no-effective-outcome
#poor-case-management

Jo Barlow:- 2017 – 2019

Summary of my Complaint to the Parliamentary & Health Service Ombudsman

From the end of 2015 I felt unwell with neck & head pains plus dizziness and saw GP's at G H Surgery on 4 different appts between January & March 2016, whilst my symptoms severely worsened. I even gave them a written list of my symptoms and asked could I have a brain tumour. Finally getting a referral to neurology (after asking 3 times) for May. But as I felt so bad and had barely moved off my sofa for weeks my parents paid for a private doctor. On examination he said I was 'drunk when I was not drunk' and needed an MRI to check my brain. Two days later (22/04/16) I had the MRI and got called back that afternoon to say I had a 3cm hemangioblastoma in my cerebellum needing urgent brain surgery. It was so urgent that my surgery was on 18/5/16 which was before the date given for the neurologist referral via my normal GP.

I wrote to the PHSO saying *"I felt my GPs failed to diagnose the fact I had a brain tumour (when I had all but 1 of the symptoms of a cerebellar tumour and had told them these symptoms), and was left for 3 months longer than I should have been. In which time my health seriously deteriorated, I suffered from horrendous blinding headaches, and hence why we paid for private doctor. I feel extremely fortunate that I do not have any major health issues now, as I was told a stroke or similar would happen if it was left much longer, and fully believe that if I had not paid privately something major would have happened. The side effects I had after the operation, and still have now, I also feel were increased due to this 3-month delay."* Plus *"The GP had a 'Significant Event Analysis Meeting' over my case. So therefore, they must know they had a significant failure!"*

I asked for reimbursement of my private costs and a contribution towards the fact I was left to suffer unnecessarily for 3 months. Adding the fact that my husband had to look after me during that time, his self-employed work suffering drastically as a result.

This initial letter was written to the PHSO on 17/2/17 & I received the reply that they would formally investigate my complaint on 6/4/17.

I expected them to agree that the GP's had failed to diagnose me (as suggested by the hospital neurosurgery staff) and at least receive money back from what we had borrowed for private consultation (£950) plus some contribution to 5 months on the sofa and my husband basically losing his business as a result. Plus get a personal apology.

It was extremely hard writing up the complaint, I felt I had no help, not really sure what to do or say but that they would hopefully understand the basics and call me. Initially I was happy when a case worker called, I felt they listened to my concerns and the GP surgery mistakes, the details being clarified for about an hour on the phone.

I was then totally confused, shocked, disgusted and tearful when the **draft report came through (15/8/17)** basically saying there was no wrongdoing.

I wrote back on 17/8/17 expressing my disappointment and asking to change the draft points, as well as adding in a lot of links to **medical websites** to show that the GP's didn't follow **their own guidelines**. I was still expecting them to have said 'sorry we misunderstood you' after this draft report, take in my concerns and re-write their report.

On 14/09/17 we received their final report, basically not changing anything from the draft report & totally ignoring the comments I had written on my last letter. The only thing they found GH failed in was not removing my staples after surgery, so they **partially upheld my complaint** but only on this one minor point - they ignored the more serious ones that almost killed me! Anything that they might have had to compensate me for... I was in tears when I read the reply. It felt like my life was worthless to both the GP & PHSO. They were lying, they almost killed me, and no one cared.

Some point after this my husband called & spoke to them and we were even more confused that the summary points they advised me to use on the phone apparently didn't cover the topics I thought they did. Plus, they would not use my added points on my second letter as they weren't in this 'original summary'!

It took me until 5/2/18 to write up my complaint to their final report. I wrote in this letter *"It basically feels like a total farce & a waste of both of our time."*

And *"I have since felt rather disheartened to start again with the complaint, as each time I need to re-read it all or I forget some of the issues that I want to make, as my memory isn't as good as it was before brain surgery and it is very emotionally exhausting re-reading how you very nearly died and just how many warning signs the GPs had, and ignored. We have also been waiting for G H to send us copies of my medical notes and also the 'significant events analysis meeting'- the last of which after several ignored phone calls we have had to formally request under Freedom of Information act and are still waiting for. We were also not made aware that I should have asked for my medical records before or during my initial complaint to you, but only got told this when we phoned to ask how do we complain about your service, the final report and the lack of response to my concerns. Surely this should be on your online guidelines or initial reply letter? After all you know what steps need to be followed as you do this every day, I have never complained to the health ombudsman before, nor had a significant illness and brain injury. Are you there to fully support the patient or not?"*

"I am not sure why I, as a patient, should be researching things like NICE guidelines on what testing should be done for the symptoms I had? Surely that should be what the health ombudsman should be doing for me... not seemingly wanting me to give all the information until you can no longer deny that the GPs made mistakes!"

It was a waste of my time as on **18/1/19 they replied back saying they would not carry out a review** as I hadn't given any new information. I was just totally disgusted, the PHSO was just a waste of my time and I felt worse knowing they had 'got away with it' than if I hadn't even bothered to complain. Possibly because I didn't know how to 'complain correctly' as none of the points I brought up after my initial letter were even considered. Even though the surgery had also not completed the correct NHS forms for their 'Significant Event Analysis Meeting' and I didn't find this out until during my complaint. Nor that my doctor is no longer a registered GP.

By the time I got the final review of my complaint it was almost 3 years, leaving it too late for a solicitor to take on my case. (I tried several, who all said they would have, but wouldn't be able to do so within 3 months we had left to complain.) I feel this was purposely left this long as they knew it was too late.

In the time my complaint was with the PHSO we had 3 different case workers (that I know of). I wrote on my final review complaint letter *"None of them called to ask if I would prefer to be called by phone or emailed. Which would have definitely been mail or email as I still struggle with memory and understanding since brain surgery, and email gives me time to digest it and reply clearly. Plus, the phone line was often too quiet for me to hear well. This is surely against your own recommendations and what your customer service said I should have been offered?"*

I am also sure when we called after the final report it was given another reference number. Why would this be?

There was NO impact to the doctor's surgery, the partner GP couldn't even be bothered to sign his OWN apology letter about the staples!

If I know anyone else in a similar situation, I would tell them to forget the PHSO and use a no win no fee solicitor as the PHSO is just a joke and will not uphold anything even if it is against all their own medical guidelines. At least that way you may get both some compensation and the knowing that things might change for others.

#misuse-of-evidence #factual-inaccuracies #delay #poor-communication #trust #bias #no-effective-outcome #poor-case-management

Liz Hallam:- 2017 - 2019

My first approach to the PHSO was dated 22/02/2017 some 15 months after my husband's death on Christmas Day 2015. I had by then exhausted the Local Resolution Process which I, unwillingly, entered in January 2015.

My husband suffered from Multiple Systems Atrophy a disease affecting all aspects of his mind and body. He had frequent falls. We had some care from Continuing Health Care but for four and a half days I was the sole carer, although there was half an hour morning and, after my husband suffered sepsis, evening care.

On 10th December 2015 a phone call from the CHC nurse forced me to accept 12-hour daily care of my husband by other carers after I refused a demand that my husband be admitted to a Nursing Home that night or I accept a live-in carer. A carer had made accusations of alcohol abuse by my family. Out of date care records led to other accusations. My true account of events, at a minuted meeting the previous day with the CHC nurse and the Community Matron, was not believed or **investigated**.

I had believed this meeting was to discuss increasing levels of care for my husband because of his falls. The meeting ended with an agreement to apply for increased care funding but increased levels could not be in place until after Christmas.

I did achieve a degree of satisfaction through SIRONA's Local Resolution Process. It was admitted that the carer's allegations were false and that the care plan was out of date. However, there was an insistence that only my acceptance of a 12-hour carer resolved the safeguarding issues because of unreported falls. However, the GP had recorded many falls and the impossibility of controlling these falls was well known. I also discovered, thanks to the intervention of my MP, that an email containing even more defamatory, untrue allegations existed on Social Services database. Even after the Local Resolution meeting no attempt was made to correct the allegations in this email. My "view" could be added. This process ended in January 2017.

I felt I had to approach the PHSO to clear our family name and challenge the process that had resulted in a distressing, stressful and unhappy period for my husband and me at the end of his life.

March 22nd 2017. I received a preliminary reply from the PHSO.

May 12th 2017. A letter informed me that as my case covered Health and Social Care I must also make a complaint against Social Services. I could then, within the 12-month window, go back to the PHSO, if necessary, and both cases could be considered together.

SURELY MANY CASES MUST INVOLVE BOTH AGENCIES. ISN'T IT TIME THAT A SINGLE ORGANISATION COVERED THE NHS and SOCIAL CARE?

6th June 2017. I made an initial complaint to Bath and NE Somerset Social Services. This triggered a report by an external Investigating Officer. After his initial report the investigation was taken back in-house by the local CCG. On November 28th 2018 it was agreed that in 12months time the defamatory email would be deleted from Social Services database. However, the local CCG could not investigate the Safeguarding Procedures in Community Health. SIRONA had lost the contract. My only way to complain about the original procedure, which had led to the defamatory, totally untrue, account of my actions being presented as fact to Social Services, was to go back to the PHSO. I was also concerned that my husband, who had mental capacity at the time, had not been consulted about his care.

February 2018. My advocate presented my case to the PHSO. Initially there were phone calls indicating a reluctance to take my case. Could it lead to any improvement in the service? At this point I began to realise the unimportance of the individual. Eventually the PHSO agreed to look at the case with a different case number.

29 June 2018. A rambling rejection letter which showed a total misunderstanding of my case. My case concerned the procedures adopted by the Community Care Nurses, not the defamatory email which had been resolved locally. The PHSO also refused to consider the matter of my husband's wishes. It stated that I had not brought up this matter locally. I certainly did in my complaint to Social Services. The letter was appallingly written. It referred to the 2004 Care Act! The PHSO letter contained a section, which must have been copied from advice received, when it referred to me as SHE not YOU.

Between June and October 2018 there were phone calls from my advocate and me to try to avoid an appeal to the review team because of the poor quality of the initial response. At one point in a phone conversation I was told that the carer's account had to be given more weight than mine as he was a health worker! That never appeared in writing.

14th October 2018. My Review Request submitted.

26th March 2019. Case rejected. I was shocked by the selectivity of the reasons which seemed to rely totally on statements submitted by the NHS Community Care team, however vague or inaccurate. My statements were ignored. This statement from the Nursing Advisor stood out **"It would not have been the role of Community Care to conduct their own investigation"**. Yet that was the whole point. They had undertaken their own thoroughly inadequate investigation, forced me to comply with their own faulty conclusions and then presented these conclusions as fact to Social Services. I would have expected the PHSO to be concerned.

And even more alarmingly from the Adviser **"There is nothing to show that the changes in care were based on the allegations made. The visit by the Community Matron and the Continuing Health Care Officer was to review Mr. Hallam's care needs......" In my file to the PHSO was a letter contradicting that view.**

30th April 2019. A letter back to the Review Team quoting from that final letter of the Local Resolution Team. It confirmed that the Dec. 9th meeting at my house had been to deal with potential safeguarding issues. That was not "conclusive" as far as the PHSO was concerned. **The case was then closed.**

I have been shown that the PHSO disregards the testimony of individuals. It puts family carers like myself at the mercy of mistaken, or even malicious, allegations while caring for loved ones. I know my husband's care was changed on Dec.10th 2015 because of the safeguarding allegations. I received the phone call telling me this. I feel it should be a matter of concern that the PHSO ignored my testimony.

An unnecessary rush to unjustified action caused great unhappiness to my husband and myself in the last fortnight of his life and caused me a three-year fight to reclaim my good name. Yet, the Community Care providers were exonerated of any blame by the PHSO. I would not recommend anyone to go to the PHSO, indeed my advocate warned me to expect disappointment. Prevarication until personnel changes make proof nigh on impossible, and the defence of the NHS seem to be the priorities of the PHSO.

#flawed-decisions #misuse-of-evidence #factual-inaccuracies #delay #poor-communication #trust #bias #no-effective-outcome #poor-case-management #external-advice

#scoping-out-key-issues

Julie Hurst:- 2015 - ongoing

I first contacted the PHSO four and a half years ago and completed their complaint form on 3/6/15. I am still awaiting resolution.

I turned to the PHSO because I believed that my mother, Mrs Betty Lythgoe, an elderly patient, had been placed on an End of Life Care Pathway at Wigan Royal Albert Edward Infirmary without justification and without relatives' consent. Mrs Lythgoe was vulnerable. Years before her death, she had been diagnosed with vascular dementia and was 'wandersome'. I also complained to the PHSO about the Clinical Commissioning Group, as my mother's care was fully funded by the NHS and also about R B C care home where my late mother was a resident. I discovered two years after my mother's death, she should have been safeguarded and a Deprivation of Liberty Safeguarding authorisation should have been in place. I believe that her death should have automatically triggered an inquest.

Before approaching the PHSO, I had naively expected that the local hospital would have agreed to meet me to discuss concerns and explore shortcomings and wrongdoings. One might have thought the public bodies would have carried out independent investigations but they haven't. I wouldn't have resorted to the PHSO had the public bodies been responsive.

My PHSO involvement is ongoing but I have to say that I feel that I have had no support from them. I am still holding out for a proper PHSO investigation but you can see from the following history the case handling tends towards closing my case down. I've had to constantly chase them up. PHSO processes are never properly explained.

My expectations of a chance of a fair investigation has diminished. I have come to the conclusion that public bodies rather than fearing a damning PHSO investigation, welcome a referral to the PHSO as a 'cop out' where the body needn't respond and PHSO's delaying tactics will provide the excuse that the complaint is out of time.

I have been given numerous case workers – the first one (20/8/15) stated they would consider investigating all my complaints as one, rather than three separate complaints as soon as all the bodies completed their own complaints processes.

Another PHSO letter dated 3/9/15 stated a local resolution meeting would be offered once the Trust had concluded their investigations. Nothing ever came of this.

A letter dated 8/6/16 stated the PHSO would allocate the case to an investigator as soon as possible. However, the next letter, two months later (dated 3/8/16), stated, *'we are therefore proposing to discontinue our investigation'*.

I believe this last action was because I had told the PHSO that I'd contacted the charity AVMA and was continuing to raise awareness regarding a group of end of life deaths at the same hospital through the local press. The PHSO do not seem to realise that where the issues raised are potentially very serious, urgency is crucial for public safety and peace of mind for the complainant. My MP Yvonne Fovargue wrote to the PHSO Customer Care team (14/9/16) to request a review of their decision not to investigate.

Some months later, I received a letter (23/2/17) from Ms Amanda Campbell, PHSO Chief Executive. In response to MP intervention, Ms Campbell wrote, '*we are now proposing to start a fresh investigation'* She included reassurances, '*We will now ensure that we provide you with the level of service that you have a right to expect from us and progress the investigation promptly.'*

Mr Behrens took over as Ombudsman in April 2017. In August 2017 I received a PHSO letter (23/8/17) which used the excuse of the police review to now stall the investigation, *'we consider that we should not proceed with an investigation at this stage'.* (and yet another Investigator allocated).

A new investigation case was set up and the PHSO letter dated 27/2/19 informed that it had been passed to yet another senior caseworker. But two years after

Ms Campbell's above reassurance of a better level of service, the following account speaks volumes. Within the same letter, PHSO Operations manager wrote to me to *'report an information security breach'* informing that the PHSO *'cannot find the paper files we held about your complaint previously*, *the loss was reported to the Head of Information ..logged as a security incident'* and the PHSO had also reported this to *'the Info Commissioners Office'*. The operations manager informed that the missing paper files, *'included your mother's records' from WWLNHSTrust'* and that the PHSO *'regret this data breach'*.

Mr Behrens had been in post almost two years by this time and I have noted how he extols the merits of the PHSO service and staff to the public. As well as losing sensitive confidential records, I see facts are now being rewritten by PHSO staff. In a recent letter dated 13/6/19, the PHSO have incorrectly stated that my mother died on the 8/3/14 instead of the 8/3/15. The PHSO have also recently wrongly stated that I became aware of lack of DOLS safeguarding in 2016 when it was verifiably shown to be in 2017 i.e. exactly two years after my mother's death. Surely the PHSO aren't rejigging facts to try to surpass some time limit for investigating? Or is it more ongoing PHSO incompetence?

I finish by referring to a recent letter from PHSO (29/8/19) which offered a proposed scope. This inadequate scope I have challenged twice in writing. Note this! The PHSO have stated that they had **not received either of those letters**! I pointed out two letters do not go missing. I have since received an email on the 22/10/19 saying quite the opposite – that the PHSO *'received your letter dated 17/09/19 and 24/09/19* (so not missing at all) *we are considering your comments on our proposed investigation scope and will be in touch again shortly.'*

It will be exactly 5 years in March 2020 since what I believe was my mother's unlawful killing in Wigan RAEI. I have still had no investigation by the PHSO and the scope has yet to be agreed. I remain concerned about the care of the elderly and vulnerable locally.   Whether complaints are taken seriously and lessons are learned depends on one man, Mr Behrens.   Would I recommend the current PHSO to a complainant seeking resolution? NEVER!

#flawed-decisions #factual-inaccuracies #delay #poor-communication #trust #bias #no-effective-outcome #poor-case-management #scoping-out-key-issues

Name withheld:-   2016 – ongoing

I complained to the PHSO on 10.6.16 because I was dissatisfied with the response to a complaint I had made to the NHS relating to dishonesty which was compromising the future safety of my healthcare. I expected an acknowledgment of this situation in order to restore my trust in the NHS and restore my own reputation among those who see me as the dishonest party.

The glossy publicity would lead anyone to think that the PHSO are impartial and supportive, but that couldn't be further from the truth. From start to finish my experience left me feeling as if they were there to obstruct the complainant by any means necessary, and protect the NHS from scrutiny. I was put under a lot of pressure to agree to a face to face meeting with NHS in order to keep the matter off the written record.

Following a year already spent by the NHS, the PHSO took another 26 months from referral to final report, just over half of which was spent resisting an investigation. I had to refer three times before they accepted my complaint without bouncing it back to the NHS. In all, I had nine different staff handling my case, and four different reference numbers. The process appears to be designed to procrastinate until the deadline for taking legal action expires. You are asked on the referral form whether you prefer to communicate by letter or phone, but although I had chosen the former they threatened to close my complaint unless I rang them.

The evidence I provided included both written documentation from my medical records and recordings of conversations with doctors which corroborated my version of events, and yet it was virtually all ignored without either explanation or justification. In stark contrast to this, the NHS version of events has been accepted at face value without question, even though it was supported by no evidence at all, and even though my own evidence, and the absence of answers to my questions demonstrated that it wasn't credible. The report uses phrases like "appear to have been…", "possibly there was…", and "may explain…", which are mere speculation. The report also claimed that GMC guidelines had been complied with, but ignored more than a dozen specific instances I cited where these rules were being flouted. In relation to the scores of questions that still remain unanswered, a caseworker told me that the role of the PHSO is to investigate complaints, not to answer questions, but the Oxford English Dictionary defines investigation as *answering questions*.

The investigation process itself is all but opaque, as the PHSO didn't disclose any documents at all prior to evaluating the evidence, despite this being a requirement of their own standards, and didn't fully disclose all the information even when explicitly requested to do so at draft report stage. Caseworker's notes, NHS complaint files, communications between the PHSO & NHS, and evidence over and above routine medical records were all withheld. There is little communication other than the procrastinating letters, so with little clue as to their thinking on the matter for two years, you find yourself given just a couple of weeks to respond to the draft report. They try to focus on the trivial and irrelevant whilst ignoring the substance, which puts you in a position of having to choose between eroding your own case by omitting minor supporting evidence, and including it only to have it used as a distraction. There were also subtle attempts at minimisation such as describing ambulance admissions as 'appointments', and referring to unrelated, irrelevant incidents in an attempt to portray the NHS in a better light.

The overall effect of the report was to spin the problem as a genuine mistake in order that they could falsely claim that it had been addressed, and then use this 'solution' as an excuse not to uphold the complaint. Even if the problem were being correctly defined it would be no defence to argue that the offending has already ceased. The final report also comes with a warning not to disclose information under threat of legal action, but only a vague explanation which information this relates to.

In summary, the PHSO ignored my evidence, accepted uncorroborated accounts from the NHS at face value, failed to investigate in any meaningful sense, failed to disclose evidence, and disregarded published standards for professional practice. The process couldn't have been more biased and unfair, and is by no stretch of the imagination *"Treating the complainant impartially, and without unlawful discrimination or prejudice"* (PHSO, Principles of Good Complaint Handling). Since there was never any agreement on the nature of the problem in the first place, it would be difficult to argue that there has been any benefit in complaining at all, indeed it has left me less safe than before I complained. I have recently applied for a review.

I couldn't recommend the PHSO to anyone expecting a fair investigation, but I would like to think that people will continue to file their complaints, if only to keep the pressure up.

#flawed-decisions #misuse-of-evidence #factual-inaccuracies #delay #poor-communication #trust #bias #no-effective-outcome #poor-case-management #external-advice #scoping-out-key-issues

Margaret Whalley:- 2014 - ongoing

PHSO's acknowledgement of the mismanagement of my case begs for proper enquiry. I question how common are the failings acknowledged in this case.

The PHSO Final Report into the care and death circumstances of my brother, Mr B R Bowdler (deceased 2012) was sent out, to all parties concerned, in March 2016.

Some months before its release, I communicated my alarm at the way the investigation was proceeding. Crucial documentary evidence, which I supplied at the outset, was being overlooked by PHSO advisers and investigators alike. My MP Ms Lisa Nandy wrote to the PHSO requesting that Deputy Ombudsman, Mr Mick Martin, provide a direct personal assurance of an *'evidence-based investigation'*.

After the release of the Draft report, I made a request that the evidence which underpinned the decision making be released to me. I didn't know, at that time, the material evidence could not be identified by PHSO staff nor could it be ascertained which advisers had seen what records. I was kept in ignorance of this internal dilemma – a dilemma that the PHSO Head of FOI was aware of at the time. Instead of the material evidence, I was sent batches of unflagged records, most of which had originally been submitted by me to the PHSO.

A few months ago, in September 2019, I received a case review letter from Mr Behrens, Ombudsman. Mr Behrens's letter conveys his apologies for *'major failings'*. Since the proposal to investigate in May 2014, nearly six years have passed yet to my mind there has been no vigorous PHSO investigation into PHSO staff behaviour or the original complaint itself.

Since the release of, what was for me, a wholly unsatisfactory Final Report in early 2016, I have been occupied these past three years in trying to secure a fair review. A PHSO 'review' did take place in October 2017 but was shut down over a weekend without waiting for the submission of all my evidence.

In November 2017, my husband and I attended a PHSO Open Meeting in Manchester. I took the opportunity afforded in a 'workshop' session to speak up about what I considered to be evidence of misconduct and poor complaint handling within my closed case.

As a result, a second review began with two face-to-face meetings in spring 2018 where only the service issues were addressed - I have still yet to comment about what is wrong with the Final Report.

Now, some 18 months following those interviews, I have received Mr Behrens' conclusion that my service complaint is upheld. Unfortunately, it appears he is not commenting on individual staff failings so I cannot know just how thorough the review has been, who on his staff has been interviewed (if any), sanctioned etc. In sum, he surmises that the original investigation findings may not be robust. The Ombudsman is proposing a fresh investigation.

Among the failings is the fact that PHSO did not meet me at outset of the original investigation, despite their original written intention to do so. As a result, the review letter informs that the investigation commenced without any clear agreement about the scope.

The PHSO Review analysis includes the following which reveals much regarding collective staff integrity:

'total failure to identify the evidence we relied on ....I think that best thing we could have done at that point was to 'come clean. While I think she would- rightly- have been dismayed to learn we had failed to identify the material evidence and may well have used this as further justification to try to halt the investigation, demonstrating our values of openness and transparency might, just, have begun to restore her confidence in our ability to 'do the right thing'.

When public servants collectively decide to do the <u>wrong</u> thing and pass off a Final report as 'robust' I wonder why this is not considered collusion? I have recently asked Mr Behrens to consider this question.

Mr Alex Robertson (10/1/2020) has recently provided one of the criteria for quashing a Final Report. He wrote:- *We will only quash a report ....If   We have missed significant material evidence which we should have considered, or significant new evidence has come to light.*

Since the PHSO have acknowledged an ' *almost total failure to identify the evidence'* then why is it I am the only one holding out for quashing?

Mr Behrens informs that the new investigation will be limited to just some of the organisations involved in the original investigation. I will be arguing that all the six organisations should be included drawing on his own points – e.g. that the PHSO declined to meet me, the scope was not agreed and the material evidence could not be identified to support decisions.

The Miller v Health Service Commissioner for England judgement ([2018] EWCA Civ 144) found that the Ombudsman must adhere to the standards of fairness. The case highlighted that where predetermination is found to exist this is grounds for quashing a PHSO Final Report.

During my service review last year, I had drawn attention to evidence of what I perceive to be clear predetermination – an email sent internally by a PHSO adviser early in the original investigation before all advice was obtained. It indicated that my case should be put to bed quickly and was effort for nothing. I will request Mr Behrens's consideration for quashing the report wholesale because of the attitude of advisers and investigators involved in the original investigation. Mr Behrens himself has endorsed his reviewer's analysis which includes comment on PHSO staff conduct – *'If we saw behaviour like this from a body in jurisdiction we would rightly be critical...'* There was clear prejudice against the complaint as shown by the reviewer comment, *'I have no idea why we did not obtain the Inquest transcript especially given that Mrs Whalley had a copy she was willing to share. Unfortunately, my suspicion is that this is precisely why we didn't obtain a copy'.*

A Final Report cannot be declared *'robust'* unless it addresses what really happened. Besides I have yet to give comment on the content of the PHSO Final Report – interview time for this has yet to be offered. It may be of note to the reader that a short article written up by a local reporter included more of the essential history of the death circumstances than the

Final Report has ever acknowledged even though the documentary evidence was held by the PHSO for the best part of two years. Only recently have the PHSO concluded that they think, *'there is a significant possibility we may find failings in the Trust's management of Mr Bowdler's placement on the ICP'*. PACAC must consider why this issue is only to be addressed now some seven years after Mr Bowdler's placement on the death pathway?

On the same day as a PHSO Open Meeting (2/10/19), the case of Mr Nic Hart was the subject of a Health Service Journal article, under the heading, *'Ombudsman probes failings of its own investigation.'* It includes the fact that the HSJ *'understands the PHSO will examine its methodology, culture and performance'*.

I feel it is of the utmost importance that the public is properly informed about a culture which has clearly been contrary to that portrayed by the body itself, online, in their own literature and communicated from the PHSO panel at Open meetings.

#flawed-decisions #misuse-of-evidence #factual-inaccuracies #delay #poor-communication #trust #bias #no-effective-outcome #poor-case-management #external-advice #scoping-out-key-issues

J Kuma 2015 - 2019

My complaint against the CSA was first assigned to an investigator on 28 May 2015. After that, it was considered by 3 more investigators.

I'm very relieved to say that, after approximately four and a half years, it has finally been resolved in my favour, but only after an almighty battle and the involvement of solicitors on both sides. I am acutely aware that, had I not involved solicitors to threaten a judicial review application, my complaint would not have been successful, despite being completely justified. Whereas the PHSO is supposed to provide a relatively pain-free alternative to litigation, I have spent thousands of hours fighting my corner and am in no doubt that the time lost has taken its toll on me, my children and wider family.

In a nutshell, in 2012, the CSA and its solicitors were negligent in relation to the enforcement of a court order for sale in that, to my dismay, they sat back and failed to take any of the customary steps necessary to protect my position in relation to the sale proceeds. As a result of this negligence, I lost the arrears of child support that had accrued due to me over a period of many years. This loss was particularly devastating as I had been told by the CSA to expect imminent payment in circumstances where I had lost my own salary due to ill health, (lupus and fibromyalgia).

Initially, K M of the PHSO upheld my complaint - I was absolutely delighted when she contacted me to let me know the good news. This was in the summer of 2015. Although she did explain that the draft would have to be submitted to the CSA, she reassured me that there would have to be exceptional circumstances for it to be changed. Ironically, I thanked her for restoring my faith in the system, a faith that had been undermined by very poor prior experiences with both the independent case examiner as well as the local government ombudsman.

To my consternation, however, following the issue of a very robust draft report, first things went quiet and I then noticed that the tone of Ms M's subsequent email letters to me had changed completely. She repeatedly referred to the need to be fair to the CSA and explained that the CSA disagreed with the report. I was told that there would be a meeting between the CSA and the PHSO to which I was not invited. I realised immediately that the findings in the report were going to be reversed. In desperation, I requested my then MP, Gavin Barwell, to intervene before it happened, explaining to him that I felt that the CSA was leaning on the PHSO and that this was corrupt. However, his response was that he was of the opinion that there was nothing untoward going on and that I should just let matters take their course and apply for judicial review, should that become necessary. I tried to explain that judicial review would be unlikely to be a realistic option, but the truth is that Barwell simply had no appetite to fight the injustice I faced.

As I had predicted, the report was, indeed, changed to my detriment. I requested the notes of the meeting, but there weren't any. What there was, however, was evidence of a phone call between the CSA and PHSO at high level during which a decision was made to alter the PHSO's findings in relation to causation: Although the amended report recognised that mistakes had been made, it concluded that I had no proof that these mistakes had caused me loss. The bar had been raised so high that I could never have hoped to satisfy the new burden of proof that was being applied to my case. Unlike the CSA's, my objections were given short shrift and the report was finalised almost before I'd submitted them.

Luckily for me, when I was on the point of giving up, I found J B of Leigh Day & Co. He was sympathetic and came to my rescue by issuing a strong letter before action threatening judicial review proceedings on my behalf. As a result, the PHSO eventually backed down and agreed to consider my case afresh. (This is a very condensed version, as there was a great deal of work involved).

Unfortunately, however, the PHSO's agreement was just the beginning of a very-long winded process indeed. I had to wait for months for my case to be reassigned. Eventually, a new investigator, D W, got involved and had to spend time familiarising himself with the case. In fairness, he was very thorough and a good investigator. The only problem was that he left the PHSO in December 2016, before issuing a draft report. He did tell me, however, that his draft, draft report had almost been finalised. I received the impression that, although he wanted to uphold my complaint and disagreed with the CSA's arguments, the CSA's lack of cooperation was a major stumbling block.

And so, I had to wait again for a new investigator to take over. The next investigator was not great: she never seemed to get to grips with the case and my impression, rightly or wrongly, was that there was no movement at all during the nine months that she spent familiarising herself with the detail. Eventually, in November 2017, she announced that she, too, was leaving. It seemed to me that the PHSO was not taking its agreement to consider my complaint afresh very seriously.

Finally, in January 2018, C P took over. She was very professional in her approach, but there were numerous interminable delays due to the CSA continuing to object strenuously to the PHSO's findings in my favour, causing the draft, draft report to be amended by the PHSO on numerous occasions.

As I told C at the time, I felt that the PHSO were bending over backwards to accommodate the CSA who were threatening judicial review. C explained that the CSA would be more likely to comply with the PHSO's recommendations if they agreed with the report. By that stage, I was so frustrated with the whole thing that I insisted that, whether or not they complied, I just wanted the report finalised. However, the PHSO remained anxious to secure the CSA's cooperation, and, as Rob Behrens explained to me at a meeting, they simply could not risk another unsuccessful judicial review.

I suppose what I found most frustrating was that, although the CSA's objections were not valid, it was permitted to drag out the resolution of my complaint for so many years without sanction. Although I am grateful to have eventually received the money I'd lost, seven years after the event, its value has been significantly eroded by inflation, a factor that was not taken into account. Moreover, whilst I had understood that the CSA would have to pay interest, I have been offered a rate of just half a percent, considerably less than the judgement rate of 8% awarded by the courts. (The CSA got to determine the rate, as the PHSO omitted to stipulate it in its report). And, if I wish to challenge the rate, unfortunately, it means a new PHSO complaint and another battle.

The crux of the matter is that, even though, given the numerous mistakes it had made, the CSA did not have a compelling case for judicial review, the PHSO was so fearful of the CSA's threats that it seemed to feel quite unable to finalise matters without the CSA's cooperation, leaving me in a state of disillusionment and limbo for many years. For this reason, I am unable to recommend the process to others.

On a more positive note, I am told that the CMS, as it's now known, will henceforth be handling orders for sale differently. Hopefully, this will mean that fewer parents with care will be deprived of the arrears of child support due to them. Having said this, however, in my view, there needs to be fundamental, systemic, change at the CSA as, in my experience, it remains highly inefficient and, for the most part, unaccountable for its mistakes, which probably explains why so many are continuing to be made.

#flawed-decisions #misuse-of-evidence #factual-inaccuracies #delay #poor-communication #trust #bias #poor-case-management

Melanie Leahy: 2015 – 2019

Paper: Complaint to Parliamentary Health Service Ombudsman in pursuant

of failings in care by North Essex Partnership University Trust directly leading to the death of our son, Matthew James Leahy

on 15th November 2012 aged 20 yrs.

Matthew died unexpectedly seven days after being admitted under section to the Galleywood ward at the Linden Center, Chelmsford, Essex.

The circumstances of Matthew's death are documented and are harrowing in any event without the subsequent events. As a family thrown into a parent's nightmare, we were offered no support or any kind of advocacy to guide us through what to expect in the aftermath of our only child's death. No effort to assist our understanding of the processes and our own role during a time of huge grief and disorientation, whilst arranging the funeral; internal investigations by the Trust; the inquest; police investigations and ultimately the complaints process.

Seven years on and we are still not able to bring this matter to a satisfying close. Closure that will finally allow us to grieve in peace. In full knowledge of how and why our son died.

We believed in the inquest procedure, confident that it would provide the answers that we desperately needed to bring peace.

The inquest itself took over two years to be heard and only served to bring up more questions and expose the complete inadequacy of all investigations into Matthew's death. Investigations and reviews carried out by North Essex Partnership University Trust, Essex Police, Kent Police, Local Ombudsman, NMC, GMC etc all lacked substance and the inquest itself clarified that vital evidence was missing, some evidence had been destroyed, significant witnesses had not been interviewed or called to give evidence and some had not even been approached. Multiple freedom of information requests; repeated letters to the Trust, attending trust board meetings; repeatedly failed to provide ourselves, as Matthew's family, any reliable answers. In point of fact, there was an absolute lack of transparency in all engagement with ourselves.

What really happened to Matthew?

The investigations? The inquest? All these had succeeded in providing was more questions but more insidiously pointed to a culture of dangerous incompetence and cover up.

How do we find out what happened to our only child?

We were signposted to escalate our complaints to the Parliamentary Health Service Ombudsman. Despite our recent experiences we still had faith that the office of Ombudsman would ensure we were treated fairly. Our complaint was accepted as meeting the threshold for investigation by the Ombudsman on the 13th March 2015. Just six weeks after the inquest. Almost five years have passed and the concluded Ombudsman's report into our complaint has not even been published.

It has been made abundantly clear to us that we should be very grateful as many families don't even get their complaints accepted. Furthermore, our complaint was upheld, we had a success. But we are no closer to the explanation of how our son died whilst under section in a place of safety, in spite of our gratitude.

To date, despite clear errors, safety recommendations that had been constantly ignored, systems and procedures designed to limit risk not being practiced, paperwork not being completed, lies and cover ups, which continue TO THIS DAY- not one individual or organisation has been held accountable for our son's AVOIDABLE death.

Would I recommend the PHSO process to a friend, or anyone else for that matter?

The answer would be an unreserved, resounding NO. It has been a long, painfully emotional road. Riddled with denial, confusion, bias and delay. We gave up taking phone calls from the allotted case worker. We found important facts discussed during calls were at times missing, ignored or taken out of context. Each time leaving us exhausted, deflated and upset, questioning why this process was draining and not helping? A cynic could be forgiven for thinking it was deliberate. Weeks would pass with no contact and then communication from the case officer would arrive on poignant days such as birthdays, the anniversary of Matthew's death or before Christmas. If this was simply coincidence, and we do give the benefit of doubt, then we would urge the PHSO office to be wary of particular case dates in the course of their enquiries. It is a small consideration that makes a huge impact.

Throughout the investigation clinical advisors were asked to give their professional opinion on certain issues. Although we were confident that they were in possession of all the evidence, many of the professional responses would be very different. Different clinicians were asked to comment on the same point and their answers conflicted with each other. Some being in our favour and some being in favour of the trust. We, as a family, had to fight for each and every favourable finding written in this report. Why was that? Why were we not able to trust due process? Particularly at a time of grieving. It is appalling, but does it serve the intention to force families to give up?

In January 2015 the inquest verdict concluded an Open Narrative.

A Coroner's inquest finds Matthew, *'was subject to a series of multiple failings and missed opportunities over a prolonged period of time by those entrusted with his care.'* The jury found that relevant policies and procedures were not adhered to impacting on Matthew's over all care and well-being leading up to his death.'

"over a prolonged period of time"

Yet the PHSO only agreed to investigate the last seven to eight days of our son's life. Considering the coroners comments why did the PHSO choose to ignore the failings that triggered Matthew's admission under the Mental Health Act? After all, it was a legal mechanism that deprived my son of his liberty to choose to be admitted into hospital, an admittance that ultimately began a trail of events that led to his death. Maybe the PHSO decided the terms of reference for this enquiry on the basis that there were no failings and therefore no lessons to be learned from the method of Matthew's admission? Nevertheless, in response to our protests we were told, "It was not within our remit" / "Outside the scope of your complaint" / "You'll need to submit another complaint". Yet we have never been offered the evidence as to why the question was not within the

PHSOs remit or why it was outside the scope of our complaint or why we would have to submit another complaint about the exact same incident?

It did not take too long to realise that the objective role of the PHSO was in reality strongly biased towards the trust and therefore not objective in any sense of the word. If we wanted misinformation changed or facts added we had to provide unequivocal evidence which, we now know, was readily shared with the trust. We were never, at any time, privy to any evidence provided by the Trust to the PHSO.

In June 2019 the PHSO presented a smaller report of our case to Parliament- Missed Opportunities. Our comments for press release were highly censored and might as well have been written by the Ombudsman himself. Crucially, those comments had to be made without seeing or reading the actual report. If nothing else this gives rise to mistrust about the process. Being asked to comment on a report without seeing it.

The Ombudsman said he agreed with all our points. The truth was he had agreed with everything he had chosen to investigate. Most of which had been covered in previous investigations. I repeat. Which had been covered in previous investigations. No doubt to be covered in future investigations.

With no imminent conclusion in sight.

Not one member of staff or witness has ever been interviewed under oath by any organisation or governing body regarding the events that led to Matthew's avoidable death.

Mr Behrens surprised reporters by being so openly critical and damning of North Essex Partnership University Trust. On camera he said, " how the family had been through review after review,". Yet despite recognising our struggles, he announced he was initiating yet another review and He ordered a government review in June 2019. It is now January 2020 and that review is still waiting for a start date.

Shortly before Christmas 2019 we received communication from Mr Behrens stating publication of Matthew's full report in the early New Year, as soon as confirmation of the NHSI review lead has received.

Another review, another investigation, another enquiry, another organisation, another government department, another diversion, another report, another paper shuffle. Another, another, another. Meanwhile another death and another death and another death.

How many deaths is each report worth? How many deaths before the recommendations of the reports and the reviews and the enquiries and the investigations are put into practice? Is there a limit? A magic number? How much more procrastination to get some straight forward answers? How much more detouring to finally arrive at where you started? **And how many more will die?**

We were pleasantly surprised that Mr Behrens went on National News in support of our call for a Public Inquiry into Matthew's death. We are also beyond frustrated that the Parliamentary Ombudsman does not have power to call a Statutory Public Inquiry or indeed even the power to enforce its own multiple recommendations onto the Health Trust.

We have lost count of the action plans, assurances, audits, inspections, processes that have been put in place by the Trust over the years, only for similar deaths to continue to this day.

'Multiple policies had not been adhered to'
or even initiated but the PHSO failed to make one single recommendation regarding improving trust policy management. We, as a family, submitted a list of suggested recommendations, which were ignored. We requested what training ward staff had received, and the PHSO responded "not in our remit".

There are many inconsistencies within the report but we have no power to respond. Learning and change is not happening fast to prevent more deaths but the PHSO has no enforcement powers. So, the question arises

What is the point of the Parliamentary Health Service Ombudsman?

After trusting due process to deliver answers, accountability and lessons in avoiding similar incidents, we have come to the conclusion that due process is at worst not effective and at best, deliberately obstructive.

Matthew is one of multiple deaths on psychiatric wards across the U.K. that are continuing to happen due to the same and similar circumstances. In order to force a public enquiry we have worked tirelessly to obtain 100,000 signatures for a UK government petition. Notwithstanding a curtailed closing date due to the general election, the petition collected 105,580 UK signatories.

We and all the petitioners wait with anticipation for the opportunity to have this case and the call for a Statutory Public Inquiry debated in Parliament, not just for Matthew, but for every person who has died in similar circumstances before and after his death.

We will be heard and every subsequent death will be laid at the feet of those who could have made a difference but chose to do nothing.

#flawed-decisions #misuse-of-evidence #factual-inaccuracies #delay #poor-communication #trust #bias #no-effective-outcome #poor-case-management #external-advice #scoping-out-key-issues

K. Scott: 2018 - ongoing

I first contacted the Parliamentary Health Service Ombudsman on 29th May 2018, this was following advice from my MP. I had spent since 2015 exhausting a farcical complaints process in regards to a grievance with my son's former Academy School. There had been serious failings to my son's education, wellbeing and breaches to policies by the school between 2012-2017, this included Safeguarding, Data breaches, and significantly suspected malpractice in regards to the GCSEs in summer of 2017. All these issues were reported to the ESFA, OFSTED, OFQUAL, NCTL, OCR, AQA, Local Authority and ICO. I had exhausted these government and public bodies and yet nobody took robust action against the academy school for failings and misconduct so I had no choice but to turn to the PHSO for help.

The PHSO told me that they could NOT look into my case as a whole, and I would have to separate each department in to separate complaints. This was totally ridiculous because that would mean I would need to send in nearly 4 separate cases. They even stated to me they had ' NO REMIT 'to investigate the Academy school , so I had no choice but to water down my son's complex case into 2 separate cases.

Case 1) was complaint against OFQUAL letter dated 29th May 2018. I was complaining that OFQUAL had dismissed my son's case from 30th Nov 2017 to the 2nd May 2018 OFQUAL complaints procedure stated that they could look into potential or actual malpractice by someone involved with an exam or assessment. I had reported a number of my son's teachers for exactly this, because we strongly believed some of his GCSE coursework had been marked with prejudice or sabotaged, this contributed to him failing over half his GCSEs. However, OFQUAL quickly tried to dismiss me by stating that they had 'no remit 'to investigate the Academy school, which was in contradiction to their own complaint's procedure. Instead they referred me back to the exam boards OCR and AQA.

On the 28th Nov 2017 I was contacted by AQA who promised an investigation into these matters (Geography / Business studies / English Oral. However, to this day I have never received an outcome to that investigation.

AQA stated in a SAR request dated 18 / 1/ 2019 that based on JCQs 13.2 suspected Malpractice the investigation is confidential between the individual involved and the awarding body.

Clearly by this statement my son has been denied answers to the investigation and this is just farcical, and outrageous !!

In regards to OCR I have seen no clear evidence that they had investigated the academy for not complying with reviews of marking so in turn I believe OCR failed to comply with their own complaint's procedure. From the evidence I have, OCR gave misleading answers in their response in July 2018 when asked why they haven't remarked/reviewed my son's GCSE Science coursework they stated to me this was not possible because a review of marking had not been requested. This was not true because a sample had been sent to them in Sept 2017 by the Academy (have evidence in writing). There was another twist because my son's GCSE coursework was not included in that sample sent back to OCR, even though I had requested this in writing to the school on the (5th sept 2017), furthermore the School had led me to believe (in writing 13th Sept / 22nd Sept 2017) that my son's science coursework was part of the sample remarked/moderated externally by OCR. On the 15th Nov 2017 in a SAR request OCR confirmed that they had never seen my son's science coursework, because he was not included in the sample for moderation or review.

OFQUAL stated to me in their response dated 9th march 2018 that they "could not compel OCR to remark the affected candidates work nor did they find any breaches to their conditions". (OFQUAL) from the letter dated 29th May 2018 the PHSO responded to me on the 14th June 2018 stating they were awaiting a case officer to look at my case. They contacted me again on the 7th September 2018 stating that after reviewing all the available information we have decided to NOT consider your complaint further.

I was shocked and upset at this decision by the PHSO and I felt totally let down so I wrote back to them and asked for a review of our case on the 17th Sept 2018. I did not hear anything back from the PHSO regarding a request for review against OFQUAL until May 7th 2019 this is approximately 8months later. In this response the 2nd case officer dismissed my request for a further review stating "we have considered the information you have given us and ultimately we do not believe this meets our review criteria". They went on to state that they understood my complaint but they had found OFQUAL considered my complaint appropriately they also stated significantly "we were satisfied and remain satisfied that OFQUAL did investigate what they were able to within their remit. Additionally, as OFQUAL did not identify any issues with OCR's moderation process they were unable to tell OCR to remark your son's work." The case officer finished the letter by stating that therefore we will not be taking further action and that marks the end of their entire complaint procedure. So, it took for complaint (1) a total of 12months and 2 case officers to dismiss my complaint without a review.

In regards to complaint (1) against (OFQUAL) I have on the 24th OCT 2019 written back to the PHSO and asked them to reconsider my case because it has been brought back to my attention through the press that indeed OCR were reprimanded and AQA were fined for non-compliance of exam regulations in regards to reviews of marking and moderation in the summer of 2017 and 2018, this clearly contradicts not only the PHSO response to me but also OFQUAL and OCR. On 30th March 2020 I finally received a much predicted response from the PHSO letter that I sent to them in Nov 2019 regarding OCR/OFQUAL. The SAME case officer replying to my letter of complaint about the way in which SHE dismissed me back in May 2019. Great work being able to investigate complaints against yourself? They clearly ignored AGAIN all the evidence I put to them.

In regards to complaint (2) against the ESFA (letter dated 29th July 2018) , the PHSO responded back to me and referred me back to the ESFA stating I needed to complete a further 3 stage complaints process at the ESFA, so they were not ready for my case yet, I wrote back again to the PHSO on the 7th Jan 2019 after completing yet another farcical process whereby the ESFA ignored the evidence presented to them and went as far as giving misleading answers in their responses. They did however partly uphold my complaint but failed to fully admit to their own failings.

The PHSO did not respond to me till I received a phone call from a case officer in (May 2019), sadly at that time my late father was terminally ill so they closed my case and suggested I took it up with them again when I was ready.

I did contact the PHSO again in (September 2019) I received an email from a case officer on the (28th Oct 2019) outlining a summary of my case that has been put forward but is still ongoing. There are at least 12 bullet points against the ESFA, but I will try to summarise this in short :

- Incorrectly closed my case in (2017)
- incorrectly stated that I had not followed the academy's complaints procedure
- misconstrued LORD AGNEWs remarks in his letter dated (23rd May 2018)
- failed to review my case because if they had then they would have seen that the academy had NOT followed their own policies or procedures

- failed to sign post me to the ESFA own 3 stage complaints procedure
- failed to evidence their own learning and actions against the academy school
- failed to demonstrate any accountability or regulation of the Academy
- failed to investigate the new evidence regarding the panel hearing held at the Academy on 18th June 2018.

In regards to complaint (2) (ESFA) I am still awaiting a case officer to see if they are going to investigate this part of my complaint, but already I am sceptical whether my son's case is going to be transparently investigated if at all. I believe The Academy School, regulators and exam boards mentioned in our case, have let us down considerably and failed my son. All I have ever asked for is accountability and an apology to the failings mentioned and evidence that they have learnt from this case, changed procedures so this never happens to another family.

I believe that the service I have received from the PHSO in regards to complaint (1) (OFQUAL) has been biased, not helpful in bringing about a resolution to my son's case.

I would also say that I do not fully understand what the remit of the PHSO is because I do not feel that it is fully explained. LORD AGNEW PARLIAMENTARY UNDER SECRETARY OF STATE FOR SCHOOLS, suggested in his response letter dated the (23rd May 2018 to my MP) that I could take my complaint to the PHSO for their review, however on the 1st OCT 2018 (letter) the PHSO confirmed that they had no remit to investigate the Academy School, so why was I advised to take my complaint there in the first instance?

In fact, in pursuing my son's case, it became evident that the regulators or public bodies that I had complained to, had no clear remit or no remit at all to investigate the Academy School. This has resulted in the Academy being only answerable to themselves and still unaccountable.

Would I recommend the PHSO to anyone I am afraid I would have to say no. Don't waste nearly 2 years of your time and energy.

#flawed-decisions #misuse-of-evidence #factual-inaccuracies #delay #poor-communication #trust #bias #no-effective-outcome #poor-case-management #scoping-out-key-issues

Anon:– 2019 ongoing

PHSO

Mr Behrens, even if contacted directly deploys the 'ignore the correspondent'. Feedback after an investigation only goes to the case worker. This means that nothing goes high enough to ensure change.

There is no facility to give feedback via the PHSO web site, no doubt intentionally.

Even if there is a partial uphold which I still believe in my case should have been a full uphold, the PHSO has no legal powers to enforce. They state on their web site that they take injustices seriously and can take action as a last resort.

In my case the escalation wasn't robust enough.

I am still waiting to find out from PHSO what 'working with the Trust on compliance' means and to date haven't received a response.

The case worker in my case commented on Duty of Candour which an operational Manager confirmed the PHSO didn't have authority to do.

This Manager also told me that the template used for the final report wasn't the standard template. She also told me that there were Quality Assurance issues during my investigation.

PHSO weren't on the ball when their 4-week deadline for the Trust to respond expired and only intervened because I held their feet to the fire.

So over two months later and the Trust still hasn't complied and PHSO did reject the initial response at 9 weeks. The Trust "action plan" was what they should be doing already and nullified any CQC monitoring which is why it was rejected.

PHSO needs legal powers of enforcement but whether, like the CQC, they would even apply them I very much doubt.

CQC

I would also add that the Patients Association need to be aware of the failings at CQC. They adopt an ignore and dismiss attitude and this includes Prof Edward Baker, Chief Inspector of Hospitals and Mr Ian Trenholm Chief Executive.

CQC have all the evidence they need to prosecute for Duty of Candour, FPPR and section 12 but do nothing. They in effect allow unsafe service delivery causing harm or even death to continue.

I was told that a local team would be looking in to possible breach of Duty of Candour but they remain silent when I ask what that means and what is happening.

Similarly, I was told they would monitor changes as a result of the PHSO report and again when I asked what that entailed they remain silent.

CQC need to start getting a much flack as PHSO because they are the regulator of the NHS (allegedly)

GMC

Hide behind the law and fall back on their expert's advice even if it differs from the PHSO report with a Consultant in the same speciality being used as the GMC did. They set the bar for investigation so high that even when they receive multiply complaints (as in the Paterson case) they don't investigate.

After rule 12 there is only judicial reviews within a month which stiches up the process for those without means to go there.

They said that the PHSO report wasn't new evidence!

I would ask that the Patients Association is aware that I would now take the stance and advise anyone just don't go there unless you have an inquest. Everything takes too long which is deliberate. Based on my experience I wouldn't even advise anyone to make a complaint to an NHS organisation as they just spin and obfuscate anyway to suit their agenda so no answers are given.

The NHS is now a Goliath which is unaccountable because of the failures of CQC and PHSO which means that scandals will continue all with common themes because even if you demonstrate failures the NHS Trust doesn't need to do anything and, in my case, hasn't.

The Patients Association should be calling these scandals out and concentrating on these instead of all the other pies they have fingers in as per their web site which they don't need to do. This means that P A appears to have lost its focus and is too cosy with the

NHS.

The laws and processes that are there to protect people don't and aren't worth burning!

To the NHS, CQC and PHSO, harm or deaths even are just collateral damage.

Duty of Candour is regulation 20 (sections 2 &3) that is law within the Health and Social Care Act and is under the jurisdiction of the CQC. It comes in to play if something goes wrong in care and should determine how the NHS responds in an open and transparent manner. Most Trusts have a policy that covers DoC but in my case the Trust conveniently decided, with no dialogue, that I came to no harm to absolve themselves of having to engage DoC and also not having to report a notifiable patient safety incident.

DoC covers physical and psychological harm.

PHSO had evidence that I came to harm but ignored it because the Trust said there was no harm so they took their word over my written evidence from a Consultant. Quelle surprise!

I was told PHSO don't have the authority to comment on Duty of Candour but they did in my final report and stated that DoC didn't apply because of no harm. This means that PHSO are straying well out of their remit which is dangerous territory and could compromise investigations.

When I got back to CQC they said that their local team would look into a potential breach of DoC but nothing more has been heard about that. My guess is that CQC don't want to act against their flagship Trust. DoC came into place after a long campaign by Will Powell who discovered that doctors had no legal requirement to tell the truth as he pursued justice for the avoidable death of his son Robbie Powell. Since then CQC haven't prosecuted one Trust and fined Bradford Trust a paltry £1200 for delayed apology to the parents of a child who died as a result of poor care.

So, by commenting about DoC and saying it didn't apply, PHSO are giving a Trust a get out jail card to vindicate their lack of action. CQC, by not properly enforcing DoC are allowing all sorts of nefarious behaviour by the NHS.

Over 4 months after PHSO produced their final report the Trust is on the 3rd action plan which awaits PHSO approval. This means that for over 31 months no change to service provision has been put in place to protect other patients. Harm to patients appears to be just collateral damage.

#flawed-decisions #misuse-of-evidence #factual-inaccuracies #delay #poor-communication #trust #bias #no-effective-outcome #scoping-out-key-issues

Anon:- 2013 – Present Day *(active PHSO work)*

I am a diagnosed autistic female. **Sussex Partnership NHS Foundation Trust** *(SPFT)* twice failed to diagnose my Asperger's syndrome, following provably substandard, non-compliant assessments by two consecutive colleagues from the same ASD clinic. When I was privately diagnosed, SPFT refused to provide me support that I am legally entitled to in accordance with the Autism Act 2009, the Autism Strategy 2010 and statutory guidance. They also committed harm against a vulnerable adult according to the Government definition, by coercing me onto medication they knew I didn't need. I had a private ASD diagnostic report which differentially assessed me for mental ill-health and stated I had none and

SPFT had several copies of this report. I had bad side-effects from the medication. There has been a lot of serious detriment to me in various ways from their negligence and cover-up. It's too much to list it here, but I have proof of it all. I first went to PHSO in 2013, with the assistance of an advocate from a well-known national charity. Although the original issue occurred in 2009, I didn't become aware of the problem *(i.e. the assessments being substandard)* until 2012, for which I provided PHSO with cast iron evidence.

I fully expected recognition of what I had been wrongly put through by SPFT and that justice and remedy would be provided by PHSO. I naively thought that's what PHSO were there to do and that they would be honest and objective. I was already exhausted and overwhelmed by the NHS complaints process, which is why I sought the assistance of an advocate to submit my complaint. At no time did PHSO offer me any reasonable adjustments and I found out later they had committed direct disability discrimination against me and abused my human rights.

I was shocked and beyond distressed that PHSO stated that my complaint was out-of-time, even though I had provided evidence it was not *(along with a supporting letter from my national charity advocate)* and the NHS would not have investigated my complaint if it had been, as they also have a 12-month limitation. The PHSO caseworker used her arbitrary opinion saying "I must have known" there was a problem. I am autistic and I had no idea, this was not only unacceptable to say to anyone, but very discriminatory to say it to me and the evidence proving otherwise along with the supporting letter seemed to not exist, as far as she was concerned. I appealed the re-scoping and they reviewed the decision, but told me it was unchanged. So, I had to go ahead with the new scope or have no investigation. The new scope meant they could avoid looking at my evidence. Because I couldn't quite grasp the fullness of what they had done, I was still sending extra evidence throughout the investigation, which I realised much later they were disregarding. My complaint was not upheld.

False statements were made in my final report. I requested a review, but this got me nowhere, these reviews I have found out are a sham. They just double-check they followed a process in the investigation, they don't look at logic, evidence, substance, fairness, detriment or anything in how they reached the decision, so they just say they got it right. It's about defending themselves, not upholding truth. By the time this process was going on, I had also obtained **incontrovertible medical evidence** of my diagnosis. So once the review wasn't upheld, I went back to PHSO to start a new complaint and they said the NHS had to investigate it first. I went back to the Trust, who refused to investigate my new evidence *(to this day it has never been investigated).* So, I went back to PHSO with my complaint. They then lost my complaint and I found they were filing communications from me in "post review" and ignoring them! When the confusion was resolved, they agreed to investigate. Then they changed their minds and lied to me saying they hadn't meant that, using a convoluted explanation that clearly was nonsensical.

I did raise service complaints during the whole mess, but of course they just defended themselves and as I hadn't uncovered all the evidence yet that I later did through Subject Access Requests, even though I knew what they had done was categorically wrong, I couldn't prove all of it.

After that, they passed my closed complaint to customer care team to deal with. Because I persisted, they obtained a 2nd clinical advice. But they still told me nothing had changed. I started doing Subject Access Requests and got a copy of the clinical advice. It was worthless because the adviser had not used any benchmark standard, yet PHSO had still accepted and relied on the advice and I would never have known, had I not got a copy. It was also full of completely ridiculous, untrue statements defending the NHS. I found so much evidence in SARs that prove PHSO are corrupt and what they have done.

PHSO admitted in writing they would not have said my complaint was out-of-time at the present time *(but still have never investigated my complaint, just a fraudulent alternative)*. I found evidence of PHSO's various lies. My advocate had suggested on the complaint form that the NHS Trust should be referred to CQC because they were ignoring NICE Guidance *(which has been tested in court must be followed)* and PHSO ignored this entirely. I found out that in my original complaint, SPFT had breached two different procedural manuals and PHSO had failed to identify this. When I contacted PHSO about it, they completely ignored this fact. I discovered PHSO had made false statements to the clinical adviser and omitted adviser statements that would throw doubt on the NHS and support my complaint, from both 1st and 2nd clinical advice. I discovered the caseworker made false statements in her "proposal not to investigate" form, completed after they had told me they would investigate, to shut the complaint down. The statements were directly contradicted and proven false in PHSO's "review proposal sheet". The 1st clinical adviser was unqualified for the job and from their own bios and/or qualifications so were the 2nd and 3rd. I found proof of collusion between SPFT and PHSO. PHSO made discriminatory comments on file about me *(see 'adverse opinions' on that link, ironically refusing to uphold my complaint of failure to diagnose ASD, whilst using my ASD traits against me!)*. PHSO has throughout, also ignored the fact that the NHS Trust had breached the NHS Constitution autism laws, my human rights, NHS rules, NHS NICE and more – all listed here: [19]

PHSO has just obtained a 3rd clinical advice because I showed the 2nd one was void. I requested a copy and have seen the person has very dubious qualifications that don't appear to be correct for the task, but worse, it's the wrong type of adviser as PHSO has hoodwinked me and tied me up with involving me in the process, so that I didn't notice it's someone in the wrong field! My new complaint was based on my medical evidence, not the clinical evidence *(which was already more than enough)*. So, it's yet another pointless advice. They have kept my

---

[19] https://brightonnhsfailings.wixsite.com/spftfailuresexposed/laws-broken

complaint closed all this time but are still doing active work on it. But J R, RaFT Operations Manager who is dealing with my case, stated before I saw a copy of the advice that it changed nothing. Six years and counting, of PHSO hell. If you want to read more, I have put it all online with evidence, the page specific to PHSO is here: [20]

Rob Behrens personally reviewed my case and sent me a letter with false statements in. I replied in detail in a 20-page report proving what he said wrong, he has not replied.

You will see from the website, PHSO has also committed gross unlawful predetermination, committed perjury, breached their own 6 principles of good complaint handling, refused to quash my report even though it meets **all** the criteria, breached NHS England's 'Ask, Listen, Do' even though they are a

---

[20] https://brightonnhsfailings.wixsite.com/spftfailuresexposed/single-post/PHSO-Lies-and-Systemic- Corruption

lead project partner of it and failed to action Section 15(1)(e) of their statutory duties as regards SPFT's behaviour. SPFT have committed criminal acts and so have PHSO.

I would advise any member of the public to **sue** the public body rather than go to PHSO. They are so corrupt it's inexpressible, you only have to read Google and Trust Pilot reviews. They are a cruel organisation, who care nothing for evidence, truth, morals or fairness. It is a mistake going to them for any reason whatsoever, other than to have the statistics of how many people are complaining. Their uphold rate is embarrassing and we the public, pay them to do this to us. They have caused me an enormous amount of work, distress, and detriment to my health, which had already been ruined by the NHS. I am now doubly disabled and SPFT continue to fail me because PHSO has helped them.

#flawed-decisions #misuse-of-evidence #factual-inaccuracies #delay #poor-communication #trust #bias #no-effective-outcome #poor-case-management #external-advice #scoping-out-key-issues

Deborah Bunn:- 2016 – 2019

My mum Patricia Bunn's 6-year Care Home residency was terminated without warning on 18th December 2015 during a meeting called to discuss concerns I had raised in a feedback survey on 21st November 2015.

Mum had suffered an unexplained injury just 2 weeks before this meeting. When I arrived, blood was dripping from her mouth, a visiting nurse checked she was OK but after she left I saw this bruising. My sister and her son came, we waited all day for an emergency GP.

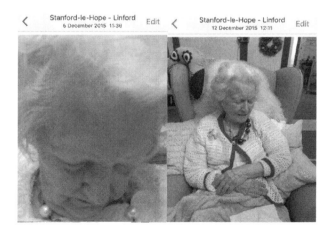

I had specifically asked by email on 2nd December *for the meeting's agenda and confirmation of who will be in attendance.*

S M, Registered Manager said *"Areas for discussion will be complaints / concerns raised, some of which you feel are repeated. Attending will be our Directors P C, N J, C D (Care Administrator) and myself."*

Also, on the 27th November the manager said *"both Directors have confirmed that they will be available at 12 noon on the 18th December so we look forward to seeing you both"*.

We were not told that a Carer would also in be in attendance or that Notice *would* or *could* be served - there is a 28 Day Notice to Quit clause in their contract.

Neither my sister and I, nor Thurrock CCG, who were funding mum's care at the time, were given any warning that her 6+ year residency was at risk.

Thurrock CCG weren't even invited to this meeting.

On 27th November the manager said: *"Due to the nature of these and previous concerns we feel it is necessary to meet before Pat's Continuing Healthcare Review"*.

Mum's residency was terminated at this meeting and an hour later Thurrock CCG carried out their review. The manager signed to say Merrie Loots were managing her Healthcare needs.

I contacted the CQC for help the next day, 19th Dec 2015 but was told they don't investigate individual or contractual issues. I was advised to contact Safe Guarding. Unbeknown to us Merrie Loots was actually under CQC investigation at this time.

We requested mediation. After the Xmas holiday on 6th January 2016 Merrie Loots Farm management and owners arranged for a meeting in the tiny bedroom of a recently deceased relative (next door to mum's). Our CCG assessor attended but only the Care Home took minutes.

Thurrock CCG organized a 2nd mediation meeting at their offices on 27th January 2016 but Merrie Loots refused to mediate and this was recorded at the beginning of the minutes. This evidence was ignored by PHSO.

Mum was denied legal representation. Mum was not examined or proclaimed fit to move by a medical professional. She was 88 with late stage dementia, unable to walk, talk or feed herself.

We practiced Contented Dementia - The Special Method is a lifelong, positive approach to managing Dementia and Alzheimer's. Routine, repetition and familiarity were of utmost importance to us. We had paid for founder Penny Garner to speak at Merrie Loots Farm 6 months before mum moved in in 2009. Merrie Loots said they agreed with these philosophies and would implement them in mum's care.

But Mum's wishes were disregarded. Her End of Life Care Plan ignored. Merrie Loots' promise of a home for life was not honoured.

On 23rd February 2016 mum was forced to leave everything that was familiar, her home and those who knew and understood her. She died 7 weeks later on 12th April 2016.

I sought the PHSO's help in February 2016 before mum was forced to leave, after reading then Deputy Ombudsman Mick Martin's blog about the barriers the elderly face when they need to complain about the NHS.

But a Final Decision was made 30th Sept 2016, 24 hrs after my response to the draft report requesting evidence, the day before new CEO Amanda Campbell started.

I engaged a leading Public Law Solicitor and the PHSO apologized. I was promised a thorough, evidence-based reinvestigation but PHSO dismissed the evidence.

Emails dated 17th November revealed CQC were investigating concerns almost identical to mine at the time. They were discovered in mum's file when we requested Full Disclosure of her care home records. Someone else thought the same as me.

I had raised almost identical concerns only 5 days later on 21st November 2015.

Merrie Loots claimed my behaviour was the cause of the termination but there is not one email or letter to me, in the 6 years of mum's residency supporting this. PHSO refused to consider the breach of mum's Human Rights in the reinvestigation:

PHSO cited Merrie Loots' minutes of a meeting 4 YEARS earlier that was called to discuss our concerns about staffing levels. But PHSO refused to consider our response that Thurrock Social Services had attended and there was no mention of this in their summary of the same meeting on 15th February 2012

I should also add that my name was mentioned more times than my mother's in the Ombudsman's Final Report. Throughout the report I was the focus of their attack.

PHSO said Merrie Loots Farm failed to act in line with NHS Values and the Ombudsman's own Principles of Good Administration but *in their view, even if they had acted correctly the outcome would "most likely" have been the same.* After 3 years and 2 investigations my complaint was not upheld.

Amanda Campbell and Rob Behrens had a chance to put this right, to ensure *The Patient* comes first in everything the NHS does but they let mum and all vulnerable, elderly Care Home residents down.

If my complaint had been upheld the Ombudsman would be admitting to their own maladministration and possible liability for my legal costs. The CQC took no action against Merrie Loots and awarded them a Good Rating.

A precedent has been set that condones care homes in the private sector evicting residents without due process and their wellbeing the priority, purely because a relative raised concerns, or considered too involved in their care, or simply not liked.

I trusted that the PHSO would act independently in line with their own Principles and with my mother the priority but believe they failed in their duty to thoroughly and impartially investigate. In not protecting and preserving a person's basic Human Rights and dignity are the PHSO not violating them too?

#flawed-decisions #misuse-of-evidence #factual-inaccuracies #delay #poor-communication #trust #bias #no-effective-outcome #poor-case-management #scoping-out-key-issues

Editor's note: There is something of an Ombudsmen's club where each supports the other by stating that their results are 'in keeping' with 'best practice' across the board. The sad truth is that all Ombudsmen systems work against the citizen as can be seen by the following two cases.

Mary Gould:– mother of Conall: NIPSO complaint

On the 28th February 2018 an online complaint to NIPSO (Northern Ireland Public Service Ombudsman) was submitted, this followed advice from an NHS Trust who had been involved in the care of our 21-year-old son prior to his death on 13th February 2017. Our complaint had not been resolved through internal processes and it was never likely to have been due to the nature of the complaint and what had occurred at inquest, therefore it was merely a formality waiting for the trust to advise us they had exhausted all avenues and the Ombudsman was the final arbiter in this process.

To add context, due to our perceived failings in our son's care we sought legal advice from three separate solicitor firms, we were told categorically that the trust did not have a case to answer by means of civil litigation, I was always sure they did, with this in mind we had no alternative but to take our case to the Ombudsman.

On 10th May 2018 we received a letter from the Ombudsman's office advising us that our complaint had been accepted for investigation and that we would receive a further response detailing the Scope of their investigation within the next two weeks. On 31st May 2018 we received a letter outlining the scope of the investigation, it included all we had complained about and indeed the scope was broad, including the care received and the way in which the Trust responded to us following our son's death.

Over the coming months we attended meetings with the investigating officer (IO), additional evidence was provided by us and we were advised that independent expert reports had been agreed as part of the investigation. During this time more information came to light regarding the care our son had received, hospital policies we were not aware of and records that had previously been withheld. Slowly and through my own investigation I became aware of anomalies in my son's records and after transcribing the Inquest myself became fully aware that the truth had not been told. I had not attended the Inquest myself mainly due to grief but also having trust and a belief there would be an honest hearing, I was wrong. I made the investigating officer aware that I knew what had occurred at inquest and the validity of some of the records.

During the meetings there was an area of our sons care that I can only describe as being brushed aside despite the wide scope of the investigation, to me it was this very action that set off a catalogue of errors, a catalyst to a series of events that eventually lead to our son's death, but we were explicitly told by the IO that this action would not have affected the outcome. This never sat well with me and was always at the forefront of my mind.

We have obviously complained to many regulators however the response (in writing so can be evidenced) from one took me by surprise, we had been told by the IO previously that they had no input into regulator's investigations when I submitted information from one of them, however one regulator responded to us by stating they had contacted the IO in our case and he had no concerns about a particular practitioner. I found this quite odd after what he had told us, it was from this moment that I lost trust in this process and did not feel that the investigation was honest, open or transparent.

We attended a meeting on 26th March 2019, we were sure the investigation was coming to a close, the IO advised that there were systemic failings in my son's care, it was at this meeting that I disclosed to the IO I intended to make an application to the Attorney General in England to have the original inquest quashed, he advised that he hoped the report would be helpful in our pursuit of this, he advised that a draft report was anticipated to be ready at the end of April 2019, in keeping with their own target of 50 weeks.

On 9th May 2019 and still no draft report. I was asked if I could share my transcript of the inquest with the Ombudsman, I advised that I didn't feel comfortable sharing it without running it past the Coroner, besides the Ombudsman had a copy of the inquest CD for quite some time before returning it to us, what value would a copy of the inquest meticulously transcribed by myself have at this stage? The inquest was not being investigated (of course it wasn't), the only organisation that would benefit from this transcript would be the Trust in light of our intention to apply to the Attorney General. I questioned at this point, if there would be a hold up with the draft, I was advised it was in hand and would be available shortly.

May and June passed, no report, we were advised that there had been a significant increase in workload and several reports were concluding at the same time, but they were progressing with the draft. End of July arrived and I decided I would avail of an independent expert report myself, after forwarding all information to the expert I received a report two weeks later, it was evident there were many failings in my son's care. I approached our Solicitor with this report in late August, he then contacted our independent expert in October where he stated unequivocally that the one area we had been steered away from was in fact negligent under Tort.

At the end of November feeling quite incensed that the draft report had not made an appearance I emailed the IO and wondered if the intention was to postpone this report until after the 3-year statute of limitation. I was asked what my intentions were and I advised that we were considering our options, not satisfied with my response I was quoted several parts of the Ombudsman's act and asked again what my intentions were, our solicitor responded and advised that we did indeed have a legal case in relation to negligence but in view of the Ombudsman's report being in the final stages it ought to be completed.

Saturday 21st December 2019 we received a letter from the deputy Ombudsman with NIPSO advising us they were discontinuing the investigation, one quote reads "While this decision was made on the basis of the information available at assessment stage, the case law in this area is clear and there is a continuing duty on the Ombudsman to keep under review throughout an investigation both the availability and suitability of an alternate legal remedy, having regard to the particular circumstances of a case". Why then, through the process of the investigation were we not informed that we could find resolution through the courts? They had exclusive access to the records, Coroners file, Serious adverse file and the IO had been a human rights solicitor (Google is a wonderful search engine if you know where to look and can throw up all sorts of interesting data) surely they would have known? Why did they allow so much time to elapse? 8 months after the draft was due for release, they have dropped the investigation.

We have been advised that learning from this case will be shared with the Trust and RQIA (CQC) but not with family, we were also advised that bringing a complaint to the Ombudsman is not meant to act as a platform for litigation, I suggest they take that up with the body complained about who referred us to the Ombudsman and after this body had ensured closure of other alternative avenues due to the actions they took post the death of our son, the way we were treated at the time and following his death and how the Coroner was misled.

I would not recommend anyone to use the Ombudsman service, I can clearly see their purpose and it is not to serve the public, sadly at the time we had no option, it was only through determination we found a way around and an alternative route. I hope our story is helpful to others who may find themselves on this journey in the future.

#flawed-decisions #misuse-of-evidence #factual-inaccuracies #delay #poor-communication #trust #bias #no-effective-outcome #scoping-out-key-issues

Celia Jones:- Welsh Ombudsman PSoW

My complaint went to PSoW in August 2018 .

I had a few acknowledgements prior to May 2019, when I was contacted by the Investigator (Ms X) who has always been very polite and courteous. No problem with her at all. She was going away but on her return in June would be writing a couple of short reports and then mine would be produced in the first week of July. I became quite nervous and had two close friends who were prepared to read it for me.

The draft report never appeared ....and at the end of the first week in July there was an apology and it was going to be the next week. It went on a week by week basis, sometimes every few days. No real explanation was given apart from an advice sent for was not back or had to be re-checked. Then the investigator went away again and I was left with the promise and apology that I would be prioritized when she got back on Aug 5th. More apology....no information back. The line manager is the problem (Ms Y).

I was then asked to meet to explain the delay with Ms X and Ms Y   I guessed something was amiss. The meeting was taped and it was explained that they had missed asking for an Advice from a radiologist which should have been asked for at the beginning...in my opinion as it was central to the case. These Advice requests take a month at least.   It was not prioritized.

In one telephone call in August the line manager said if I was depressed then she could give me the Samaritans phone number. I felt this was totally inappropriate.

The line manager of the investigator had blamed the investigator for not managing expectations!

Anyway, after a lot of stress I got my advice which was on a CT scan in 4 days!   I had my answers.

The Draft report issued at beginning of October. The hospital notes were wrong but amazingly the analysis and conclusions were correct more or less.

It was painful reading. The line manager took over and I was to be contacted in 3 weeks. I had no idea of the procedure. They are supposed to guide you through it.

The deadline for comments was 25th October. I was told as I happened to ask about next steps in an email that the hospital was not happy and wanted a month extension. They met the Health Board. I was not happy. I said nothing.

It is now a waiting game. They have no idea when the report will be issued. The Line Manager (Ms Y) who is so unpleasant is doing the Final report!!

When I gave them a deadline, they immediately put me on a restriction which I have been told to appeal about. I am to be phoned once a week. I have no reason to email them as they have all my information now.

The person who imposed the restriction on me has no idea of the timescales. This is over 450 days. I have been told that no complaint should take longer than 50 weeks. They have apologised in September. I am left confused and unhappy as the draft report I am told is only provisional can be reversed. So, the upholds can be non-upholds.

I am seriously wondering if I should get a solicitor. A very helpful Community Health Council has told me that the length of time between Draft to Final is very unusual as so long. Also unusual in the meeting between the parties.

I have to ask the question what is the point of a draft report if it is all changed. Very cruel in my case as most of my complaints were upheld.

In my opinion the system is fundamentally flawed. There is no disclosure. It is one-sided. They mediate with the Health Board (trust) but fail to offer the complainant the same. There are only 7 LHBs in Wales and they must know them all. Bias.

Eventually, I did get the final report. Although the analysis and conclusion remain the same the report has the Health Board hallmark stamped all over it with their opinions and mine not noticed. The Health Board have again swiped at me and in a very derogatory manner. Hence the report has dates and times that are not correct. I have asked for corrections to be made. Last night received an email having had no contact with them, telling me that my contact was again restricted. Just felt it was bizarre and unnecessary. I am left having no trust in them at all. I would not recommend this service to anyone.

#misuse-of-evidence #factual-inaccuracies #delay #poor-communication #trust #bias #no-effective-outcome #poor-case-management

Editor's note: This is just a snap shot of the harm caused by the poor Ombudsman process. Procrastination serves to weaken the resolve of the complainant and reduces the opportunity for them to take legal action. Can it just be inefficiency, lack of training or poor oversight which allows so many errors to occur? Given that people tell fundamentally the same story, it must surely be by design.

Chapter 3. Is PHSO corrupt by design?

Editor's note: Many take objection to the use of the word corrupt. **Mr Behrens,** specifically asked PHSOtheFACTS not to link #phso with #corruptbydesign on social media. Corrupt is indeed a harsh word, but after years of monitoring, it is the only one which accurately describes the way in which the Ombudsman repeatedly and systemically fails the public. The extraordinarily low uphold rate tells its own story. It would be logical to expect something of a spike in upholds for public bodies since they have all been hit by a decade of austerity cuts. But the uphold rate has actually fallen under Rob Behrens's leadership to under 3% of all complaints. [21]For parliamentary complaints it has fallen to just 0.6%.[22] How can this be?

The following article, posted in November 2018, sets out what we mean by 'corruption' which is essentially a 'corruption of purpose' and how this was deliberately 'designed' into the Ombudsman legislation by parliament.

---

[21] See Fig. 1. PHSO data table 2016/17 to 2018/19 p6
[22] See Fig. 2. Parliamentary complaints 2018/19 p7

PHSO is #corruptbydesign

November 20th 2018.

Corruption can take many forms and in relation to the Ombudsman (PHSO) the corruption referred to is, 'systemic corruption of purpose'.

A generic definition of an Ombudsman as supplied by Wiki:

> *An ombudsman, ombudsperson, ombud, or public advocate is an official who is charged with representing the interests of the public by investigating and addressing complaints of maladministration or a violation of rights.*

Yet here in the UK our Ombudsman does the very opposite and represents the interests of the state against the public. This article will provide evidence that from the very inception and throughout various amendments the UK Ombudsman is **#corruptbydesign.**

Systemic corruption (or endemic corruption) is corruption which is primarily due to the weaknesses of an organization or process. It can be contrasted with individual officials or agents who act corruptly within the system.

Factors which encourage systemic corruption include

- *conflicting incentives,*
- *discretionary powers;*
- *monopolistic powers;*
- *lack of transparency;*
- *low pay;*
- *and a culture of impunity.[23]*

Birth of the modern Ombudsman:

Sweden is the birthplace of the modern Ombudsman initiating their Parliamentary Ombudsman in 1809 "to safeguard the rights of citizens by establishing a supervisory agency independent of the executive branch." No doubt many citizens needed such safeguarding in the UK at that time but it took the resignation of a Cabinet Minister in the **Crichel Down Affair** of 1954 to persuade the British Government to adopt the Ombudsman model. This scandal culminated in the first resignation of a Minister since 1917 and was marked by a very public scrutiny of a Minister carrying out his discretionary duties.

"In the history of modern parliament, the Crichel Down affair takes on momentous significance, and has been described as a 'political bombshell'. The public inquiry

---

[23]

wikipedia.org/wiki/Corruption#Government/public_se ctor

into the Crichel Down events revealed a catalogue of ineptitude and maladministration and resulted directly in the resignation of the Secretary of State for Agriculture (Sir Thomas Dugdale), then a senior cabinet position, and was the first case of Ministerial resignation since 1917. Whilst the underlying case was, in the scale of things, trivial, involving the transfer of some seven hundred acres of mediocre agricultural land in Dorset, the ramifications for subsequent government procedure have been enormous, and it is regarded as one of the key events leading to the creation of the post of Ombudsman. Crichel Down was probably the first instance of close and very public scrutiny being directed at a Minister of the Crown in the execution of his duties." Crichel Down affair[24]

#corruptbydesign 1.

The motivation for the creation of a UK Parliamentary Ombudsman sprang from a desire to protect Ministers and not a desire to protect the public. This can be seen in the drafting of the legislation.

The fundamental flaws of the 1967 Parliamentary Commissioner Bill:

---

[24] en.wikipedia.org/wiki/Crichel_Down_affair

- A failure to include discretionary decisions made by Ministers or government departments for scrutiny by the Ombudsman or by other means.
- A failure to define 'maladministration' leaving it to the Ombudsman's discretion on a case by case basis.
- A failure to provide direct access to the public forcing them to appeal through their MP who can decline their request.
- A failure to give the Ombudsman powers of coercion over public bodies.
- A failure to make the Ombudsman accountable except by judicial review, beyond the means of most citizens but within the means of government departments with funded legal teams.

The Whyatt Report, The Citizen and the Administration: The redress of Grievances (1961)

Written after the Crichel Down Affair, Whyatt quite rightly determined that much injustice was delivered to the citizen due to the inappropriate use of administrative discretion and that independent tribunal was necessary for public redress. Failure to act in a timely manner or failure to take the most appropriate action is often described in public inquiry reports as 'missed opportunities'. These actions undoubtedly led to the ensuing disaster, but often fail to be judged as maladministration. When policies and procedures are only guidelines, proving maladministration is extremely difficult. There is rarely a smoking gun, more often a trail of error and ineptitude. Providing the opportunity for citizens to seek redress for poor administrative decisions through independent tribunal was always more likely to provide redress than the cumbersome investigation process, yet this key aspect of the Whyatt report was never implemented.

The debate in the Lords in 1967 identified the difficulties with providing redress when there was no clarity over what constituted 'maladministration' and was therefore within the remit of the Ombudsman and what would be determined as 'discretionary decision making' and consequently beyond scrutiny.

Lord Harlech

"But, my Lords, let us look for a moment at those Departments listed in Schedule 2 which do have a more direct and frequent impact on the lives of the general public. To what extent does the Bill provide a means of redress of grievance by the general public? It seems to me that it would depend very much on how we define and interpret the word "maladministration". I think that the noble and learned Lord conceded that this was a point of difficulty. Certainly this was a point which gave rise to long debate in another place without, it seemed to me, anyone being very much

wiser at the end of it. Speaking for myself, I should be immensely grateful if we could be given, first, a simple example of a grievance likely to be submitted by an individual for investigation by the Parliamentary Commissioner; secondly, an explanation as to in what respect the action complained of might be due to maladministration and, thirdly, even if it was due to maladministration, how it could be determined that this was not due to the exercise of a discretion vested in the department or authority". I have taken those words, of course, from Clause 5(4) a subsection which, as the noble and learned Lord said, was inserted by the Government at a late stage in the passage of the Bill through another place, and which seems to me to give the Bureaucracy a loophole as large as the Round Tower of Windsor. If it is not the case, I, for one, should be most grateful to have it explained to me."

Equally**, Quintin Hogg** leading for the Conservatives on the Ombudsman legislation of 1967 referred to it as a *"swiz"*: *"We on this side always knew that the whole thing was a swiz, but that was not spelt into the Bill. It did not write down in so many words in a schedule, "this is a swiz"....The bill was always drafted to be a swiz, and now it is spelt into the bill."*[25]

---

[25] Parliamentary Commissioner Bill – Hansard 8th February 1967 vol 279 cc 1384

#corruptbydesign 2.

The government paid no attention to the debate in the Lords and in fact set up the office of the Parliamentary Commissioner before the debate even took place. Maladministration has never been defined and can be anything the Ombudsman considers it to be, offering no consistency or predictability. Discretionary decisions are still beyond the remit of the Ombudsman and it is for the Ombudsman to decide which evidence falls under such a heading allowing him to 'cherry-pick' through the evidence. The MP filter has not been removed giving Parliament continued control over access to the Ombudsman for parliamentary complaints.

There has been a failure of parliament over 50 years to reform the Ombudsman which was originally considered to be something of an 'experiment'. Despite much discussion on the subject, successive governments have failed to tackle the fundamental flaws in legislation which prevent citizens from achieving redress.

Lord Lester in one such debate (January 2000) put forward the notion that, *"Of course it is convenient for Ministers to have a rusty machine that takes a long time and does not deal very effectively with citizens' complaints."* [26]

---

[26] Lords Hansard text for 17 Jan 2000 (200117-06)

#corruptbydesign 3.

Recent draft proposals for reform, serve to further disable the Ombudsman from upholding complaints, indicating that Government have no intention of reforming this body for the benefit of the citizen.

In December 2016 the Cabinet Office finally released a draft proposal for reform of the Ombudsman. It is clear from this proposal that parliament has no intention of removing any of the barriers to justice and in fact, clause 8 effectively nullifies the Ombudsman's investigative process by removing any requirement on public bodies to act on the findings of an Ombudsman's report.

> *(8) designated authority must have regard to any recommendations contained in a statement under subsection (1)(c) in respect of the authority (but is not required by virtue of anything in this Act to give effect to any such recommendations). (p16)*[27]

Although the Cabinet Office drew on a report entitled **'Better to serve the Public'** the proposal ensures that the public would continue to be stymied by

---

[27]

https://assets.publishing.service.gov.uk/government/uploads/syste m/uploads/attachment_data/file/575921/draft_public_service_omb udsman_bill_web_version_december_2016.pdf allowing the continuation of the following flaws in the legislation.

- The Ombudsman must determine harm caused by maladministration when there is no definition of either term and the Ombudsman has the discretionary powers to decide that the harm would have occurred in any event, leading to no uphold.
- The Ombudsman investigates in private resulting in an inability to challenge false evidence or assumptions until after a decision has been made.
- The Ombudsman is under no obligation to apply statutory regulations but can decide which regulations to apply on a case by case basis without challenge.
- The Ombudsman can determine which parts of a complaint to investigate and which to 'scope out' of the investigation without challenge from the complainant.
- The Ombudsman can continue with an investigation even when the complainant loses confidence and withdraws from the process. This can produce a flawed report which effectively prevents the complainant from taking legal action.
- The Ombudsman can only investigate the complaint when the designated authority has had a 'reasonable opportunity' to carry out an internal investigation and respond. The 'reasonable opportunity' is not time-bonded and can continue for years, wearing down the

ability of the complainant to pursue the case. It gives the authority under investigation every opportunity to review the evidence and gather legal advice before the 'independent' Ombudsman investigation takes place. Evidence can and has been removed, destroyed or altered.

"In no other area is one party allowed to have complete control over evidence that might prove the complainant's allegation while the other party has to beg for access to information." [28]

- There is no requirement of the Ombudsman to hold evidence for longer than 12 months. Evidence is then destroyed making it impossible to detect repeated patterns of poor performance/emerging scandals.
- All complaints about the Ombudsman are handled internally by the Ombudsman themselves. No external scrutiny.
- The governance structure allows for political appointments to the board such as Sir Alex Allan who is simultaneously an advisor to Ministers, creating a conflict of interests for the 'independent' Ombudsman.
- There is 'free-flow' of personnel from the civil service into management positions at the

---

[28] *control of the evidence – Telegraph article 2013.*

Ombudsman's office. Amanda Campbell moved from the Home Office to become CEO in 2016 and in 2017 Rob Behrens moved from Office of the Independent Adjudicator (OIA) to become the new Ombudsman.

- The Ombudsman can decide the level of transparency, delaying or avoiding the publication of minutes from board meetings, staff survey results and performance stats on the PHSO website.
- The board has no powers of control over the operation of the Ombudsman.
- PACAC is unable to examine individual complaints on behalf of parliament resulting in no oversight of the investigation process

#corruptbydesign 4.

Returning to our definition, it can be seen that the Ombudsman has **conflicting incentives** as it is funded by parliament, with key appointments through parliament and regularly meets in confidence (no meeting minutes) with government departments such as the Cabinet Office and Department of Health. It also has no powers of coercion over the public body 'stakeholders' so must negotiate with them for compliance. The Ombudsman has significant **discretionary powers** which make legal challenge virtually impossible for members of the public. The Ombudsman is the only body who can investigate parliamentary and health complaints giving it **monopolistic powers**. There is a significant **lack of**

transparency with private investigations, no external review of the investigation processes or decisions and control of data released into the public domain. There is a **culture of impunity** as it is impossible for a member of the public to hold the Ombudsman to account either by direct complaint to PHSO, appeal to parliament or appeal to the criminal justice system. **The Ombudsman meets virtually all of the factors for systemic corruption**.

This should cause a public outcry but the situation is unlikely to change while those in power are protected and other interested parties benefit from the failure of the public sector complaint system. **'Patient safety'** is a multi-million-pound industry, spawning conferences, think-tanks, charities, publications and the servicing of citizen-funded legal claims.

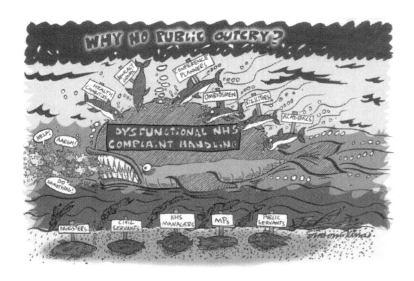

Editor's note: Credibility of the Ombudsman relies upon public acceptance that it is both independent and impartial. The following blog post from June 2018 demonstrates how the government uses the so-called 'independence' of the Ombudsman to have a show of clean hands, whilst at the same time holding tightly to the reins of power.

Just how 'independent' from government is PHSO?

June 20th 2018

If you consider that anyone in the pay of government is not truly independent of government, then PHSO is not independent at all. The use of the term 'independent' is, however, a most useful one and we can see it in action in these two recent examples.

The first is part of a letter from **Rob Behrens,** the Ombudsman to a complainant who recently attended the PHSO Open Meeting in May 2018. He is inviting her to take part in an 'independent' review into the way PHSO uses clinical advice. For context, PHSO does not reveal the identity of their clinical advisors and advisor's single, anonymous opinion, can override medical expertise provided by the complainant, legal advice and hard evidence in the form of medical records and reports.

> *However, to signify my respect for your concerns, I need to tell you that I am in the process of commissioning an independent review into the way in which PHSO commissions and uses clinical advice. It is clear that clinical advice was particularly important in the investigation relating to your father's death, and therefore I am writing to invite you to make a submission to the independent review which is being chaired by Sir Alex Allen. Sir Alex is an independent Non-Executive member of the PHSO Board, and he will be receiving advice from a nationally known and respected clinician, whose name will be disclosed when we publish the Terms of Reference.*

The chair of the review will play a pivotal role in shaping the scope, deciding which evidence to include and which to discard and framing the final recommendations. So how independent is **Sir Alex Allen**? He has previously been **Chairman of the Joint Intelligence Committee,** so an expert in keeping secrets and is currently, according to the PHSO Conflict of Interests Register, the **Prime Minister's** (David Cameron) **Independent Advisor on Ministerial Interests.** No doubt a paid role but it would seem this one man can serve two governors for he is also on the Non-Exec board for PHSO which is an organisation totally independent of ministerial involvement. Just how does he keep the two interests separate?

In 2015 he was clearly working for the government in his failed attempt at the High Court to prevent disclosure from ministerial diaries, in accordance with FOI law.

The rulings are also embarrassing for the Government because the High Court concluded that evidence by the Prime Minister's adviser on ministerial standards was "way below" what the public were "entitled to expect" of a senior civil servant. Mr Justice Charles said the testimony of Sir Alex Allan, a former chairman of the Joint Intelligence Committee, had "lacked objectivity" and should be "roundly rejected".

The judge also accused Sir Alex of demonstrating a "determination to avoid directly conceding the indefensibility of things he had said" and a "keenness to repeat generalised lines... rather than give direct answers to questions". He said the evidence was a "reminder of the secretive culture of the public service" that the Freedom of Information Act was meant "to change for good".

The Government, via Sir Alex Allan, had been attempting to overturn a ruling by the Information Commissioner that the contents of official ministerial diaries should not be exempt from requests under the Freedom of Information Act. [29]

So, a defender of 'the secretive culture of public service' is put in charge of a review regarding the secretive culture of PHSO clinical advisors. Not a good omen.

The Ombudsman is appointed by the Queen under the recommendation of parliament and the funding for PHSO comes directly from the treasury. It is for all intents and purposes a government paid organisation which holds government departments to account. There is an inherent bias in this arrangement compounded by the fact that parliament sets the legislation under which the Ombudsman operates, conveniently tying his hands by failing to provide 'own initiative investigative powers' or 'legal powers of compliance'. The strings are firmly held by the

---

[29] independent/whitehalls-secrets-to-be-revealed-as-ministers-ordered-to-produce-diaries-to-the-public

Cabinet Office – the centre of government, who confer regularly with the Ombudsman in meetings which are not minuted or recorded in the public domain. Yet, when it suits, which is most of the time, the Ombudsman is totally independent of government in a 'nothing to do with us' shrug of the shoulders manner. Take this recent example from Hansard 14th June 2018.

Roger Godsiff Labour, Birmingham, Hall Green

To ask the Secretary of State for Work and Pensions, whether additional resources will be allocated to the Parliamentary and Health Services Ombudsman as a result of the increase level of caseload from WASPI complainants.

Guy Opperman The Parliamentary Under-Secretary of State for Work and Pensions

The Parliamentary and Health Service Ombudsman (PHSO) is independent of Government and is accountable to Parliament through the Public Administration and Constitutional Affairs Committee for its performance. The DWP plays no part in allocating resources to the Parliamentary and Health Service Ombudsman's Office.

4,000 WASPI (Women Against State Pension Inequality) complaints are on their way to PHSO having passed unsuccessfully through the complaints process at DWP and the Independent Case Examiner

(ICE). This massive increase in complaints is due to a government decision to delay pension payments to 1950's WASPI women and failing to give sufficient warning to allow them to make other arrangements. Many women in their early sixties are destitute as they wait a further 6 years for their expected pensions. PHSO have had a 24% cut in funding, a government decision to save money and a relocation to Manchester has seen a loss of experienced caseworkers and senior management. All the work of the Whitehall boffins, yet when PHSO have to pick up the pieces and will clearly fail to do so to the satisfaction of the public, they are 'totally independent of government' who cannot interfere with their decision. How convenient. A show of clean hands for parliamentarians as the Ombudsman diffuses the anger caused by their poor policy decisions.

Editor's note: Creating toothless quangos is something of a speciality for UK governments. Listen to any breaking scandal and you will have a regulatory body bemoaning the fact that much of the called for **'action'** is outside their remit. When organisations have shown themselves to be effective, it doesn't take long for the government to step in. Why, it's almost as if they don't want them to do a good job.

How the voice of the patient has been deliberately diminished.

9th November 2019

You can forget all that 'listening and learning' stuff when it comes to the NHS. History shows that successive governments have deliberately diminished the voice of the patient when dealing with complaints about healthcare. Let's start with this reference to the **'complaint monitoring panels' (1999)** who, according to this extract from the **Mid Staffs review,** would have been better placed to prevent the national scandal from harming so many before the citizen-led **'Cure the NHS'** campaign brought it to light.

135. The Trust also had the benefit of complaints monitoring panels, which Ms Llewellyn introduced from around 1999. She said the system worked extremely well. Non-Executive Directors chaired the panels, and the Chief Executive would also attend. The panels reviewed every complaint, challenged service managers and reviewed action points from previous meetings to try to ensure that change had taken place. Quarterly reports were prepared for the directorates so that learning could be shared. Funding could be sought from outside the Trust where particular action was required.[193]

136. In 2004, the complaints regulations changed, local independent review panels were abolished and the HCC took on responsibility for second stage complaints. However, she said: "The Healthcare Commission was completely overwhelmed by complaints after they had been established and there was quickly a backlog of hundreds of cases." Sometimes the Trust would have to chase the HCC on complainants' behalves due to the HCC's inaction. There was also no follow up

Unfortunately, these panels were abolished in 2004 so were unable to detect the horror of neglect which featured in the report from 2005 to 2009.[30]

---

[30] Mid-Staffordshire-Trust-inquiry-how-the-care-scandal-unfolded.html

- **Key Points:**

- **The system worked extremely well.**

- **The panels reviewed every complaint**

- **They reviewed action points from previous meetings to ensure change had taken place**

When the **Healthcare Commission** took over in 2004 they were 'overwhelmed by complaints and there was no follow up. This body was in turn abolished in 2009 with the bulk of the monitoring role going to **CQC** who have no powers to investigate individual complaints.

Community Health Councils acted as effective, local complaint monitoring panels from 1974 to 2003. They were abolished by **Tony Blair** who declared 'war' on complainants who were bringing the NHS into disrepute.

Blair's bully-boy gag on patients

By George Jones, Political Editor
https://www.telegraph.co.uk/news/uknews/1382627/Blairs-bully-boy-gag-on-patients.html
12:01AM GMT 25 Jan 2002

DOWNING STREET declared war yesterday on patients who make high-profile complaints about mistreatment in National Health Service hospitals.

The full weight of the Government's publicity machine will be used to help hospitals rebut allegations by members of the public that ministers believe are unjustified or create an unfair picture of the health service.

As the row over the treatment of Rose Addis, 94, intensified, Tony Blair said he had "no regrets" about the use by his officials of personal information about patients.

He told the Cabinet that the Government was engaged in a "full-scale battle" on the public services and that he was determined to win.

Downing Street said that hospitals were being authorised to take a "robust" approach to patients' complaints, including the discussion of information about their condition and treatment.

Blair used the 'full weight of the Government's publicity machine' to help hospitals rebut complaints whilst at the same time abolishing those bodies which effectively spoke out on the patient's behalf. **Rhion Jones** gives a warning as the Welsh government consider abolishing their **Community Health Councils.**

Insofar as the replacement body will cover both the NHS and social care, the change is very welcome, but if the 'abolition of CHCs' sounds familiar, it is because fifteen years ago, the English tried the same trick. Managers were fed up with those they saw as local interfering busybodies inspecting NHS facilities (unannounced – what affrontery!) and generally being unco-operative when it came to service changes, that the then Labour Government was persuaded to wind them up. What followed was a case study in how not to manage change. First, they invented Public & Patient Forums, which were not Forums but Committees, only for them to be castrated in infancy and replaced by something called Local Involvement Networks – called LiNKS – which were Forums – but actually couldn't be called that!

LiNKS was hobbled from the outset. Ministers decided not to specify how these new creations would work. Each one therefore spent about eighteen months trying to work it out, and some never managed it. In no time, they were gone – to be replaced by Healthwatch, which seven years later, are still just about finding their feet. For about five years, the NHS was not subject to effective public/patient (as opposed to Council) scrutiny. It is this mistake that the Welsh Government risk repeating.[31]

Essentially, bodies who use their powers to effectively work for improvements are replaced by government quangos who have only 'advisory' powers.

Kelvin Hopkins MP and member of PACAC thinks he knows exactly why the staff at PHSO are having difficulty improving first-tier complaint handling and took the time to inform **Rob Behrens** and **Amanda Campbell** at the scrutiny meeting held on 22nd January 2019.

> **Kelvin Hopkins:** What you both say is most interesting. Some 15 years or so ago, the Government introduced changes to complaints systems at local level. They abolished the Community Health Councils and I was one of those who had a suspicion that this was a deliberate attempt by Government to weaken complaints handling at local level—I do not know if you feel the same—and the suspicion was supported by the fact at that time. The Government tried to encourage private

---

[31] *wales-to-abolish-community-health-councils-can-it-avoid-the-mistakes-made-in-england*

companies to come in and provide those services, and the private companies did not want strong complaints procedures that might make life more difficult for them. Do you feel that the Government are still reluctant to introduce strong complaints systems at local level?[32]

Kelvin Hopkins was extraordinarily outspoken in his view that the government were in fact spiking the complaint system, but then he was stepping down as an MP at the next election.

So, there we have it. A simple formula. Take away all the bodies who have teeth and represent the people. Replace them with quangos who are starved of resources and power. Any harm caused by cuts to the NHS, inadequate staffing levels or lack of suitable resources can all be swept under the carpet.

Rob Behrens, Ombudsman accepts that he has the role of 'igniting' the momentum across the NHS to improve complaint handling. His apparent lack of enthusiasm for the task [given his flat tone of voice at the PACAC meeting] was no doubt due to his awareness that as he

---

works to ignite, the government works to extinguish and so the wheels turn.

Editor's note: Rob Behrens has been a civil servant for many years and knows that controlling the narrative is vitally important. He takes every opportunity to state that the Ombudsman service is independent and impartial, though there is no external evidence to support this view. He introduced 'radio ombudsman' as a way of interfacing with his stakeholders. In these podcasts Mr Behrens interviews people he finds interesting, asking them questions he finds relevant. The locus of control is firmly in his grasp. He also introduced the annual open meeting. In the first of these Behrens made the mistake of holding 'workshops' in the second half and a member of PHSO staff regretted asking a room full of angry complainants to describe what 'good looks like' Subsequently, the event is packed with so many official 'speakers' there is little time for questions from the floor.

Controlling the narrative is important to maintaining 'public confidence'. If you take a glance at **Dame Julie Mellor's** wiki page, there is no mention of her sudden demise from the role of Ombudsman. Equally, the Patients Association wiki page contains virtually no information about the work of **Katherine Murphy**, who as CEO released three damning reports into the failings of the Ombudsman. Why it's almost as though it never happened.

Chapter 4. The Pursuit of Justice

Editor's note: We are all familiar with the media referring to 'the fight for justice', yet they seldom ask who are we fighting? We are of course fighting the state. The very people we pay to protect us. As children we are brought up to believe in justice, truth and the benign nature of authority; who may be inept, but never deliberately corrupt. If you are fortunate enough not to suffer a personal trauma, you can probably drift through life with those fundamental notions in place. However, for those of us who have reached out to our 'benevolent authorities', it comes as a shock to find they lie, cheat and collude together to protect the state. Because we believe in justice and democracy as core values, many citizens continue to battle over many decades to force the state to accept responsibility and deliver justice for their loved ones. But the state provides a rigged complaint system resulting in victims exhausting their time and money in a largely fruitless task. If you are tenacious you might break through and cause a ripple or two, but the state is the only real winner. Here we see how the Ombudsman plays its part in maintaining the 'justice illusion'.

The pursuit of justice

15th August 2018

Justice – definition:
just behaviour or treatment

'a concern for justice, peace and
genuine respect for people'
Oxford English Dictionary

A common belief is that a civilised society designs systems by which justice can be delivered and injustice punished as a mark of **'genuine respect for people'**. Administrative law is just such a system created to protect citizens from the abuse of government power. It operates through courts, tribunals, ombudsmen and commissions with access via a complaint process which must be followed according to the stages laid down. Given that there is a pre-determined right to justice in our civilised society, why is it that the pursuit of justice is such a lengthy and soul-destroying fight?

Who are we fighting and why is it so difficult to win?

Public confidence.

Here in the UK, we live in a democracy which operates through legislation, delivered by consent of the people and monitored by state-funded regulatory bodies. At least that is the given narrative but in fact, UK democracy relies not on the actual delivery of rights but on **'public confidence'** that the state will honour our rights. It is vital that people believe themselves to be safe and believe that those in authority are benign (possibly inept but not deliberately malicious, which is why the word 'corrupt' sets their teeth on edge). Public confidence relies upon shared values, so concepts such as justice, truth and honesty are reinforced through family, education and religion from an early age. Such notions become so fundamental to our health and well-being that we will defend these ideals even when the evidence suggests otherwise. Justice only exists as a belief system, (much like the tooth fairy) because we want to believe in it. Which is helpful to those in positions of power who are required to **'restore public confidence'** when some unfortunate scandal seeps into the public domain. Restoring public confidence should not be confused with putting things right. Public inquiries rarely put things right but they defuse the heat of the moment with words of regret and sweeten the future with the promise that **'lessons will be learnt'**.

Twitter -

an angry pool of justice seekers

Twitter is awash with people calling for justice. They will explicitly use this word to head up their campaigns and it is clear that they expect the state to deliver on their promise. By the time they turn to Twitter they will have found that the official complaint process has failed to deliver anything which looks like justice, in fact, it has likely delivered the very opposite with hostile attacks aimed at discrediting the victim in order to defend the public body from reputational damage. Our deep-rooted belief in the notion of justice has not prepared us for this shock and many never recover their emotional and physical health as a result. We are convinced, because we have evidence of wrongdoing, that we have a right to justice and when it is not forthcoming we reach out far and wide to find that someone, somewhere who can deliver it. The rhetoric of justice is so pervasive that it can take many, many years to accept that justice will never be forthcoming no matter how strong the evidence or how great the determination. It is a bitter pill to swallow and it requires a most painful re-evaluation of our core beliefs.

Accountability theatre.

What if 'justice' doesn't exist? What if it is nothing more than a social construct which has been instrumental in ensuring public compliance with rules and regulations? Is there any evidence to support such a theory? Historically there is a plethora of gross injustice to choose from where the powerful take unhindered advantage of the powerless. The first to spring to mind is **slavery**, which allowed a select group to build fortunes from free labour and the continued discrimination along ethnic lines which remains with us today. Then there are the **Inclosure Acts** which gave the rich the right to take and own common land; an aspect of history often neglected in the school curriculum. The **subjugation of women** is an injustice which blights over 50% of the population. Women were denied the right to vote through 40 years of peaceful campaigning and there has been a continual fight for equal pay and opportunity since. It is interesting to note that although the Suffragettes are said to have 'won the vote' for women the change in policy came at the end of the first world war when women had proven themselves to be both essential and cost-effective in the workplace.

More recent injustices would include **Hillsborough** and **Gosport** where campaigning families have sacrificed years of their lives to reveal the truth about the way in which their loved ones died, and who are now raising funds to fight their own court cases. (Why isn't the state doing this on their behalf?)

Campaigning for justice involves the powerless taking on the powerful with nothing more than;

'the simple sword of truth and the trusty shield of British fair play'.

But when 'truth' is a matter of interpretation and British fair play is nothing more than a cover for colonialism then, just as **Jonathan Aitken** discovered, they prove to be sadly lacking. In contrast, those who benefit from maintaining the status quo hold much more valuable weapons such as possession of the most damning evidence which must be prised from their hands and can be redacted beyond use; unlimited funds for legal representation from the public purse; the ability to interpret the rules and regulations in whatever way they see fit; the knowledge that other organisations will follow their lead to provide circular assurance; complex legal processes designed to prevent examination of the evidence; the silence of the media and a lack of opposition from the academics.

It is so difficult to win because whenever they lost in the past they rewrote the rulebook to ensure it didn't happen again. That's what they mean by 'lessons have been learnt'. But it would be foolish of them to win all the time – that would most certainly give the game away. At the present time, about 65% of people feel there is no point in complaining. Without a few victories for the little guy this figure would be much higher and public confidence would take a significant hit. So, every now and again a campaigner breaks through and is honoured for their 'brave fight' and applauded for their 'determination' and 'selflessness' for the common good. These select few can then be held up like trophies to prove that campaigning is a worthy cause. This is no more than **accountability theatre** and delivers a cruel blow to those still suffering, who have just as much fight, just as much determination and just as much right to justice. They are left swimming round in the angry pool of authoritarian control as new recruits are added daily by a bureaucratic system which has no intention of delivering justice but knows how important it is to pretend that they do.

Editor's note: Below is a letter which appeared in response to a **Telegraph article in 2013.** It clearly explains the way in which the various 'authorities' collude together to prevent the true facts from being examined. Although we can see an acknowledgement that evidence has been suppressed, neither the Coroner nor the Police appear to have any concern. When did we normalise such widespread corruption?

The whole #NHS #PHSO complaints process is corrupt by design.

4ᵗʰ April 2018

This response to a Telegraph article in 2013 accurately describes the way in which the complaint process is deliberately stacked against the complainant at every turn making it 'corrupt by design'. And this single sentence captures the problem in a nutshell.

"In no other area is one party allowed to have complete control over evidence that might prove the complainant's allegation while the other party has to beg for access to information."

The problem is the burden of proof.

Comment on Telegraph article 27 January 2013 by "romeolima"[33]

This is a long comment from me but I hope people will read it. I absolutely agree with your sentiment but the problem is the burden of proof. Before the police can investigate, complainants often have to go through a tortuous multi-layered system that allows an internal investigation into an incident by the hospital itself without the complainant or their legal representatives

[33] http://www.telegraph.co.uk/health/heal-our-hospitals/9828966/Stafford-scandal-hindsight-isa-luxury-we-can-ill-afford.html

being allowed to question the witnesses. Staff do not have to swear or affirm and their version of events frequently reads like a novel. Notes go 'missing' (this is a common event) and staff are 'helped' to make statements by their legal department although this is meant to be a process without lawyers on both sides. Hospital legal departments often regard this as a 'dry run' of a possible court case and can prepare their defence whilst obstructing the availability of medical data to the police, should they be involved, the complainants and their legal team. There is no organisation of any credibility that can carry out an investigation into an individual complaint even if this is about a patient death. The Ombudsman has proved ineffective and the system is such that the hospital already has prior knowledge of the details of the complaint as the complainant must have already gone through the hospital system prior to reaching the Ombudsman. It's a terrible catch 22. In no other area is one party allowed to have complete control over evidence that might prove the complainant's allegation while the other party has to beg for access to information. Almost all the Incident Reporting Protocols that I have read say

194

that in the event of any incident that all notes, statements etc should be immediately captured electronically but this wealth of material, which cannot be altered, is almost never made available to the complainant. In all cases of death, the Coroners Officer would appear to be the proper person to immediately seize and hold originals of all patient records whether paper or electronic while a decision to proceed to an Inquest or not is being made. In my own family's case, the notes were held at the hospital's litigation department for nearly six weeks before the Coroner requested a copy. This is highly unsafe as an evidential chain and we have never received all the material requested and are fairly certain that the Police would be told that material was missing and therefore the Crown Prosecution Service could not proceed.

Editor's note: Many people suffer burn out, mental health issues or PTSD from years of battling with the authorities. **Mr Hawkins** was one of those who managed to persist for over a decade with the support of his MP, **Andrew Gwynne** who brought the matter to the House at a 'backbench' meeting in January 2018. The story of Mr Hawkins, so eloquently described by Mr Gwynne, is a case-study in the way in which the publicly-funded legal teams deny access to justice and how all parties, including Ministers collude with this arrangement.

The state V the citizen
The ultimate catch 22

12th February 2018

A primary responsibility of the state is to protect its citizens from harm. So, what happens when the state is the body causing harm and those in authority collude together to cover it up? In the UK we like to believe in **'British fair play'**; a somewhat bureaucratic but essentially benign system of checks and balances to put things right.

Yet anyone who has made a complaint about a public service will have learnt that the machinery of the state is used against the citizen, not for the citizen. Those who have not made a complaint will not want to know this bitter truth and will likely not believe a word of it.

And there is the dilemma. What right-minded person would go about telling all and sundry that various government authorities have conspired against him? Clearly, only a delusional trouble-maker would dream up such a tall story.

Meet **Mr Hawkins.** A brave campaigner for truth and justice who told such a story to his **MP Andrew Gwynne,** shadow minister for communities and local government. In an unusual twist of events not only did **Mr Gwynne** believe his constituent, he felt so strongly that **Mr Hawkins** had been let down by multiple agencies for over a decade that he brought it to the attention of parliament at a 'backbench' meeting on 30th January 2018.[34] Sections of **Mr Gwynne's** statements to the House are recorded in italics below.

> *"Sadly, I have to publicly outline how my constituent, Mr Hawkins, has been let down by public authorities. The law and NHS rules have been abused to avoid giving him the justice that*

---

[34] ://www.theyworkforyou.com/whall/?id=2018-01-30b.288.1

is rightfully his. His attempts to seek that justice, along with some semblance of honesty and humility, have already passed the decade mark, so I shall be grateful for the Minister's reply after I set out the case."

Did you get that – '...the law and NHS rules have been abused [by the state] to avoid giving him the justice that is rightfully his.'

Mr Hawkins was given surgery on his ruptured Achilles by a junior doctor instead of the allotted clinical surgeon in order to **'meet government targets'** and following a serious clinical error, which left him in great pain, he was discharged prematurely also to **'meet government targets'.**

"Mr Hawkins immediately made a complaint through the hospital trust's internal complaints procedures. He believes that on receipt of his letter of complaint, the trust should have called him in for an examination and a scan. It should have admitted that a serious problem had

occurred and carried out a further operation to release the Achilles tendon from the rear of his leg. In Mr Hawkins's mind, the matter would then have been resolved. However, the trust decided to take a different route: it instantly instructed Hempsons solicitors."

So easy to put things right at this early stage yet the state used public funds to protect itself against a genuine complaint. Clearly, Mr Hawkins wasn't expecting this.

"Although, obviously, Mr Hawkins is concerned about the clinical errors that have caused him lasting damage, he is rather more appalled by the actions of a variety of organisations afterwards. He believes that those actions were deliberately designed to cover up the fact that a clinical mistake had been made, caused primarily by the replacement of a consultant surgeon with a junior doctor."

'He believes that those actions [by the state] were deliberately designed to cover up the fact that a clinical mistake had been made...' **Why would the state deliberately design such harmful actions?**

Now that the complaint is in the hands of a legal team **Mr Hawkins** has little option but to appoint his own solicitor who then uses him as a cash cow and appears to work in cahoots with the NHS legal team.

> *"In 2008, Mr Hawkins instructed a solicitor, who requested disclosure of all full medical records. The trust passed his request on to Hempsons. However, in the immediate period after his request he received only a very selective number of his own medical files from Hempsons. Mr Hawkins's solicitor failed to ensure that all full medical evidence was disclosed within statutory time limits and failed to apply for a court controlled disclosure, while knowing that the records he had listed were missing. Mr Hawkins's solicitor instructed a clinical litigation medical*

expert, who produced a case-closing report that failed the objectivity test and was therefore invalid. The trust and Hempsons initially failed to disclose relevant medical records, doing so only after continued and considerable pressure from Mr Hawkins."

'Mr Hawkins's solicitor instructed a clinical litigation medical expert, who produced a case-closing report that failed the objectivity test and was therefore invalid.' State corruption providing lucrative work for 'the legal teams' who could act with impunity knowing that there is no effective mechanism for a member of the public to hold a solicitor to account.

"In 2013, the trust eventually conceded and his remaining medical records were fully disclosed. On analysis of the records, it was plain to see that there were omissions and that pre-action protocol time limits had been exceeded. In response, Hempsons sought the opinion of a

medical litigation expert. A report was produced, but it was based on the selected medical records that I mentioned earlier, as well as on the falsified information. Mr Hawkins believes that that report would fail any objectivity test and is therefore invalid."

Let's just get this straight. The NHS Trust deliberately and wilfully withheld medical records demanded under the legal pre-action protocol time limit and falsified other information. A criminal offence, yet no-one is held to account. Instead, the solicitors working [from the public purse] to protect the trust were able to produce a 'whitewashed' report in order to deny justice.

Withholding records is a breach of the **Data Protection Act 1998** but the state body responsible for protecting the citizen from such breaches, the **Information Commissioner's Office** (ICO) is slow and cumbersome with no real powers of coercion.

"Mr Hawkins also believes that the Limitation Act 1980 *was breached from 2008 and that rules 31 and 35 of the* Civil Procedure Rules 1998 *were breached in compiling medical reports, because the medical experts failed in their duty to the court to be objective."*

More breaches of the law and regulation by the trust and their legal team which required action from the state to protect the citizen, but the body charged with finding against such 'maladministration' the **Parliamentary and Health Service Ombudsman** (PHSO)refused to investigate leaving him high and dry.

"The delays in disclosure of information meant that Mr Hawkins's complaint to the Parliamentary and Health Service Ombudsman *was ruled out of time. My constituent believes that that makes a mockery of the trust's failure to disclose his medical records within statutory time limits, which he believes the*

ombudsman ignored while upholding the strict time criteria regarding his making a complaint to the ombudsman. Mr Hawkins appealed the decision on several occasions when the evidence was retrieved through the Information Commissioner. However, he was unsuccessful in overturning their original view that a letter from the trust indicated that the complaint was closed in 2007, which he utterly refutes. Hempsons later apologised and admitted that that letter did not clearly state that the local complaints procedure was closed. However, the ombudsman still refused to investigate the complaint and, in doing so, Mr Hawkins feels that the ombudsman has assisted the trust to conceal the cause and effects of a clinical error."

The Ombudsman has total discretion to investigate a case which is outside the normal 12-month time limit yet it refused to do so and even refused to accept the evidence that their initial decision to time-out the complaint was flawed.

To recap, unrealistic and inflexible NHS targets caused harm to the citizen. Then publicly funded legal teams dragged their heels, refusing to release records and fabricating evidence in breach of legal protocols. The Ombudsman then 'assisted the trust' by refusing to investigate clear breaches of policy and procedure.

Clearly a believer in justice, **Mr Hawkins** then appealed to the **NHS Litigation Authority** only to find that they too were in cahoots with the trust and the legal team.

"In 2013, Mr Hawkins wrote to the NHS Litigation Authority, *as the trust was not reporting clinical mistakes. Initially, the NHS Litigation Authority would not get involved and requested my involvement, as Mr Hawkins's* Member of Parliament, *which I duly offered. Two replies were received that indicated that the NHS Litigation Authority was involved in the case, despite previous assertions and written evidence that it was not involved. Mr*

Hawkins was notified in writing that the trust, on receipt of his letter of complaint, had instructed Hempsons in January 2007, *with the NHS Litigation Authority directly instructing Hempsons and the trust from* November 2007 *to* February 2009.*"*

"Hempsons was aware of a breach of the Limitation Act 1980 and the Data Protection Act 1998 when it disclosed to Mr Hawkins his missing medical records in October 2009. *This means that the trust and Hempsons had illegally avoided disclosing all full medical records within statutory time limits and successfully passed the three-year limit for litigation. Mr Hawkins believes that indicates that the NHS Litigation Authority was aware that rules had been broken, yet failed to take retrospective action based on the strength of the evidence that he had disclosed to it in 2013."*

'... the trust and Hempsons had illegally avoided disclosing all full medical records within statutory time limits and successfully passed the three-year limit for litigation.'

A state body and a state-funded legal team committed illegal actions in order to deny justice to the citizen with the support of the **NHS Litigation Authority** and the complicity of the Ombudsman.

> *"The actions taken by the trust, assisted by Hempsons and the NHS Litigation Authority from January 2007 to* December 2013, *clearly indicate that the trust was covering up a clinical incident and its cause. With so much time having passed since my constituent first exited the operating theatre in the summer of 2006, I hope that today the* Minister *of State will be able to afford Mr Hawkins guidance and support in this matter, and finally bring to some closure what has been a dreadful episode for my constituent."*

You may expect the Minister to be horrified that various state-funded bodies had conspired to deny justice to a citizen harmed by the state in the first instance but **Stephen Barclay,** Minister of the Department of Health and Social Care was having none of it. He used the usual caveats which allow politicians to show a clean pair of hands by stating that the NHS complaint system and the work of the Ombudsman are independent of government. Also, that it was not for the DoHSC to discuss individual cases.

If the bodies set up by government fail to protect the citizen, who is to take them to task when they are all deemed to be 'independent'?

Then **Mr Barclay** casts aspersions on the validity of the claims and in doing so discredits the complainant. Here is his statement below.

"As you are well aware ... the NHS complaints process operates independently of Government, to prevent political bias in the handling of individual complaints. However, a number of points arise from the hon. Gentleman's remarks, in respect of his contention that Mr Hawkins was let down by a number of individuals and organisations within the NHS. Specifically, it is alleged by Mr Hawkins that the hospital failed him by prioritising then Government targets, which delayed his operation; that the clinician failed him through clinical error; that the duty surgeon failed him by falsely reporting that his wound had healed; that the hospital failed him by not correcting the alleged mistake and by instructing lawyers; that Hempsons solicitors failed to disclose full records; that his own solicitors failed him by not obtaining his records; that his own clinical medical expert failed him; that the hospital failed him, regarding his report; that the Ombudsman failed him; and that the NHS Litigation Authority failed him."

"Although the Department of Health does not comment on individual cases, and it is not for me to adjudicate whether all of those claims by Mr Hawkins are valid, it is worth noting that a very wide range of both individuals and organisations are alleged by Mr Hawkins either to have conspired against him or, indeed, to have failed him in this matter."

'... it is not for me to adjudicate whether all of those claims by Mr Hawkins are valid, it is worth noting that a very wide range of both individual and organisations are alleged by Mr Hawkins either to have conspired against him or indeed, to have failed him in this matter.'

Mr Hawkins provides us with a case study of state corruption and the misuse of power. This happens to thousands of people every year. But if they speak out about the deliberate corruption and collusion of state bodies it marks them as delusional fantasists or vexatious troublemaker. Who would believe that state-funded bodies would conspire in such a concerted and prolonged manner? Yet, to not speak out is to be complicit in the state violation of human rights. So, the brave or the foolish, speak out and become victims of the state all over again.

Let's give the final word to the Minister, **Stephen Barclay.** *"It is equally important that patients and their families are listened to and their concerns taken seriously and addressed".*

That would be all the concerns which don't indicate a deliberate cover-up and collusion by the state then Mr Barclay.

Editor's note: At PHSOtheFACTS we know that the experience of Mr Hawkins is not an unfortunate set of circumstances but a deliberate and systemic attack on his human rights by the very organisations charged with protecting him. In 2016 PHSOtheFACTS put out the following 'guideline' as a warning to others. Complain at your peril!

Thinking of making a complaint?

5th April 2016

10 things you need to know:

1. Although you are the one asking for an investigation you will have to find all the evidence yourself.
2. You will have to access and read all the policy documents to identify the breaches.
3. Having done so you will be told that policies are only 'guidelines', so no breaches occurred.
4. You may find that the law has been broken. You will be told to take your complaint to court and fund yourself while the public body is funded by the taxpayer.
5. Your complaint will be dealt with by the legal team who have no duty of candour and will do and say 'anything' to protect their client.
6. If you object to the manipulation of the facts you will be told to take your complaint to court.
7. There will be endless delay. Like a boa constrictor, the complaint process will slowly suck the life force from you.
8. Truth and evidence are irrelevant. Linguistic manoeuvrings will absolve all guilty parties.
9. Any internal review process is merely a rubber stamp of the first decision made by a colleague.
10. The 65% of people who say they wouldn't make a complaint because it won't make any difference are right. Listen to them.

Editor's Note: The Ombudsman would not normally investigate a complaint when the first-tier complaint process has not been fully completed and neither would the Ombudsman investigate if there is an alternative legal remedy (ALR) available. But, to the confusion of many complainants, the Ombudsman has total discretion on these matters, so no matter whether injustice is caused as a result of the Ombudsman's actions (or inactions) the Ombudsman has breached no legal requirement, so cannot be held to account. The case of the **WASPI** (Women Against State Pension Inequality) women is of interest as the Ombudsman uses discretion to alter its position on whether to investigate 6 sample cases.

Have WASPI women been let down by PHSO?

6th November 2019

When PHSO decided in 2017 to intervene on behalf of the WASPI women to 'speed up' the maladministration cases, many believed that action was finally being taken to deliver justice. Two years later and PHSO have yet to commence any investigations on behalf of these women. What went wrong?

Changes to state pension age were originally brought in by the **Pensions Act 1995** and at that time it was stated there would be 15 years notice for changes to pension arrangements. But the **Pensions Act of 2011** brought forward the timetable and increased state pension age to 66 for both men and women. Little or no notification was given by the **Department for Works and Pensions (DWP)** to those who were affected, in particular 50's born women, many of whom were expecting to receive their pension at 60.

As realisation grew, complaints were made to the DWP regarding the way they handled the changes to pension arrangements and seeking recompense for the hardship caused as consequence. Approximately 3.3 million women have been affected and many have become destitute due to lack of income.

In November 2017 the DWP had fully processed just 6 complaints from a total of 4,557 submitted. [35]

The DWP's **Independent Case Examiner (ICE)** set up a team of just three case managers from existing resources to deal with these complaints and as they made slow progress, thousands more joined the end of the queue. ICE was clearly overwhelmed. On 30th November 2017 it was reported that the **Parliamentary and Health Service Ombudsman (PHSO)** would intervene in order to 'speed up' the process; this coupled with a vote of support in the House for improving transition arrangements, gave encouragement to many WASPI women that their long fight was coming to an end.

> *THIS WEEK HAS turned out to be a hopeful one for the Women Against State Pension Inequality (WASPI) campaign, with an intervention from the Parliamentary and Health Service Ombudsman to speed up its*

---

[35] Commonspace article 27.11.17

maladministration case against the Department of Work and Pensions (DWP), followed closely by a unanimous vote of support in the House of Commons.[36]

It was unusual for the Ombudsman to step in at this stage as they regularly state that they cannot intervene in cases which have not completed the first stage investigation and neither are they permitted, by legislation, from investigating cases where there is an alternative legal remedy. A FOI request in December 2017 [37] asked PHSO for confirmation that their decision to intervene at this stage was permitted by law. They were, after all, working alongside the very body [ICE] they would later be holding to account.

Prior to this announcement by PHSO **#backto60 One Voice** campaign announced (18th November 2017) that **Michael Mansfield QC** agreed to represent them and fund raising began in earnest to judicially

---

[36] commonspace 30.11.17
[37] whatdotheyknow.com/request/ombudsman_legal_remit#outgoing-720131

review the actions of the DWP. Despite access to alternative legal remedy and a possible conflict of interests, PHSO agreed to work with ICE to identify sample cases for investigation as part of a bid to 'streamline' the DWP case handling process.

Given that the Ombudsman's intervention was intended to hasten the delivery of justice, it has done just the opposite. A year was apparently 'lost' in negotiation as it was not until **October 2018** that PHSO announced they would investigated 6 sample cases. In the meantime, ICE closed down all the WASPI complaints waiting for attention. Now all hopes for recognition of injustice rested with the Ombudsman. Just one month after selecting the 6 sample cases PHSO put all investigations on hold when in **November 2018** it was announced that a Judicial Review had been granted.

We considered the impact of the judicial review on our proposed investigation and reached the view that it would not be practical or proportionate for us to investigate while similar and related issues were being considered by the court.[38]

The Ombudsman is generally very strict on its observance of access to alternative legal remedy. It will close down cases on the basis that the complainant has or had an opportunity for legal recourse even when the complainant has made no mention of any such intention. It is a value judgement on the part of the Ombudsman as to whether or not it is 'reasonable' for the complainant to resort to legal remedy due to the discretion allowed in their legislation.

The PHSO promise of intervention in 2017 gave false hope to WASPI women that action was being taken on their behalf.

Why did PHSO use Ombudsman's discretion in 2017 to become involved in cases which, at that time, had

[38] Ombudsman.org

not fully completed the internal complaint process and which would most likely be the subject of legal action? Perhaps this article from **Civil Service World,** January 2018 explains the motivation. Speaking about government departments such as the DWP **Rob Behrens, Ombudsman** says;

...there is "goodwill towards us because people recognise that the ombudsman is the last in the line for complaints, and departments understand they rely on the ombudsman for relieving them of issues they can't deal with".[39]

It was clear that both DWP and ICE could not deal with the continual flood of WASPI complaints. Having 'relieved them' of their burden PHSO then 'paused' all activity due to impending legal action. PHSO could have used their discretion to scope investigations to look specifically at aspects of DWP/ICE 'maladministration' as this matter was not subject to legal scrutiny, but they chose not to. WASPI women should note that historically,

---

[39] Civil Service World Jan 2018

PHSO uphold very few cases against either the DWP or ICE as can be seen below.

[2018/19 Ombudsman data - from 1,553 complaints about the DWP the Ombudsman investigated 30 cases and partially upheld 4. They also resolved 2 cases without full investigation which gives an uphold rate of 0.3%. For ICE complaints the uphold rate was 0]

Editor's note: Early in 2020, just days before the WASPI campaign group were given the go-ahead for a legal appeal, PHSO contacted the 'sample cases' and offered to go ahead with their investigations. This was despite the fact that legal action was still pending – in fact the appeal date has been given as 21st July 2020. The Ombudsman put out the following statement on their website.

Why are you proposing to investigate when an application to appeal the judicial review is pending with the Court of Appeal?

We have now seen the judicial review judgment and know what issues the High Court made decisions about. We have considered this and we are able to proceed with our investigation while the application for appeal is ongoing.

Are the issues that the Court looked at and the Ombudsman proposed to investigate the same?

Not all of the issues we propose to investigate were considered as part of the judicial review, in particular DWP's and ICE's complaint handling and the communication of changes to National Insurance. Our investigation looks at the issues from a different perspective. We are proposing to investigate whether there was maladministration, where an organisation does something wrong or provides poor service.

Editor's note: We can see that the odds are not stacked in favour of a successful outcome for these women. The uphold rate is extremely low and even with a positive outcome they are likely to receive very low levels of compensation for the many years of hardship suffered. Is this what justice looks like?

Even with a supportive MP, Mr Hawkins didn't achieve justice in his ten-year struggle, which took him to every UK authority. We can see in the Hawkins case that all those 'independent' bodies worked together to actively deny him justice. New complainants are like lambs to the slaughter. With a belief in truth and justice citizens spend many hours gathering evidence to support their complaint. Naively, they battle to be understood by a system which is deliberately deaf and blind to them. Frustrated but determined, they are easy prey for unscrupulous solicitors. So where are the advocacy groups to lead and protect the citizen as they attempt to navigate a system which is stacked against them at every turn?

Chapter 5. Whatever happened to the Patients Association?

Editor's Note: We saw in chapter one that under the leadership of **Katherine Murphy**, the Patients Association were actively speaking out on behalf of the patients to reveal the ordeal they were suffering as they tried to pursue complaints through the Health Service Ombudsman (PHSO) Shortly after **Rob Behrens** took up the office in April 2017, the Patients Association selected **Rachel Power** as their new CEO. Her response in 2018 to the new PHSO strategy can be seen in chapter one and it provides a good summary of the key issues identified by her predecessor, in the three damning reports.

As part of his initial 'meet and greet' strategy Rob Behrens agreed to meet with members of **PHSOtheFACTS** and a seminar was held in October 2017. Group members who were still struggling through the complaint process at PHSO and those who were dissatisfied with previously closed (now historic) cases attended in the hope that the new management would be able to deliver remedy and justice for both current cases and those mishandled under the previous administration. Although Mr Behrens informed us that he was 'horrified' at the evidence we presented to him, shortly after this meeting he communicated that he no longer recognised PHSOtheFACTS as a group and stated that he would only communicate with individuals in the future. As a consequence, PHSOtheFACTS had no influence during the transition process and historic cases were soon relegated to 'outside PHSO remit'. We were therefore dependent on organisations such as the Patients Association, who still had the ear of the Ombudsman to speak on our behalf.

There was a 'honeymoon' period for the new Ombudsman, as he settled into a role which also included moving the Ombudsman's office from London to Manchester with a loss of senior staff and a budget cut of 24%. Individual group members continued to communicate their concerns with senior staff and a small number received apologies, financial compensation or the promise of a reinvestigation. For the majority of those in attendance, no further action was taken. Those who were provided with a reinvestigation found many of the same problems as before with caseworkers limiting the scope, failing to understand the facts and ignoring their evidence.

In June 2018 the Patients Association put out an expression of 'shock' at the findings of a review into the avoidable deaths at **Gosport War Memorial Hospital**. Members of PHSOtheFACTS were concerned that the PA summary made no mention of the role of the Ombudsman in allowing the deaths of 450 people to go undetected until their families managed to raise public concern through a lengthy campaign.

> **Rachel Power, Chief Executive of the Patients Association, said:**
>
> "It is deeply shocking to read the conclusions of Bishop James Jones's review, that the lives of hundreds of people were cut short by one doctor's inappropriate use of drugs. We have heard of many instances of poor care over the years, but to shorten the lives of patients represents the very worst betrayal of patients that any doctor can commit.
>
> "The scale of the failures and the culture at Gosport War Memorial Hospital is in some ways even more appalling. The report makes clear that leaders, clinicians and nurses at the hospital were all aware of what was happening, but that the failure to act ran from top to bottom.

Why are the Patients Association shocked at the Gosport findings?

26ᵗʰ June 2018

In response to the **Gosport Inquiry findings,** the Patients Association released the following headline:

Gosport War Memorial Hospital:

Patients Association expresses

shock at findings

For many years the **Patients Association** have been listening to people who have lost loved ones through avoidable NHS neglect, who report to them on a daily basis the difficulties of pursuing their complaint against a body which uses legal might and a lack of transparency to deny justice and learning. So why the 'shock' and why no mention of the role played by the **Health Service Ombudsman (PHSO)** who once again has failed to alert the authorities to a crisis which lasted more than a decade? The **Gosport Inquiry** will deliver many words and many promises but who will actually deliver the change?

The response of PHSOtheFACTS member Nicholas Wheatley can be read below.

Dear Ms Power,

We read with interest your statement about the Gosport War Memorial Hospital scandal and the shock you felt at the number of lives cut short. You state:

"we should pay tribute to the tenacity and determination of the families who stood by their belief that things were not as they should be, even when the NHS was telling them otherwise"

Our pressure group, PHSOtheFACTS, has been campaigning for several years for reform of the Parliamentary and Health Service Ombudsman, which has been described as not fit for purpose by the Patients Association itself. Many of our members, whose loved

*ones have suffered avoidable or unexplained deaths,
have the same "tenacity and determination" you
praise in the Gosport families, and the same belief
that "things were not as they should be, even when the
NHS was telling them otherwise".*

*You also stress "the effects of such serious betrayals of
trust, first in the improper care itself and then again in
the way the NHS closed ranks against them." Our
members have experienced the same betrayals of trust,
compounded by the failure of the Health Ombudsman to
take their concerns seriously or to investigate their
complaints thoroughly and impartially. You will be
aware that a number of the Gosport families took their
complaints to the Ombudsman and were badly let down
when their cases were not upheld.*

*You state "When patients and their families raise
concerns in future they must be properly listened to and
given full and open answers". Sir Robert Francis QC,
President of the Patients Association stated:*

*"Once again we hear of a lack of transparency which left
the truth hidden" and "in future when serious concerns*

228

are raised they are properly examined in investigations in which patients and families can play a full part"

Our members are only too aware of the "lack of transparency", "the truth hidden", not being "properly listened to" or "given full and open answers" in the complaints process.

The Parliamentary and Health Service Ombudsman is the final tier of the complaints process and yet it fails hundreds of complainants every year by failing to investigate their complaints properly or to take their concerns seriously. We believe that it is of vital importance that the Ombudsman is reformed so that it becomes a service that acts on behalf of the public to hold public bodies to account. The existence of a properly functioning Ombudsman would represent a major step forward in patient safety. No Trust or doctor currently need fear the threat of "taking a complaint to the Ombudsman". That must change.

Since the resignation of your predecessor Katherine Murphy, the Patients Association has ceased campaigning for Ombudsman reform and has also ceased to engage with us or indeed to reply to any of our requests for help. If you are indeed serious in your comments about the failures at Gosport War Memorial Hospital and the associated investigations, then please let us know that you will be willing to help us in our campaign for Ombudsman reform. It may help prevent a repeat of the terrible events at Gosport.

This letter will be published on our website and we look forward to your reply.

Editor's note: Quite possibly as a result of this blog post the Patients Association released a position statement with regard to PHSO. This can be seen in the following PHSOtheFACTS blog post, which was published in July 2018.

Can complainants rely upon the Patients Association to be their strong voice?

25th July 2018

The Patients Association defend their position on PHSO following criticism from PHSOtheFACTS members. But it is not clear from their actions just **how** they will monitor or challenge the performance of the Health Service Ombudsman on behalf of patients. Representing patients and not organisations should be their core role.

Position statement: PHSO

The Patients Association has for some years been highly critical of the performance of the Parliamentary and Health Service Ombudsman (PHSO). This has been for good reason: we have received abundant evidence of PHSO letting patients down, and making things worse when they needed it to help them right a wrong. In particular, we issued three reports: 'The People's Ombudsman – How It Failed Us'

(November 2014); an immediate follow-up, 'PHSO – Labyrinth of Bureaucracy' (March 2015); and a final follow-up report in December 2016.

With this work, we called for change. And we succeeded in getting change. PHSO has recognised the scale of both its problems and the action needed to correct them. It has set out a strategy for how it will improve its performance across a period of years. We have welcomed this, and the organisation's new leadership as of 2016-17.
However, at present PHSO is only part-way through this change programme. It has not yet produced the transformation that is needed. For now, we continue to receive calls to our helpline from patients, carers and families who are unhappy about PHSO.

We recognise that achieving change on the necessary scale will take time, but we hope PHSO will be able to show progress as soon as possible, with reference to patients' experiences of their service. This should include closing gaps between PHSO's casework process assurance and complainant feedback against the same measures on its Service Charter.

We will judge PHSO's reform programme on the results it achieves for patients. During its implementation period, we will continue to raise concerns with PHSO when things have not been good enough. We will also work with PHSO to help it become a patient-focused organisation that delivers a high quality service. Some patients and bereaved relatives who have been let down by PHSO have gone so far as to suggest that it is corrupt, or for some reason intentionally providing a bad service. We do not believe this to be the case. PHSO's service has been bad: this problem has not yet been solved, and it has work to do to rebuild trust with patients. But we do not attribute these failures to malice, and we wish to work with the new leadership team at PHSO, providing constructive challenge. In this way, we hope that PHSO will achieve the transparency to give patients confidence that allegations of this nature are untrue.

Nicholas Wheatley describes in his letter to Rachel Power, some key ways in which the **Patients Association** could actively monitor the progress at PHSO during their 'change programme' and make this information available to patients and complainants. He also points out how retrograde steps taken since the arrival of the new Ombudsman **Rob Behrens** will impact negatively on transparency and trust.

Dear Ms Power

Thank you for your reply to my email and your offer to deal with our requests for help. We simply ask that when people contact the Patients Association to complain about the PHSO, that they are made aware that there is a user group, PHSOtheFACTS, to which they can turn if they so wish. One of the most distressing things about being a victim of mistreatment by the PHSO, as I am only too aware, is the sense of helplessness and isolation at having nowhere to turn to. Knowing that there are others who have been through the same ordeal is a great comfort and empowers one to believe that it is possible to fight back and not simply be a victim of injustice.

It would also be helpful if you would publish or record and make available statistics showing the number of complaints you receive about the PHSO on a monthly or quarterly basis, as this would give a good idea of any ongoing improvement in the service provided by the PHSO.

It would also be of help to publish details of the issues discussed at the regular bilateral meetings between the Patients Association and the Ombudsman, to give people an idea of how the Patients Association holds the Ombudsman to account. I believe the most recent meeting occurred on 25 June.

It is disappointing that the Patients Association is not actively campaigning for further reform of the PHSO. We have no confidence that the current strategy will result in an improved service. It is not the transformational change required to create an Ombudsman service fit for purpose. Of great concern is the fact that the Ombudsman has removed the possibility of external review of complaints. You may be aware that external reviewers were instrumental in overturning incorrect decisions for the cases of Scott Morrish, James Titcombe, Nic Hart, and Maggie and Janet Brooks amongst others. This retrograde step will make it much more difficult for complainants to achieve justice through the PHSO.

I'm sure you will also be aware that the Service Charter performance has shown no significant change over the past year while the most important indicators for gathering information and explaining decisions have actually worsened slightly to just 42% and 57% respectively for the first quarter of 2018. At the same time the performance statistics have fallen through the floor with 537 investigations completed in the final quarter of 2017, a drop of nearly 50% from the previous year, and the report withheld for the first quarter of 2018. At some point questions will need to be asked about *whether the Ombudsman's strategy is working or whether the problems at the PHSO require a more rigorous and fundamental approach.*

You will be aware that from Gosport to Mid-Staffs, via Morecambe Bay, Southern Health, Bristol, and many others, the complaints system failed to pick up on health scandals which cost many lives. There are likely to be other scandals currently occurring and lives being lost. A properly functioning complaints system, with a robust Ombudsman as the most important tier, would likely identify systemic failings at an early stage and prevent them from developing into full blown scandals, saving lives in the process. This is the kind of Ombudsman we would like to see, but without campaigning pressure this will never be realised. We hope you will re-evaluate your position with regards to the PHSO and adopt a more proactive and critical approach to Ombudsman reform.

Yours sincerely

Nicholas Wheatley

PHSOtheFACTS

It is clear from their position statement that the Patients Association is 'working with the Ombudsman' through a series of pre-planned meetings.

What is not clear is how the Patients Association is working with complainants in order to evaluate the results achieved from the patient's perspective, nor how it will raise the concerns of patients when service delivery falls short.

Note the change in approach from the following correspondence with Margaret, another PHSOtheFACTS member.

In March 2016 the PA was willing to 'work together' with Margaret in order to help prepare for and attend a meeting with PHSO.

Dear Margaret,
I am sorry that we have let you down and not responded or supported you through a very difficult time. I can well understand you frustration with the PHSO and LGO and not having the energy to struggle on.

What I can do is support you at a meeting with the PHSO and LGO so that you can voice your concerns to them face-to-face. It appears that neither organisations have taken your concerns seriously and have avoided responding to your questions. If you would like to take this forward to a meeting with the PHSO and also the LGO, please let me know. We can then work together and give them specific questions prior to the meeting, which you want addressed.

Let me know how you would like to proceed.

With kind regards,

Diane
Helpline Manager
The Patients Association
PO Box 935 | Harrow | London | HA1 3UJ
Helpline: 0845 608 4455
Email: helpline@patients-association.com

By January 2018 their position had changed and no support was offered.

> *Thank you for contacting The Patients Association. I was sorry to read that your complaint remains with the PHSO and that it has not been resolved, this must be very frustrating for you and your husband.*
>
> *Margaret, we have had a number of personnel changes and structural changes since you first contact the charity. These changes have meant that we have been unable to continue engaging in casework, which includes having the resources to*

attend meetings to support complainants. Regrettably, until we have adequate resources we would be unable to support you by attending the meeting proposed by the PHSO-please accept our apologies for this. It is encouraging that the PHSO wish to meet to discuss your complaint and I hope that the outcome will be a positive one for you and your husband.

If you wish to keep us informed about the progress of your complaint please feel free to do so as we are keen to hear from patients about their experience and whether their complaints are resolved to their satisfaction.

If you have not engaged with an advocate you may find their services helpful. Information about how you may find an advocate in your area can be found in our downloadable advice leaflet, How To Make A Complaint, which you can select here:

Margaret, I wish you the best of luck in your meeting with the PHSO.

Please do not hesitate to contact us if we may be of assistance.

Working only with the Ombudsman will not reveal evidence of deliberate poor service or a corruption of purpose when conjecture replaces evidence-based decision making. Members of PHSOtheFACTS are concerned that the Patients Association cannot be relied upon to be the voice of the patient unless they continue to work closely with patients throughout all stages of the process.

Editor's note: It would appear that the Patients Association can do no more than 'wish you the best of luck' as they direct you to seek help elsewhere. Given that in July 2018 Rachel Power stated that the Patients Association would

'continue to raise concerns when things have not been good enough'

Janet and Maggie Brooks, wrote the following letter in August 2018 asking for support. Unfortunately, there has been no response from the Patients Association to this correspondence.

Dear Rachel Power,

My sister and I have been members of the Patient's Association since 2014.

We are extremely grateful for the support the Patient's Association gave us from 2014 — 2017.

We were fortunate that your predecessor, former CEO, Katherine Murphy, published the account of our experience with the Parliamentary and Health Service Ombudsman (PHSO).

In 2011, we had taken our case to the Ombudsman, hoping they would investigate the death of our mother in King George Hospital in 2010. But the Ombudsman allowed the Trust to provide a set of our mother's medical records which had all the crucial records missing.

Despite our providing the Ombudsman with many of these missing records at the Draft stage, the Ombudsman disregarded these and produced a report which gave a totally false and misleading account of the facts of our mother's death.

For the next two years the Ombudsman refused to review its investigation or to withdraw its report. This risked perverting the course of justice as an inquest was opened on the suspicion that our mother had not died a natural death.

The Ombudsman reassured the Trust that, although the Trust had failed to supply over 100 of my mother's records to the Ombudsman's investigation, the Ombudsman would not investigate this until after the inquest. This gave the appearance of collusion between the Ombudsman and the Trust.

The inquest was compromised by the Coroner's acceptance of the Ombudsman's report into evidence.

In 2015, the Ombudsman's External Reviewer issued his findings that the 2012 investigation report had been seriously flawed due to the Trust not supplying crucial medical records to the Ombudsman's investigation He pointed out that this shortfall of records should have been addressed at the Draft stage in 2012. And that the Ombudsman should have made the Coroner aware of this.

The Deputy Ombudsman apologised for the Ombudsman having left the flawed report in circulation for three years — but it was too late. The damage had been done.

The Ombudsman still continued to thwart our every attempt to get the report withdrawn.

It was only once the CEO of the Patient's Association, Katherine Murphy, intervened and highlighted the inadequacy of the Ombudsman's processes in our case, that the Ombudsman began to cast around for a way to quash the report.

In 2016, the Ombudsman's Director of Investigations, Russell Barr, held meetings with us attended by Katherine Murphy, Dr Bill Kirkup and the Rt Hon Margaret Hodge MP.

He said that the Ombudsman's office had drawn up a 200 page dossier about the complaint handling of our case, which he described as `terrible', and that the Ombudsman's office would be sending this dossier to an external barrister for legal opinion.

He said he would tell us the outcome and that **if the Ombudsman found it was able to quash the flawed 2012 report into our mother's death in the High Court, they would do so.**

These promises were recorded and transcribed by the Ombudsman's officials so we believed they could be relied upon.

The Ombudsman's meeting with the barrister took place but its outcome was not shared with us, as we had been told it would be. Instead, the Ombudsman stalled and would not answer our inquiries.

Three months after the meetings with Russell Barr, Katherine Murphy, Bill Kirkup and Margaret Hodge, we were still unable to find out what advice the outside barrister had given about this.

We needed to know this because we were seeking a second inquest and the Ombudsman's report was likely to stand in the way of our application.

We instructed lawyers to send the Ombudsman a Letter before Claim.

Our lawyers asked the Ombudsman whether it was possible within their legislation to quash the report in the High Court or not.

The Ombudsman's lawyer told our lawyers categorically that it was not possible, the Ombudsman's lawyer, Helen Holmes replied:

> *"Our legal view is that while there is wide discretion for the Ombudsman to conduct her own procedure during an investigation, once she has done so, her report of that investigation is not capable of being withdrawn.*

However, six months later in January 2018, the Deputy Ombudsman announced publicly to PACAC that it WAS possible for the Ombudsman to quash our flawed report in the High Court. She said:

"What we can do is apply to a court to have the investigation quashed

We had spent £17,500 on legal fees to oblige the Ombudsman to give us a definitive answer and **now the Ombudsman was giving the exact opposite answer to PACAC** than the answer it had given to us.

We felt like the Ombudsman had defrauded us.

The Ombudsman later wrote to us saying that although he had the capability to quash the report in the High Court, it 'didn't seem right' that he should have to do so.

The Ombudsman said that, instead, he would give himself powers to personally 'quash' our 2012 report — powers which he admitted he did not currently have

He said he would write to the Trust telling them he had 'quashed' the unreliable report asking them to shred it or return it. Although, he added that the Trust did not have to take any notice of this.

We had been this way before. The previous Ombudsman had written to interested parties such as the GMC, asking them not to use the report because it was unreliable. The GMC had simply ignored the Ombudsman.

If an Ombudsman's process is, like most judicial processes, functus officio, then a report which has been produced by means of an illegal process **can only be quashed in the High Court.**

If so, then this personal 'quashing' of our report is a sham and the Ombudsman is taking us and PACAC for a ride.

Why does this matter?

Because two judges in the High Court have recently quashed the inquest into our mother's death and have ordered a second inquest.

The Trust's lawyers are likely to argue at the second inquest, as they did at the original inquest, that the Ombudsman has already conducted an investigation in 2012 and that therefore, the State's obligation to investigate has been met.

Since March 2018, we have been asking the Ombudsman to tell us whether the Trust has accepted that the report is actually 'quashed', but the Ombudsman declines to answer us.

If the Trust is allowed to use the Ombudsman's 2012 report to compromise the second inquest just as it did the first, we fear it will prevent the facts of our mother's death from ever coming to light.

We have heard that the Patient's Association has said that it will continue to raise concerns with the Ombudsman's office 'when things have not been good enough'.

"Things have not been good enough" in our case. The Ombudsman claims to give a voice to the voiceless, but it has ridden roughshod over our human rights for the last eight years.

Without your former CEO, Katherine Murphy, fearlessly championing us against this all-powerful yet unaccountable organisation, we have no-one to fight our corner unless you are prepared to do so.

We would be grateful if you would ask the Parliamentary and Health Service Ombudsman to explain the status of the `quashed' report and the legality of this informal 'quashing'.

We also ask you to, please, ensure that each member of your board and your staff have the opportunity to read this letter.

Yours sincerely,

Janet Brooks
Maggie Brooks

Editor's note: The correspondence from the Brooks family describes in great detail their concerns about the 'quashing' of their report by Mr Behrens. They have been unable to obtain a satisfactory response from the Ombudsman, who is now silent on the matter. It is telling that the Patients Association have not raised this important concern in line with their position statement but have also remained silent. Is anyone now defending the rights of the patient?

From the time Rob Behrens took office (April 2017) PHSO have taken actions which served to close down access to justice, not least of which was a major reduction in the number of investigations. (From 4,239 in 2016/17 to just 1,617 in 2018/19). Early on there was the removal of the external reviewers and in September 2018, the five external quality assurance associates were removed, resulting in no external evaluation of the PHSO process.

In January 2019, PHSO quietly reduced the time to request a review of their decision from three months to one month. As PHSO rarely send the evidence relied upon with the final report, it is necessary to make a Subject Access

Request to review the material evidence and this would take a month to arrive. Consequently, the complainant must apply for a review in an impossibly short time-frame. In contrast, PHSO take many months to decide whether to go ahead with a review and many more to actually complete it.

The Patients Association did not report on any of these detrimental changes, nor did they apparently lobby on behalf of the complainant to ensure that they were given adequate time and opportunity to dispute the findings of the Ombudsman. In October 2019, Rachel Power was invited to talk to Rob Behrens as part of the Radio Ombudsman podcast. This rather 'cosy' chat did not reassure complainants that the Patients Association was in a position to effectively hold the Ombudsman to account.

Rachel Power reveals that as she was taken on as CEO of the Patients Association there was a high turnover of staff in her own organisation, as there was at PHSO.

> *"We secured a team. There had been quite a high turnover of staff for a while, so we're pretty much a brand new team since the beginning of 2017. With a large turnover of trustees, mainly because*

a number of the trustees had been there for a number of years and it was time for the change. So, pretty much a brand new trustee board as well. "

PA then set about a new three-year strategy which Rachel Power describes using a number of well-used memes.

"Yes. Our strategy is completely about listening to patients and using that information that we've received through our helpline, and through our survey work and our project work, to inform the changes that we think need to happen within the health and social care system, to ensure that patients are truly at the heart of their care and that they're equal partners within that care. "

During the interview Rachel Power is asked a direct question about the removal of the damning PHSO reports from the Patients Association website.

Rob Behrens: *"Now, we asked for questions from followers on Twitter. One question to you is this: Why did the Patients Association take down the three damning reports into PHSO from their website? These should be the baseline from which we measure improvements."*

Rachel Power: *"They are the baseline from where we measure improvements. We took them down. We launched a new website in 2018, and had to make a decision about what remained on* *the website, because we wanted something that was more up to date. Our position statement on the PHSO remains on our website.*

Our position is that we recognise the extent of change that PHSO has embarked on, and we agree it is extremely necessary. We will judge the results for patients on their merits, and would hope to see substantial benefits from this process in the next year or so. "

The interview rattles on with more homilies about the importance of 'listening' 'learning' 'leadership' and 'culture' but Rachel runs out of soundbites when Rob Behrens asks the following question.

Rob Behrens: *"What do you think is the best way of ensuring that patients' voices are heard and acted upon by those in power? "*

Rachel Power: *"I think the best way... The solutions are... Solving it will be hard ..."*

Concerned that our patient voices were not being heard by either PHSO or the Patients Association, PHSOtheFACTS member **David Czarnetzki** instigated a series of communications with the Patients Association, centred on the difficulties he was experiencing with his own complaint with the Ombudsman, which culminated in this final response to **Ms Lucy Watson, Chair of Trustees** sent on 17th February 2020. He refers also to correspondence from **Margaret Whalley**, another PHSOtheFACTS member who appealed to the Patients Association for support.

Ms. Lucy Watson
Chair of Trustees
The Patients Association

Dear Ms. Watson

Parliamentary and Health Service Ombudsman

I refer to your letter of 7th February, note the contents and make the following observations. As indicated in our conference call, your letter has been shared with people in our support group PHSO-thefacts as will this response.

From my perspective, as a patient, the lack of timeliness by the Patients Association in dealing with the issues raised has been extremely frustrating. It is right that your organization seeks to 'up its game' when dealing with the issues patients raise with you. I trust my negative experience will not be repeated in future patient contacts.

A major point of concern to me is the timeline of events. My first contact with your CEO, Rachel Power, was by letter dated 1st September 2019. You confirm that, with her, you met the Ombudsman in October, yet Ms. Power's conversation with me did not take place until 4th November. I do not recall her informing me that she had met the Ombudsman the previous month.

Our group of complainants who have received, and continue to receive poor treatment at the hand of PHSO thought it might be useful if a conference, outlining continuing patient concerns, could be arranged under the umbrella of the Patients Association. This need not be an expensive exercise. Ms. Power declined to do this but did say she would 'give some thought' to helping us find a venue. My letter of 3rd December to you was as a result of hearing nothing further from her.

Patients Association Position Statement regarding PHSO

I take the following key messages from the position statement:

"For now, we continue to receive calls to our helpline from patients, carers and families who are unhappy about PHSO".

When I spoke with Rachel Power and asked how many PHSO complainants have contacted the Patients Association, the response was "a few". She did not elaborate further. Perhaps you can now do so.

"We will continue to raise concerns with PHSO when things have not been good enough".

The valid question raised is how does the Patients Association know when things have not been good enough? Failure to look at individual cases and retain documents to establish commonality and for future reference will undoubtedly continue to leave complainants in an isolated and vulnerable position if it is only PHSO who decides when to apply their own discretion and movable criteria.

It is time for the Patients Association to say whether it believes, based on evidence and testimonies received, things are now good enough at PHSO or not.

"Some patients and bereaved relatives who have been let down by PHSO have gone so far as to suggest it is corrupt. We do not believe this to be the case".

My understanding is the evidence recently forwarded to you by Margaret Whalley, in addition to my own, challenges that belief.

This brings me to the heart of the problem with the Patients Association position statement. Thus far, it is based on belief and not on hard evidence. The definition of corruption, according to the Oxford English Reference Dictionary is:

"Affect or harm by errors or alterations"

It is easy for both the Patients Association and PHSO to associate corruption with dishonesty or actions in pursuit of personal gain. That is not what I, and other critics of PHSO mean by corruption.

Factors encouraging systemic corruption include conflicting incentives, discretionary powers, lack of transparency and a culture of impunity. Though I know little of her case, Margaret Whalley has communicated to you that PHSO have pointed out the Trust continue to hide behind a police report which itself had failed to factor in the correct procedure at end of life. The PHSO themselves recognize the negative impact of the continued existence of a flawed report giving rise for the possibility of significant injustice.

I have provided the Patients Association with a complete case file which includes PHSO errors and, therefore by definition, a file containing corrupt documents. Despite this, Mr. Behrens refuses to quash a flawed report and has chosen to leave it in the hands of the NHS Trust concerned. Your letter of 7th February 2020 states you did not know the Ombudsman could quash a report approved by a previous Ombudsman. What the Patients Association seem to be saying is that no report, no matter how incorrect, can be quashed if it was circulated by a previous Ombudsman. I would urge the Patients Association to think again regarding this spurious argument.

I am aware Margaret Whalley has made contact with you regarding her case. I suggest all Trustees at the Patients Association read her valid submission before formulating your future policy.

You state the Patients Association has accepted an invitation to meet the PHSO case work assessment team. I would be concerned as to the level of access and openness your Trustee was given. It is a fact that all PHSO investigations are conducted in private. It is therefore questionable as to how effective such limited access given to the Patients Association could be. You should also note the recently formed PHSO Expert Advisory Panel will only provide advice as a non executive function to the Ombudsman when he decides they should be involved. They are not a decision making forum (see terms of reference on PHSO website).

The Patients Association might better serve patients by examining PHSO Trust Pilot, an avenue I mentioned during our conference call and to which you have not referred in your letter. From over 90 comments, the only positive one is dated 22nd December 2019. I question whether this was actually a PHSO case due to the fact the complaint concerned a Practice Manager – something PHSO would not generally be involved in investigating.

When the original legislation was making its way through Parliament, Quintin Hogg MP made the following comment in the debate on 24th January 1967 (Hansard):

"As the House knows from my speech on Second Reading, I have always regarded the ombudsman as a 'swiz'…The Bill was always drafted to be a 'swiz' and now it is spelt into the Bill. I shall vote against it"

The Patients Association, rather than acquiesce to the status quo should now actively campaign for change, seeking the result of an independent element to oversee Health and Social Care complaints at the initial stage and taking investigations out of the hands of NHS Trusts who cannot be trusted, as evidenced by scandals from Mid Staffs, Morecambe Bay, Gosport and many others which now have come to light.

Conclusion

The Patients Association current position appears to be, thus far, based on belief – not evidence. It cannot be right you have moved from the severe criticism of PHSO expressed in 2015 to the current position without taking evidence from patients and their families.

By not hosting or lending the Patients Association name to a conference of patients adversely affected by PHSO's conduct of investigations, your organization has declined to receive such evidence.

The position statement has been issued without any independent survey of complainant satisfaction by the Patients Association and

The Patients Association prefers to rely on what it is told by the Ombudsman rather than the patient as being factually correct. Patients need reassurance the Patients Association has their interests at heart.

I hope the Patients Association Trustees will now fully address these serious issues at their next meeting and have sight of all the exchanges of correspondence that have taken place between the Patients Association, Margaret Whalley, myself and any other patients who may have shared their experiences with you since I wrote on 1st September 2019.

I will be grateful for the return of the case file sent to you if you do not wish to retain it as evidence. The thought of this file being shredded is abhorrent to me and it may be useful elsewhere.

I would like to thank you for taking a personal interest in the issues and leave you with the following quotations which, on current evidence, certainly apply to PHSO:

"Power tends to corrupt and absolute power corrupts absolutely". (Lord Acton)

"Not everything that is faced can be changed but nothing can be changed until it is faced"
(James Baldwin)

Yours sincerely
David Czarnetzki

Editor's note: below is the letter sent to the Patients Association on the 15th February 2020 by Margaret Whalley. In this correspondence Mrs Whalley lays out the catalogue of errors in the handling of her case by PHSO and it would appear that we citizens know more about the Ombudsman's ability to 'quash' a flawed report than the Patients Association do, despite the earlier correspondence they received from Maggie and Janet Brooks on this subject. There is much to be learnt from the facts revealed in this correspondence.

Chair of the Patients' Association

Dear Ms Watson

Mr David Czarnetzki has shared, with members of PHSO-the facts support group, the contents of your recent correspondence (7 February 2020).
I note that you included this paragraph which is concerned with the quashing of PHSO Final reports:-

'On our phone call you set out your concerns, in particular you said that the Ombudsman had agreed that the final report into your case published in June 2015 was flawed. You remain concerned that the PHSO has refused to quash your report and this is still the report that the NHS Trust holds. You raised the problems that you had with the quality of case management, and you were concerned about the way in which your public questions to the Ombudsman at the public meeting in Manchester were published on the PHSO website and responded to. We said that we did not know that the Ombudsman could

quash reports approved by a previous Ombudsman. We will follow this up and ask the Ombudsman if this is the case and if so, clarify the criteria used for deciding when to quash a final investigation report.'

My Case Also Flawed

My Final Report into the care and death circumstances of my brother, a vegetative state patient, was published in March 2016. As in Mr Czarnetzki's case, my Final Report is flawed. This is finally admitted by the PHSO but only after years of sustained effort on my part. The PHSO have not automatically quashed the report. Instead they are offering a partial re-investigation.

With respect, from your correspondence with Mr Czarenetzki, it is clear that the Patients' Association – the body who the public expects to support and guide – appears ignorant of the circumstances which trigger a quashing. I infer this from your comment, *'we did not know that the Ombudsman could quash reports approved by a previous Ombudsman'.*

In order to be of help, I would like to provide a recent email response (dated 10/1/2020) sent to me by Mr **Alex Robertson** Executive Director for Strategy and Operations for the PHSO. I am forwarding his email now, which you can see below this one. I am copying Mr Robertson into this email. I understand he has a role in Communication, and is therefore in a strong position to clarify for the PA what does/does not deserve to be quashed.

You will see that regarding quashing, Mr Robertson explains:-

73. *We will only quash a report or decision we have made in exceptional circumstances given the strong public interest in certainty around our decisions. These circumstances are;*
- *We have missed significant material evidence which we should have considered, or significant new evidence has come to light, and/or;*
- *Our decision is incontrovertibly and significantly wrong for some other reason, and;*
- *There is no other way to resolve the matter, and;*
- *It is in the public interest for the report to be quashed, for example because the existence of the report and its findings are having a demonstrable adverse impact.*

Taking each of his four bullet points in order, I would like to relate them to examples from my case so you will see how a case is judged against these criteria. I feel this is important for the Patient Association to learn about PHSO procedure to be in a position to inform complainants. :-

1 of 4 'Missed Significant Material Evidence' (Mr A Robertson Guideline)

Mr Robertson communicates that the PHSO will quash a report if they have, *'missed significant material evidence'*.

Not only was the material evidence not in place in my case, PHSO staff knew it was not in place but continued forward to publication, despite my protest and despite written representation by my MP, Ms Lisa Nandy. Ms Nandy had requested that Mr Martin (the then Deputy Ombudsman) provide a *'direct personal assurance that this will be an evidence based investigation'* (10 Dec 2015 and Post release of Draft)

The PHSO Service Review Analysis (obtained Nov 2019) includes: -

Should we be subject to JR (judicial review) *on this case there is a significant risk we would be criticised...it is tricky to say with any certainty what we (and our advisers) did or did not consider...I think the best thing we could have done at that point was to 'come clean'* (my highlight)

Shortly after their group realisation (revealed in internal emails) that PHSO staff collectively couldn't identify (or satisfy my request for) the relevant material evidence, the investigator wrote this to me dated 9/02/2016. (Note this was in the period between the Draft and publication of the Final Report.) :-

'We are satisfied we have completed an appropriate, thorough and robust investigation based on relevant evidence. '

One might think, that now this behaviour has come to light, this would trigger an across-the-board automatic quashing of my case and an enquiry into staff conduct. However, I am now offered only a partial re-investigation. Without inviting my comments on the Final Report, the PHSO are proposing that only the 3 of the 6 original bodies are to be re-investigated. Since the same staff (plural) - who disregarded a respect for evidence - handled all facets of the investigation then it is difficult to see how any part can be upheld without re-investigation? Moreover the PHSO acknowledged that they failed to factor in the correct advice and did not draw on essential evidence e.g. issues revealed at inquest, x rays etc.

2 of 4 'Our Decision is Incontrovertibly Wrong' (Mr A Robertson Guideline)

The 2016 PHSO Final Report includes this confident statement:-

114. From the advice we have received, it is clear that the decision to start Mr Bowdler on the ICP was correct in the circumstances, and that decision was communicated appropriately to the family and Ms A.

In the 2019 PHSO's Service Review Analysis, the PHSO quote the Police report. Regarding the excerpt shown above (i.e. that the family were in agreement with the commencement of the end of life pathway) the PHSO note the Police observed, *'this comment appears to be factually incorrect'*.

Most significantly the 2019 PHSO Analysis, written by a PHSO Reviewer includes,

'It does seem that we relied on the wrong GMC guidance (for patients lacking capacity rather than for patients in a permanent vegetative state like Mr Bowdler. The correct guidance does indeed say that any decision to withhold nutrition and hydration should be referred to court. I think that both the Inquest and the Police shied away from addressing this. Of more concern to us is that when Mrs Whalley recently asked the Trust for the rationale for their decision they too 'hid' behind the comments in the Police report rather than answering her question. ..We also did not address this in the original investigation.'

Even Lasca/NHS England (one of the parties I am told will not to be re-investigated) has, since publication of the Final Report, written independently to the PHSO pointing out that facts included in the Final Report are quite wrong.

Since almost four years have passed since the publication of an inaccurate and unreliable document, you can see my utter frustration that the parties are allowed to hide behind the flawed PHSO Final report.

One of the principle reasons I approached the PHSO was for them to explore <u>why</u> Mr Bowdler was placed on the LCP (twice within a week and each time with nutrition and hydration entirely withheld, the second time to death). The Final Report does list this as a complaint they were going to investigate as can be seen by their statement in the Final Report - *'Doctors' decisions regarding end of life care, specifically the decisions to put Mr Bowdler on an end of life care pathway, take him off it, and put him back on it.'* The Final report went on to conclude this:-

114. From the advice we have received, it is clear that the decision to start Mr Bowdler on the ICP was correct in the circumstances, and that decision was communicated appropriately to the family and Ms A.

However, the recent PHSO Service Review Analysis reveals that :-

'consideration of the second admission was far too brief.' 'we simply accepted that it was correct to put Mr Bowdler on the pathway and that this decision was clinically sound.... *'at the time of the decision, there was no clinical evidence that her brother had aspiration pneumonia...there is no clear evidence to support either of the reasons given to explain the decision to place Mr Bowdler on the ICP'*

It is clear that this crucial issue has yet to be investigated.

3 of 4 'There is no other way to resolve the Matter' (Mr A Robertson Guideline)

Some may argue that allowing a flawed and incomplete report to remain in existence for years is not a <u>resolution.</u>
To my mind, quashing the first Final report in its entirety and beginning afresh is the commencement of what one hopes will be a resolution.

Additionally, there is the significant issue of not referring the decision to the Court of Protection. It does seem that we relied on the wrong GMC guidance (for patients lacking capacity rather than for patients in a permanent vegetative state like Mr Bowdler). The correct guidance does indeed say that any decision to withhold nutrition and hydration should be referred to court. I think that both the Inquest and the Police shied away from addressing this. Of more concern to us is that when Mrs Whalley recently asked the Trust
for the rationale for their decision they too 'hid' behind the comments in the police report rather than answering her question. I can fully understand why this adds to Mrs Whalley's concerns. We also did not address this in the original investigation. Clearly, this raises the possibility of a significant injustice (even more so when factoring the uncertainty about the reasoning for the placement) and is an issue that should be considered very carefully to judge any impact.

4 of 4 'It is in the Public Interest for the Report to be quashed..findings having a demonstrable adverse effect' (Mr A Robertson Guideline)

The demonstrable adverse effect is that all readers of a flawed report which purports to be robust and quality assured, are in essence being knowingly duped by the PHSO.

The quote from the Service Review Analysis (shown above in green text) explains that the continued existence of the report allows the Trust to hide behind such flawed reports and is an ongoing *'significant injustice'* to me.

The issues which should have been speedily addressed in the interest of ongoing patient safety have been allowed to lie since my MP's intervention in 2015.

Monitoring the Numbers of Quashed Reports

You will see below that Mr Robertson's January email (below) includes,

'Executive Office will have arrangements for monitoring the number of occasions where reports are quashed.'
I wonder if the Patient's Association is aware of the number of cases already quashed by the Ombudsman?

The number of cases could be taken as a performance indicator but we all have to concede from the criteria (which my case according to Mr Robertson fails to meet) that the bar seems set exceedingly high. My PHSO Reviewer wrote in his Analysis, *'we blatantly failed to cover ourselves in glory'.* Surely to get a balanced picture, there would be strong public interest and curiosity in any quashed Final Reports to set against the public profile promoting integrity?

I would be most grateful if on your intended approach to the PHSO you could determine how many such quashed cases there actually are and provide details to me and to phso-thefacts group. This would better help you and I understand PHSO process.

Patients Association Support Sought

Where the Ombudsman chooses to re-investigate, after admittedly poor prolonged complaint handling, to whom can a complainant turn for external support to try to ensure better service? Is this where the Patient Association would step in?

When you do approach the PHSO, I wonder if you would find out (for your organisation and our support group) just who is an acknowledged flawed Final report serving for those years between its publication and necessary amendment? Is it the complainant, the PHSO, the parties central to the complaint, for it seems it cannot be for patient safety?

The PHSO, in this case, have set the rules for an investigation, which to the best of my ability I have followed repeatedly for years but am dismayed that they did not follow their own rules for investigation. Mr Robertson writes about the *'strong public interest in certainty'* regarding PHSO decisions. The PHSO have admitted to <u>uncertainty</u> due to knowledge of a lack of identifiable material evidence, sources not taken up, incorrect conclusions and to my mind dishonestly touting a report as 'robust' when they knew decisions lacked underpinning.

I noted in the PHSO Review Analysis (2019) there was an unwarranted suggestion that a personal dislike of me had influenced an investigation manager - someone I hasten to add I had never met or spoken to, and with whom all written correspondence was polite. Over 9 weeks ago I wrote to Ombudsman Mr Behrens, to counter these suggestions with contemporary written evidence. I also pointed out a serious data breach (sensitive unredacted data - not my data - lay amongst my subject access request material). Inexplicably I have yet to receive an explanation (though the correspondence was acknowledged received by Mr Behrens's secretary well before Christmas).

After reading the criteria Mr Robertson has provided, and considering how it is being applied, here is an opportunity for learning for those in advocacy. I would be interested to hear if the PA judge the bar for quashing may be set too high and whether they feel the input of another body to oversee the PHSO process may be useful to assure fairness and integrity. I would be most grateful to receive your feedback which I will gladly share with Mr Czarnetzki and others within the phso-thefacts group.

Yours sincerely

M Whalley (Mrs)

Reply from the Patients Association. 25th February 2020

Dear Mrs Whalley

I am writing in reply to your email sent to me dated 15 February 2020, following your review of my correspondence with Mr David Czarnetski in respect of the Parliamentary Health Service Ombudsman (PHSO). I am sorry to hear about your experiences in your dealings with the PHSO.

First of all thank you for sharing the criteria for when PHSO will quash final investigation reports that was provided to you by Mr Alex Robertson Executive Director for Strategy and Operations at the PHSO. We will make sure our Helpline staff have this so they can share these criteria with other complainants who contact us for advice in this respect. You have set out a number of concerns about the way in which your own case has been handled by the Ombudsman. I note that the PHSO is now undertaking a partial reinvestigation into your case. Whilst this may not be the full reinvestigation that you were hoping for, I hope that this may achieve some resolution to your concerns and a better experience for you of the Ombudsman investigating your case.

With regard to your enquiry about the number of cases where final reports are quashed by the Ombudsman, the Patients Association is not currently aware of this number. I agree that it would be interesting data to monitor but I suspect the overall numbers are likely to be too small to provide a reliable performance indicator. It is also difficult to comment on whether or not the bar for quashing final investigation reports has been set too high, but we will explore this and the number of reports that have been quashed when we next meet with the Ombudsman.

Finally, you have asked who complainants can turn to for external support to try to ensure a better service when the Ombudsman chooses to reinvestigate a case. This is not a role the Patients Association can take on. Although we are a national charity and speak up on behalf of patients to influence national policy, we are a small organisation. We have nine employed staff which includes a small Helpline team and are not in a position to take up individual cases in the way that some charities can. There are local independent complaints advocacy services in each area that may be able to help although some are stronger than others. The role of our Helpline team is to provide advice and access to relevant information and signposting to relevant sources of help and advice to assist patients and their families including people who wish to complain to achieve the resolution they are looking for. Our Helpline can be contacted on Tel: 0800 345 7115.

Thank you for bringing this information to my attention and I will ensure that this is shared with the Governance Sub Committee of the Board of Trustees.

Yours Sincerely,

Lucy Watson, Chair

Cc Archie Naughton Trustee, Chair of the Governance Committee

Editor's note: The Patients Association will often be referring distressed patients to other organisations who have already failed them such as PALS (Patient Advice and Liaison service) or to organisations such as CAB (Citizens Advice Bureau) who do not have the funding or expertise to assist. Compare the work of the Patients Association, with their nine employed staff and corporate donations of £167,501[40] with that of the charity **'Compassion in Care'** which is run, virtually single-handedly by **Eileen Chubb** on a budget of less than £10,000. Eileen is a one-woman powerhouse, writing books, reports and submitting evidence to government while supporting individual whistle-blowers through stressful court cases. She has visited over 300 care homes undercover and was instrumental in a Panorama programme which showed footage of serious abuse in a care home, which at the time of the undercover operation was passed as 'fit' by the CQC. Where there is a will there is a way.

From Eileen Chubb's second book, **'There is no Me in Whistleblower'** published 2020.

---

[40] Charity Commission 2018 Accounts for Patients Association

"Compassion in Care is a registered charity which exposes abuse, raises awareness on whistle-blowing and has published comprehensive evidence in support of our work. We have helped, advised, supported thousands of families who have a relative in a care setting who has suffered abuse. We have helped over 7000 Whistle-blowers, supporting them as best we can with the small resources we have throughout the trauma, hardship and smearing that follows doing the right thing." P163

Editor's note: This final letter to the Patients Association is from **Della Reynolds**, the co-ordinator of PHSOtheFACTS.

Lucy Watson,
Chair of Trustees,
Patients Association.
20th February 2020

Dear Ms Watson,

As co-ordinator for PHSOtheFACTS I have been party to the correspondence between yourself and a fellow group member Mr David Czarnetzki. I quote below from your response to Mr Czarnetzki on 7.2.2020.

> *Rachel Power CEO and I met with the Ombudsman and with the PHSO CEO in October 2019 and the quality of case management was the main topic of our discussions. The PHSO set out wide ranging actions taken to improve the quality of case management. Our*

principal question to the Ombudsman was that whilst a number of sensible strategies have been put in place to improve casework, and quarterly performance data against the service charter is published, we were still concerned that there was limited evidence about what this meant for patients' actual experience of going through the investigation process and their satisfaction or dissatisfaction with this, and with their final investigation report. We asked for more detail on patient experience of PHSO. In response we were offered the opportunity to meet the case work assessment team. One of our Trustees undertook this last month.

It strikes me (and others in the group) that if the Patients Association wish to know about the **'patients actual experience of going through the investigation process and their satisfaction or dissatisfaction with this'** then you need to speak to the patients and not the Ombudsman. Since the Patients Association ceased supporting individuals through the complaints process you have lost an opportunity to monitor the process at close quarters. This is regrettable. Particularly when you note that you have only met with the Ombudsman twice and the first visit in 2018 was **'an introductory meeting'.**

We have met twice with the PHSO in June 2018 and in October 2019. The meeting in June 2018 was an introductory meeting. We will be reporting on our October 2019 meeting to the Governance Committee and Board of Trustees in March 2020. This will inform an updated position on the PHSO which we will provide on the Patients Association website for our members and the public. This is likely to be in April 2020 after the Easter break.

It is also unfortunate that the Patients Association has not done more to deliver on the recommendations from your 2014 report. With a new Ombudsman, the move to Manchester which saw a major change to staffing and the implementation of a new strategy the Patients Association could have used their influence to deliver on these important recommendations which are listed below. Perhaps progress towards these could be part of your report, to be released in April 2020?

Recommendations from Patients Association 2014 Report:

1. It is time for an independent review of the role and accountability of the Ombudsman.
2. A more publicly accountable PHSO.
3. Legislation applied to the PHSO should be reviewed.
4. The statutory duty for NHS Trusts to adhere to the principles of being open should be extended to the PHSO handling of complaints.
5. Clearly defined organisational boundaries and jurisdiction must be established.
6. A review of case by case costings by the National Audit Office.
7. PHSO's paper-based procedures need to be completely overhauled.
8. An independent appeal process for PHSO investigations.
9. A code of practice for investigators.

10. Terms of reference for each investigation must be agreed with the families at the commencement of an investigation.
11. A review of time lines for the completion of investigations.
12. Face to face meeting with the complainant/s at the commencement of an investigation.
13. Agreed regular face to face meetings with complainants at each stage of the investigation.
14. Independent advocacy support available for all complainants.
15. Time lines for submissions of appeals must be extended.
16. It should not be under the remit of the PHSO to recommend monetary settlements to complainants.
17. To ensure learning the PHSO must influence change and ensure Trusts adhere to recommendations following appropriate investigations.

I am also wondering if you have taken up with the Ombudsman the discrepancy in responses between the complainant and the public body as recorded in the latest Service Charter data (September 2019) from the PHSO website. Such wide discrepancies in satisfaction levels between the public body and the complainant indicates a level of bias in the process. I attach screenshots.

Following an open and fair process

Commitment	Quarter 2 (July-Sep 2019)		Change from Quarter 1	
	Complainant feedback	Organisations we Investigate feedback	Complainant feedback	Organisations we Investigate feedback
5. We will listen to you to make sure we understand your complaint	69%	84%	-5%	+2%
8. We will gather all the information we need, including from you and the organisation you have complained about before we make our decision	48%	88%	NC	NC
11. We will explain our decision and recommendations, and how we reached them	47%	90%	-6%	NC

You may also like to take up with PHSO the reasons why they have not carried out and/or published an independent complainant survey since the arrival of Rob Behrens.

Complainant feedback surveys

We regularly commission independent research with people who bring complaints to us to help measure our performance.

Here you can read the most recent reports based on their feedback.

- 2015-2016
- 2014-2015

At PHSOtheFACTS we regularly hear from people who are mystified and distressed by the PHSO complaint process. Their experiences of delay, scoping out of key aspects of the complaint and denial of the evidence, suggests that nothing has fundamentally changed at PHSO since the arrival of Rob Behrens, which will be three years in April 2020. We are currently compiling a book about our efforts to hold the Ombudsman to account which contains new case studies of complaints closed since Mr Behrens took office. We aim to publish this early in March 2020. Unfortunately, your updated report on progress at PHSO will not feature as it will be released too late to be included but correspondence with our group members will make up one of the chapters.

You may be aware that Mr Behrens will not respond to correspondence from PHSOtheFACTS which prevents us from directly challenging PHSO on any of the issues raised in this letter; effectively making your organisation our only voice. I hope you find this information useful for future discussions with PHSO.

Yours sincerely,
Della Reynolds
Coordinator PHSOtheFACTS

Editor's note: At this point let us look at how the work of the Patients Association has changed since its conception in 1963. This statement is from the Patients Association accounts, as published on the Charity Commission website.

Objectives and Activities

The Patients Association is one of the oldest and most distinctive health and care charities in the UK.

It was first established in 1963 by Helen Hodgson, a part-time teacher who was motivated by recent events concerning the drug thalidomide, and reports of patients receiving the wrong treatment and tests being carried out on patients without their informed consent. Our remit is not condition or organ-specific, but covers all issues that affect patients -including social care and public health. We work with patients directly: they are our members and supporters, and also the people who benefit from our help and advice services. We also speak to government, the NHS and others about patients' priorities and concerns, to ensure the patient voice is heard and acted upon.[41]

Editor's note: It now appears that the Patients Association **works** with the government, NHS and others and **speaks** to patients, something of a reversal of roles. Considering the Patients Association first came into being in order to challenge the injustice caused by the use of the drug thalidomide, it is worrying to see that two sponsors for the PA helpline are themselves major pharmaceutical companies and the third is a solicitor who specialise in taking clinical negligence cases forward against the NHS.

Helpline sponsors

41

https://apps.charitycommission.gov.uk/Accounts/Ends33/0001006733_AC_20181231_E_C.pdf

Is it by chance or by design that following the very public criticism of PHSO by the Patients Association, which no doubt contributed to the early departure of the Ombudsman **Dame Julie Mellor,** both bodies take on new leaders, new staff teams and new three-year strategies? With significant staff change there is a loss of organisational memory. Fewer people will notice if reforms are detrimental to the established core role of the organisation. We can see that the Patients Association has been reduced to little more than a 'finger-wagging', after the event, mouthpiece as in their recent response to the **Marmot Review,**[42] which highlighted severe health inequalities.

Marmot Review 10 Years On

Patients demand action on health inequalities, as report shows how government policy has degraded the nation's health

The Patients Association is calling for decisive action by the Government in the wake of the publication of the ten-year review of Sir Michael Marmot's landmark report on health inequalities.

---

[42] https://www.patients-association.org.uk/news/marmot-review-10-years-on

Rachel Power, Chief Executive of the Patients Association, said: "Today's report makes for truly shocking reading. It shows that improvements in life expectancy have stalled for the first time in over a century, and that people across England are now spending more of their lives in ill health.

"It is time for the Government to take its responsibilities for stewarding the nation's health seriously, so that ten years from now we are not once again reflecting on a decade of disgrace and failure.

"The Patients Association will be taking the findings and recommendations of this report as our starting-point for our own work to drive improvements in the health and wellbeing of people who suffer most as a result of health inequalities, and can find it hard to access the support and services they need."

Editor's note: Brave words from the Patients Association but unfortunately, there is every possibility that PA will do no more than continue to be shocked at the damage caused by government bodies. The correspondence from the Patients Association sadly confirms that those who *'find it hard to access the support and service they need'* will be disappointed in turn by the Patients Association, who will 'wish them luck' as they refer them onto somebody else.

Let us give the final word to **Eileen Chubb**, from Compassion in Care. Whether 'whistleblower' or 'complainant' it is the same story.

*"We now have authorities that are so dysfunctional, dishonest, complacent, self-serving and totally incompetent that the abuse and suffering of vulnerable people has reached epidemic proportions. Whistle-blowers do not have authorities they can go to in order to report abuse, **instead they have authorities that aid and abet the abusers.**" There is no Me in Whistleblower P90*

NO MALADMINISTRATION HERE

Chapter 6. Holding the Ombudsman to Account
Part I – Parliamentary Scrutiny

Editor's note: We expect public bodies to be accountable but who holds them to account? Since 2013 members of PHSOtheFACTS have attempted to use the tools of democracy to hold the Parliamentary and Health Service Ombudsman to account for the harm caused by repeated failure to uphold valid complaints about government bodies and the NHS. Although there are mechanisms built into the legislation to engender public confidence that the Ombudsman is accountable, in reality none of them are effective. PHSO is a secretive, self-regulating body, dealing in-house with all complaints about the delivery of its service and restricting public access to data through the questionable use of Freedom of Information exclusions as can be seen in this example below.

> M.A from the PHSO Data protection writes (to his peers), 'I think this would be best dealt with as a material evidence request. However, if there is any issue with this I'm happy to write and refuse the request under the Data Protection Act 2018. Let me know if this is suitable for you,' and, **'I've given this to her earlier so we're covered on that as**

well.' COVERED on WHAT 'AS WELL' and why does the PHSO need to be 'covered'? Does the PHSO make arbitrary data provision decisions based on what is 'suitable' for its employees and 'covering' its employees?

Having received nothing but ghosting or deflection from direct attempts to raise our concerns with PHSO, we started to lobby Parliament. Initially we had a degree of success, as reform of the Ombudsman was on the political agenda.

As described in chapter 3, the **Cabinet Office** drafted the original legislation which created a body that would then hold themselves and other government departments to account. With such an obvious conflict of interests it is unsurprising that the legislation included a series of loopholes which ensured that most government departments were let off with no more than the occasional slap on the wrist.

Key among those loopholes was the inability of the Ombudsman to examine 'discretional' decisions, which covers a lot of ground. In order to uphold a complaint, the Ombudsman must determine there has been 'harm' caused by 'maladministration' where neither 'harm' nor 'maladministration' have been defined. Members of the public might expect that breaches in procedure and policy would be deemed maladministration and go to great lengths to prove such breaches. But according to PHSO, there is no compulsion to follow procedures and policies and a failure to do so is deemed nothing more than a shortcoming.

The public may consider that 'harm' would include the avoidable death of a patient, but this can be dismissed with the statement that even if procedures had been followed it was likely that the same outcome would have occurred.

It is for the Ombudsman to decide the merits of a complaint, on a case by case basis, resulting in a lack of consistency and predictability. The Ombudsman has discretion to determine which standards to apply and which to ignore, making it is impossible to hold the Ombudsman to account for what the public may see as 'irrational behaviour'. The Ombudsman's decision is final and can only be challenged in court via judicial review. All records are destroyed after 12 months making it impossible to detect repeated patterns or brewing scandals.

At the time of writing (March 2020) PHSO has just released 2018/19 parliamentary complaints data. An extraordinarily long delay given that this information has been held by PHSO since April last year and their Annual Report was released in July 2019. A recent FOI[43] request has revealed some overall figures which demonstrate the fundamental ineffectiveness of the Ombudsman to hold government departments to account. Just 38 upheld complaints from a total of 5,744 submitted cases about government departments gives a 0.6% uphold rate. If you include the 35 cases resolved through intervention then the upheld figure rises to a heady 1.2% but there is no guarantee that the complainant was satisfied with the intervention and no investigation report is written to determine the nature of these 'resolved' complaints.

Here are the relevant figures for each of the items you've requested:

1.   There were 5,744 Parliamentary complaints received in 2018/19

2.   There were 38 Parliamentary cases upheld or partly upheld at investigation in 2018/19 (3 upheld, 35 partly upheld)

3.   There were 52 Parliamentary cases not upheld at investigation in 2018/19.

43

whatdotheyknow.com/request/complaints_against_government_de_2

The Ombudsman primarily comes under the wing of the Cabinet Office, but in nod towards impartiality it is monitored by a select committee set up for that purpose which is currently called the **'Public Administration and Constitutional Affairs Committee' (PACAC)** but was previously called the **'Public Administration Select Committee (PASC).** **Sir Bernard Jenkin** was chair of this committee from 2010, stepping down at the 2019 general election.

Since the Ombudsman combines the roles of both Parliamentary Commissioner for Administration and Health Service Ombudsman (since 1993) the **Health Select Committee** also monitors the work of the Ombudsman. Periodically, reform of the Ombudsman comes to the top of the political agenda and like visiting comets all three bodies orbit in a display of concern and debate. But once the noise and light die down, you find that nothing has fundamentally changed.

The release of the **Francis Report** following the **Mid Staffordshire NHS Foundation Trust Public Inquiry in 2013**, was the trigger for debate on reform of the complaints system, including the role of the Ombudsman. As in other health scandals, it was not the Ombudsman who lifted the lid on the deaths of over 1,000 people due to NHS neglect and abuse, but persistent and dedicated citizens from **'Cure the NHS'** led by **Julie Bailey.**

The following blog post from November 2015 (a time of naïve optimism) gives an historical overview of the many words spoken about Ombudsman reform. It can be seen that the select committees certainly did their bit by interviewing witnesses, carefully summarising the faults in the present system and putting forward detailed proposals for the shape of future reform but unfortunately change depended upon government action.

The creation of the **Healthcare Safety Investigation Branch (HSIB),** driven forward by Sir Bernard Jenkin with a sense of urgency rarely seen in Parliament; is notable as a single, tangible result. Bear in mind when you see the catalogue of ignored reports that Ombudsman Rob Behrens, recently stated in a UKAJI article[44] concerning

---

[44] ukaji.org/2020/04/29/a-manifesto-for-ombudsman-reform/

Ombudsman reform, that there was a *'lack of hard evidence to support the need for reform'*. It would simply kick the reform can down the road a little longer if there were to be yet another review of the Ombudsman process.

DEEDS NOT WORDS

17th November 2015

A review of the (lack of) progress in Ombudsman reform.

For the first time in 48 years there is an opportunity to reform the Ombudsman service. Oliver Letwin and the Cabinet Office are currently compiling draft legislation to lay before the house in the spring of 2016. At this point the debate opens and it has been made clear from the many words written on this subject (not all recorded here) that there is great public concern, shared by parliamentarians, who have been anxious for some time to reform this key pillar of democracy.

When the public and parliament are in agreement, then great things are possible. If we work together we can ensure that in 2016 the new Public Service Ombudsman has the statutory powers to drive reform plus the clarity of responsibility to be held to account if it fails to do so.

History of Ombudsman reform:

Life was breathed into the **Parliamentary Ombudsman** via the controversial **Parliamentary Commissioner Bill** of **1967.** Before parliament or the Lords were given time to debate the merits of the legislation, those in 'another place' had gone ahead and set up the office, hoping for a rubber stamp passage through both houses. Not an auspicious start. According to **Lord Harlech** speaking in the House of Lords, the primary purpose of the legislation was as follows;

"It seeks to redress the balance of power between the Government and the governed in the latter's favour;

However, the failure to determine a definition of maladministration and the total discretion given to the Commissioner (later Ombudsman) did indeed provided a loophole as large as the Round Tower of Windsor (as stated in the Lords debate) which has served to protect the balance of power in the government's favour ever since. The Ombudsman was also given no powers of enforcement and no statutory responsibility to monitor improvements following investigation uphold.

Flawed from the outset, nevertheless this legislation has stayed largely untouched for the last 48 years. Not to say that the subject hasn't come up for discussion. There have been a great many words spoken and recorded regarding the shortcomings of the Ombudsman service, but for all the good intentions, action has been thin on the ground.

This fruitless process was well documented in **2003** by **PASC**, in the hope of reigniting the debate.

The Review of the Public Sector Ombudsmen—A History of Delay

4. In 1996 our predecessors, the Select Committee on the Parliamentary Commissioner for Administration recommended "the thorough revision of the [1967] Act to remove the omissions in the Ombudsman's current jurisdiction, to implement the past recommendations of the Committee on the extension of his jurisdiction, and to ensure that the Ombudsman has comprehensive and effective powers". Despite numerous reviews and consultations and general agreement on both the need for reform and on the basis for the necessary changes, the Ombudsmen system has not been reformed. We set out below the whole series of events. It is a roll-call of talk rather than action.

The Timetable of Events

- **1996** Select Committee on the Parliamentary Commissioner for Administration recommend review of the Ombudsman.

- October **1998** the public sector ombudsmen submit a paper to Government proposing a comprehensive review of the organisation of the public sector ombudsmen in England.

- April **2000** *'Review of the Public Sector Ombudsmen in England'* or the **Collcutt Report**, published.

- June **2000** the Government publish a consultation document.

- August **2000** Public Administration Select Committee publishes its report *'Review of the Public Sector Ombudsmen in England'*

- July **2001** Government respond by way of a written Parliamentary Question agreeing with the review's recommendations and announcing that detailed proposals would be published in due course.

- January **2002** Memorandum from the Government to the Public Administration Select Committee announcing that it will be undertaking a further consultation exercise.[45]

---

[45] PASC historic review of Ombudsman reform 2003

2000 was the 'nearly year' with **Collcutt** producing a very comprehensive report calling for the following reforms.

- In line with the Ombudsman themselves, Collcutt called for a single commission with a common gateway for improved access to Ombudsman services.

- Collcutt also determined that the MP filter was obsolete and should be replaced with direct access.

- That the powers of the Ombudsman be strengthened in order to meet the needs of increasingly complex casework and the growing demand for resolution from the public.

The government responded to this report in broad agreement and concluded that the Ombudsman should be able to work in a more flexible manner than that allowed by the present legislation making the successful resolution of complaints possible using informal methods such as mediation. However, the need to change primary legislation led to interminable delay frustrating the PASC committee.

We endorsed the calls for a thorough review of the jurisdiction and powers of the Ombudsman, with an emphasis on increasing rather than reducing those powers. In conclusion we urged that the programme of reform should not be allowed to slip, adding that "We hope that restrictions on parliamentary time will not prevent an early opportunity being found for this important legislation to be enacted. It will bring important benefits to the public and should be seen as an integral element of the Government's programme of public service and modernisation"." PASC

Those 'important benefits to the public' are still in the pipeline 17 years later, not helped by the tendency of government responses to be **'in due course'** and despite the Select Committee throwing their full weight behind the call for reform.

This Committee supports the need for reform. Without clear, credible pathways for complainants, public services will never be adequately reformed. We reiterate our concerns and once again recommend that the Government produce a draft bill to implement the review of the Ombudsmen and actively seek an early solution to the problem of legislative delay. PASC 2003

In **2005** the **National Audit Office** released their review of government complaint handling and concluded that it was virtually impossible to evaluate either the true cost or the effectiveness of complaint handling due to the piecemeal fashion (and poor record keeping) of departmental complaint and appeal processes. [46] Around this time a number of white papers were published which tinkered at the edges of reform, unable to alter the original legislation.

In **June 2011, The Health Select Committee,** who monitor the Ombudsman in relation to NHS complaint

---

[46] NAO report 2005

handling, released a report entitled **'Complaints and Litigation'** [47] which confirmed that the legislative remit of the Ombudsman was ineffective in meeting public demand. This was closely followed in **July 2011** by a **Law Commission** report calling for legislative change, plus a wide-ranging review of public service ombudsman independence and accountability in order to improve public access and flexibility.[48] Unfortunately, neither of these reports were sufficient to secure parliamentary time for further debate.

Failure to heed previous warnings led to the **inevitable scandal**, the Mid Staffordshire inquiry and the **Francis Report of 2013**[49] which found that the complaints

---

47

https://publications.parliament.uk/pa/cm201012/cmselect/cmhealth/786/786i.pdf

48

https://assets.publishing.service.gov.uk/government/uploads/system/uploads/attachment_data/file/247386/1136.pdf
[49] https://www.rcgp.org.uk/policy/rcgp-policy-areas/~/media/Files/Policy/A-Z-policy/RCGP-Francis-Report-Overview-2013.ashx

process had failed to alert those in authority to the estimated 1,200 unnecessary deaths due to NHS neglect. Following this report, **PASC** held an inquiry into public sector complaint handling which culminated in their report **More Complaints Please!** in March 2014.[50]

This report focused primarily on changing the culture of complaint handling, seen by so many in authority as just a nuisance to be closed down rather than as valuable feedback. It also took the opportunity to once again call for the single portal.

*As so often in our Reports, we highlight that success depends on the right leadership. Government must ensure that **leadership of public services values complaints** as critical for improving, and learning about, their service. We welcome the Minister for Government Policy's review of complaints handling in Government, and recommend that:*

---

[50] http://www.ajustnhs.com/wp-content/uploads/2012/05/PASC-Report-Complaints-W-B-April-20141.pdf

- *there should be a **minister for government policy** on complaints handling;*
- *the primary objective of the Cabinet Office review of complaints handling in Government should be to **change attitudes and behaviour** in public administration at all levels in respect of complaints handling;*
- *in respect of **complaints from MPs handled by ministers,** replies must be accurate, clear and helpful. Confidential information should not be shared with third parties, and responsibility for responding cannot be delegated (which contributed to the blindness about Mid Staffordshire NHS Foundation Trust);*
- *the Government should create a **single point of contact** for citizens to make complaints about government departments and agencies; and*
- *the Government should **provide leadership** to those responsible for various parts of administrative justice, to ensure that there is a clear and consistent approach to sharing, learning and best practice. Achieving change of this nature is a difficult but vital challenge, and one that must be addressed now if we are to avoid*

the "toxic cocktail" poisoning efforts to deliver excellent
public services.

This report puts emphasis on the fact that successful public service complaint handling requires the cooperation of MPs, Ministers and responsive government departments. To call for a Minister with responsibility for complaint handling indicates PASC's desire for government to take complaints seriously and act upon them. No doubt a Minister for Complaints will be considered **'in due course'**.

This honest account of poor government department complaint handling (identified by Francis as a major contributor to the scandal of Mid Staffs) was followed by a hard hitting report into the specific performance of the **Parliamentary and Health Service Ombudsman (PHSO) 'Time for a People's Ombudsman'**,[51] which

---

51

https://publications.parliament.uk/pa/cm201314/cmselect/cmpubadm/655/655.pdf

was published in April 2014 following a further PASC inquiry.

Unsurprisingly, given their previous attempts to reform the Ombudsman in 2003, PASC confirmed that the Ombudsman service was **'outdated'** and **'stuck in time'**. Calling once again for a single, unified Ombudsman service and the removal of the MP filter; PASC went further by calling for a strengthening of **accountability** for the Ombudsman service and the introduction of **own initiative powers** of investigation.

- *As a priority, the iniquitous restriction on citizens' direct and open access to PHSO, known as the **"MP filter"**, must be abolished, as is already the case in respect of NHS complaints.*
- *PHSO must be **able to receive complaints other than in writing:** such as in person, by telephone or online, just as is expected of any normal complaints system.*
- *PHSO should have **"own-initiative" powers to investigate** areas of concern without having first to*

receive a complaint.

• Parliament should **strengthen the accountability of PHSO***. PASC, along with other Departmental Select Committees, should make greater use of the intelligence gathered by the PHSO to hold Government to account.*

• In the longer term, there is scope to change the way that ombudsman services are delivered. **(flexibility)***.*

• A consultation on the creation of a **single public services ombudsman for England***.*

• At the same time, there must be a distinctive ombudsman service for **UK non-devolved matters.**

* *In our Report,* **More Complaints Please***! we raised our concern that a "toxic cocktail" in respect of complaints handling—a combination of a reluctance on the part of citizens "to express their concerns or complaints" and a defensiveness on the part of services "to hear and address concerns"—so often*

poisons efforts to deliver excellent public services. An effective ombudsman service can help to address this but change is urgently needed if PHSO, or any future public services ombudsman, is to ensure that it delivers a more effective service that is responsive and proactive. Complaints must make a difference and they must be welcomed and used to help to improve public services for everyone. **(PASC 2014)**

We recommend that Parliament should strengthen the accountability of the Parliamentary and Health Service Ombudsman (PHSO). The Public Accounts Commission, or a similar body should take primary responsibility for scrutiny of PHSO, including examining corporate plans, budget and resources. **(PASC 2014)**

In 2015 PASC was renamed **Public Administration and Constitutional Affairs Committee** (**PACAC**) in recognition of its new role. **Bernard Jenkin** continued to be the chair. The standing order for **PACAC** is rather limited but it remains the only parliamentary body with any remit for scrutiny of PHSO.

2014 was a difficult year for **PHSO** who were also under inquiry from the **Health Select Committee (HSC)** following the release of a damning report from the **Patients Association.** Inundated with complaints from the public, the Patients Association released case studies detailing distressing accounts of service users' experiences. **'The Peoples Ombudsman – How it failed us.**

> *The evidence we have gathered gives a public perception of the PHSO as lacklustre, weak, secretive, unaccountable, untouchable and ineffective. The emotional cost for many families left exhausted and distressed through their experience with the PHSO far outweighs the huge financial cost. [£40 million PHSO funding]. The Patients Association therefore continue to be drawn to the conclusion that the PHSO remains unfit for purpose.*

Coming from **service users** this report focuses directly on the **investigative process** of the Ombudsman and on **public accountability**; giving specific recommendations for system change. It did not call for a single Commission, nor changes to the MP filter which have been set as key objectives by parliamentary bodies. Instead it called for **clearly defined jurisdiction** and a **code of practice** which could then be used to hold the Ombudsman to account. **Cost effectiveness** was also called into question.

The Patients Association report, addressed the thorny issue identified in the House of Lords back in 1967, that in **order to be effective and accountable the Ombudsman must have a clearly defined jurisdiction and the statutory power to drive reform.**

In response the **Health Select Committee** took evidence in 2014 and released their own report[52]

52
https://publications.parliament.uk/pa/cm201415/cmselect/cmhealth/350/350.pdf

'Complaints and Raising Concerns' in **January 2015.** With an emphasis on service users and NHS whistle-blowers the HSC looked at progress in complaint handling since their 2011 report **'Complaints and Litigation'** and the impact poor complaint handling had on the individual concerned.

HSC concluded that;

> *There have been a number of significant reviews of the complaint system which have urged a change in the culture of the NHS in responding to complaints. There is little firm evidence to date of the moves to change culture having a wholesale positive effect either on the behaviour of NHS providers which give rise to complaints or on the satisfaction of service users about how their complaints have been handled.* ***(Paragraph 13 HSC Jan 2015)***

They called for a government review and for a number of recommendations to be implemented:

- A single portal for complaint handling.

- This should integrate complaints regarding 'social care' under a single Health and Social Care Ombudsman.

- Local resolution at first-tier level.

- A review of advocacy arrangements.

- Vindication for whistle-blowers

- External accountability for PHSO.

The serious criticisms of the Ombudsman from the Patients Association are of grave concern. We recommend that an external audit mechanism be established to benchmark and assure the quality of Ombudsman investigations. In her response to this report we ask the Ombudsman to set out how her organisation is seeking to address problems with its processes, and a timetable for improvements. ***(Paragraph 91 HSC Jan 2015)***

Accountability for the Ombudsman was now firmly on the agenda, due largely to public demand. In **March 2015** the **Patients Association** published a follow up to their previous case studies with an analysis of the types of issues faced by complainants using the Ombudsman service. **'PHSO – Labyrinth of Bureaucracy'** Using survey data the Patients Association determined that there were common weaknesses in the investigation process which needed to be addressed, and called once again for the recommendations from their previous report to be implemented.

> *The Patients Association has collated the responses which evidence that the PHSO:*
>
> *• **Does not investigate complaints fairly** – Evidence is ignored.*
>
> *• **Takes sides with the organisation they are supposed to be investigating** – Even when there is clear evidence to do the contrary.*
>
> *• **Does not make the process straightforward** – They ask many questions*

that the complainant has already answered or cannot answer. They change case worker/investigator without informing the complainant. They take weeks to respond and then ask a question which could be answered by looking in the submitted paperwork.

• **Produces reports that aren't thorough or the product of comprehensive investigation** – Final reports are full of inaccuracies despite the inaccuracies being highlighted by the complainant when the report is in draft format.

• **Fails to make a difference through the complaints process** – Trusts aren't asked for assurance that recommendations are acted upon and so change is not implemented and improvements are not made.

• **Does not put patients central to process** – Patients are made to feel like they are a nuisance for complaining, that they are wasting the PHSO's time and that there are others worse off.

Prompted by a paper from Carl Macrae and Charles Vincent **'Learning from failure: the need for independent safety investigation in healthcare'. PASC** had instigated a further inquiry to establish an expert panel to investigate clinical incident with the same robust measures as those used by the aviation industry. This was reported in **March 2015, 'Investigating clinical incidents in the NHS'**[53]

This report provides a good overview of the chaotic NHS complaints process with over 70 different bodies involved, yet no single body with overall responsibility to drive improvements. It concluded that;

> *There is no systematic and independent process for investigating incidents and learning from the most serious clinical failures. No single person or organisation is responsible and accountable for the quality of clinical investigations or for*

[53]

https://publications.parliament.uk/pa/cm201415/cmselect/cmpubadm/886/886.pdf

*ensuring that lessons learned drive improvement
in safety across the NHS.*

Highly critical of the role of **PHSO**, the report called for
an **internal change programme** to be drawn up by the
Ombudsman and placed in the public domain as a
matter of urgency. The inquiry confirmed **low public
confidence** and that **expectation outstrips current
capacity**, particularly in relation to complex clinical
investigation. A further recommendation was that the
National Audit Office (NAO) assist in an inquiry
regarding **value for money** of the Ombudsman
services, which cost **£37 million in 2014/15** (£8,644
per investigation carried out).

*Complainants deserve an Ombudsman they can
have confidence in. There are serious questions
about the capacity and capability of the
Ombudsman's office, in particular in relation to
complaints involving clinical matters. We are
aware of considerable anguish and disquiet
where Parliamentary and Health Service*

Ombudsman investigations fail to uncover the truth, and of pain inflicted by the Ombudsman's defensiveness and reluctance to admit mistakes. This underlines the need for improved competence and culture change throughout the system, including in the PHSO. PHSO leadership is aware of the need for this change, but it is proving more challenging than expected. We welcome the PHSO's aim to improve the quality and accessibility of its services. However, the Ombudsman's office is under considerable strain. Fundamental reform of the Ombudsman system is needed.
(Paragraph 75)

We can see from this summary that there has been concern in parliament for many years that the Ombudsman is failing to deliver justice and drive reform in public services. This concern is shared more vociferously by members of the public with the presence of an **active pressure group, damning reports from the Patients Association** and over **96,000** signatures collected by a **Which?** **campaign** to improve public service complaint handling.

Finally, after 48 years and much debate there is an opportunity to take action.

Editor's note: After the many stirring words the action fell to the Cabinet Office. They were charged with drawing up the legislation for the creation of a new **Public Service Ombudsman** (PSO) combining both PHSO and LGO into one effective and accountable body. The work of the Cabinet Office was guided by **Robert Gordon's** review of the Ombudsman's landscape, euphuistically entitled **'Better to Serve the Public'**

The Cabinet Office Review of the Ombudsman Landscape

In the Queen's speech of September 2015, it was confirmed that time would be set aside to discuss the **draft Public Services Ombudsman Bill**

This is the one draft bill to feature in the Queen's Speech. It proposed to reform and modernise the Public Service Ombudsman sector to provide "a more effective and accessible final tier of complaints redress within the public sector". It would absorb the functions of the Parliamentary Ombudsman, the Health Ombudsman, and the Local Government Ombudsman and potentially the Housing Ombudsman.[54]

In **October 2014, Robert Gordon CB** presented to **Oliver Letwin,** Cabinet Office Minister for Government Policy, a proposal to restructure the Ombudsman landscape following a review of the current position. **'Better to Serve the Public: Proposals to restructure, reform, renew and reinvigorate public service ombudsmen'**[55] A glance

---

[54] https://www.bbc.co.uk/news/uk-politics-32898443
[55]
https://assets.publishing.service.gov.uk/government/uploads/system/uploads/attachment_data/file/416656/Robert_Gordon_Review.pdf

through Appendix B will demonstrate that most of those consulted were service providers. Despite the fact that the primary objective was to improve accessibility and effectiveness for citizens, they were not consulted.

The Gordon review starts with the acceptance that;

- a citizen centred Ombudsman is a vital part of the redress landscape, but that the present **legislation** diminishes the role that the Ombudsman can play.
- the current Ombudsman landscape is **complex** and poorly understood.
- strong need to consider the most **cost-effective** means of delivery whilst maintaining public confidence.

Using reports from the PASC inquiries and others; notably that of the **Law Commission** (July 2011) the Gordon review put forward the following recommendations:

318

1. *That the Ombudsman be the final tier of complaint redress for citizens as it is now.*

2. *New powers to **champion and monitor complaint handling standards**.*

3. *New responsibility to be an **agent for public service delivery improvements**.*

4. *Agreement to **removal of the MP filter.***

5. *Agreement to giving the Ombudsman **own initiative powers of investigation**.*

6. *That legislation provides for a new **single Public Service Ombudsman (PSO)** encompassing UK Parliamentary Ombudsman, Health Service Ombudsman, Local Government Ombudsman and Housing Ombudsman.*

7. *PSO jurisdiction is defined in statute to follow the **'public pound'.***

8. ***Accountability** to parliament should be divided between Public Accounts Committee (PAC) for costs, performance against targets*

and budget setting and Public Administration and Constitutional Affairs Committee (PACAC) for delivery and dissemination of reports to drive public sector reform.

To date too little attention has been paid to the issues raised by the **Patients Association** reports which highlight the distress of service users whose poor experiences were confirmed by the many individuals who submitted evidence to the PASC inquiries in 2014 and since. This review suffers from a lack of consultation with service users at the earliest stages. For instance, one recommendation is that the Ombudsman themselves act as advocates to assist the citizen to navigate through the system. There is clearly a conflict of interests here and this role must be given to an independent body. Scant reference is made to the **level of expertise** required by the Ombudsman staff to bring it in line with the new **Healthcare Safety Investigation Branch HSIB**] All mentions of accountability are related to parliament with no reference to strengthening accountability to the public. There has been no recognition of the importance of **defining the terminology of 'maladministration', determining** a code of **practice** and **replacing total discretion with clear performance criteria** which would all work towards **holding the Ombudsman to account.** Equally, no reference is made to introducing **an external audit** of Ombudsman reports and decisions as recommended by the **Health Select Committee.** There is a tendency for the Cabinet Office to leave key principles of reform to the Ombudsman themselves; a condition which has brought us to the present state of affairs. By supporting the continuation of wide-ranging discretion, the Gordon report goes a long way to maintaining the status quo.

> *"...that the ombudsman alone must have the power to decide whether or not a complaint is within jurisdiction and then have the power to determine it; that the ombudsman's determination should be final and should not be able to be overturned other than by the courts and that the ombudsman should be accountable*

to a body independent of those subject to
investigation. I consider that these criteria
should apply to any public services ombudsman
arrangements for the future and that the core
functions of the ombudsman should not
alter." **Robert Gordon p15**

The court, via judicial review, does not hold the Ombudsman to account as it has proven to be (virtually) impossible to prove that the Ombudsman has acted unreasonably given the wide powers of discretion gifted by parliament. The draft legislation will be based upon this report and to date it does not go far enough to meet public expectations or restore public confidence. Much active debate will be needed if we are to make the most of this opportunity.

The PHSO Pressure Group are calling upon all interested parties to combine together and convert the very many fine words into effective deeds for 2016 and beyond.

Editor's note: Due to this great flurry of interest in the work of the Ombudsman members of the PHSOtheFACTS group were able to attend a plethora of meetings held in Westminster. Thanks to the generous work of the late **Michael Meacher MP** we were granted a meeting with **Oliver Letwin** who was Minister of State for Government Policy based in the Cabinet Office and **Robert Gordon**; unfortunately, too late to have any impact on his review. We were ushered into a classic drawing room at number 11 Downing Street where Letwin sat at one end of a fine, oval table. I attended to represent PHSOtheFACTS, **Katherine Murphy** from the Patients Association along with **Gary Powell**, a campaigner from the **Local Government Ombudsman Watch.** I can recall that as I spoke about our concerns Mr Letwin rubbed his chin in serious contemplation. He looked concerned as I informed him that the Ombudsman was totally unaccountable to the public, try as we might, there was no mechanism available to us. He repeated my words slowly, as if actively listening. He seemed to be somewhat perplexed by the story unfolding before him. Then the knock came on the door, he was needed at another meeting and we all said our thanks and left. Naïve as I was back then, it took many months for me to realise that we hadn't told him anything that he didn't already know.

We attended the meeting at the Cabinet Office in 2014 however, the draft legislation for the new 'Public Service Ombudsman' was not published until December 2016, nearly a year after the expected date. Much momentum for change was lost in the long delay but crucially publication after the Brexit referendum in July 2016 meant that no parliamentary time was made available to discuss the draft plan, which still sits today on a dusty shelf somewhere in the Cabinet Office.

In January 2017, after analysis of the draft proposal, it was impossible to see why the delay had been necessary as the majority of the document was mere 'cut and paste' from the previous, flawed legislation. Essentially, after promising to **'Better to serve the public'** the proposal significantly reduced the powers of the Ombudsman to hold public bodies to account, making it even less effective. A detailed analysis is given below.

Fatal extraction: New Health Service Watchdog has all teeth removed.

16th January 2017

After a prolonged wait, the draft legislation for the new **Public Service Ombudsman** has been released by the Cabinet Office.

They have taken their time to slowly extract any teeth the already deficient Ombudsman had and present a proposal for a combined Health, Parliamentary and Local Government Ombudsman that will have fewer powers than any other UK Ombudsman Service. Most significant is the fact that public bodies will only be required to **'take account'** of investigation findings and have no obligation to take any action. All the old loopholes have been retained such as finding harm caused by maladministration without definition, total discretion of the Ombudsman to act as she sees fit and no external audit of the investigation

process. An Ombudsman better to serve the public?
See the facts for yourself.

Review of the draft legislation for the proposed Public Service Ombudsman [56]
January 2017

The establishment of a new Public Service Ombudsman (PSO) fifty years after the original legislation provides government with a rare opportunity to 'better serve the public' as heralded by the preliminary Robert Gordon review. Unfortunately, after the long wait for this proposal it is seriously deficient in terms of reform and appears to be no more than a money saving merger between PHSO and LGO which will result in a single ombudsman appointment and a reduction in staff.

Members of PACAC will be only too aware of the anguish caused to the public by poor investigation

---

[56]

https://assets.publishing.service.gov.uk/government/uploads/system/uploads/attachment_data/file/575921/draft_public_service_ombudsman_bill_web_version_december_2016.pdf

326

processes and the frustration of trying to hold the current ombudsman to account. All the deficiencies of the previous legislation, which have facilitated this state of affairs, have been transferred into the draft legislation for the new PSO. On this basis, the current proposal will do nothing to improve service delivery or public satisfaction and requires significant amendment.

Chris Skidmore, Minister for the Constitution suggests in the foreword that the proposals will deliver an,

> *"independent and strong ombudsman who can launch an impartial investigation."*

However, an analysis of the draft legislation does not support this statement.

Harm caused by maladministration:

1. *The purpose of an investigation by the Ombudsman is to establish—*

   a. *whether the matter complained of involved **maladministration** or a failure on the part of the authority to which the complaint relates, and*

   a. *if it did, whether the person by or on behalf of whom the complaint was made **suffered injustice or hardship as a result of the maladministration or failure.** (p7)*

An investigation based on harm caused by maladministration is a flawed model and should not have been transferred wholesale without consideration of how this requirement has consistently failed the public.

- There is no definition of maladministration so the public are unable to assess the validity of their case against given examples.

- Although 'maladministration' cannot be defined this woolly concept is used to determine uphold. Without uphold no learning takes place.

- There is no consistency as 'maladministration' is decided on a case by case basis.

- Breaches in statutory and non-statutory policies are not considered to be automatic maladministration. These policies should be mandatory as they exist to ensure safety and good service delivery to the public.

- The connection between maladministration and harm is a subjective one and it is possible for the ombudsman to determine, with an insight beyond human powers, that the harm would have been the same in any event.

- Finding maladministration does nothing to check systems and processes, which may be flawed and dangerous. Following a flawed process leads to flawed outcomes but without maladministration.

Discretion:

4. *The functions referred to in subsection (3) include, in particular—*

   a. *those involving the exercise by the Ombudsman of a discretion relating*

to any of the following— 30

1. *whether to investigate a complaint;*

2. *how to carry out an investigation;*

- *how and when to conclude an investigation;*

1. *what action to take following an investigation, and*

   (p8)

- The discretion of the ombudsman has not been balanced with a requirement to apply the most appropriate statutory or non-statutory regulations to an investigation. The ombudsman can apply whichever regulations she/he sees fit.

- There is no obligation to ensure that the key concerns of the complainant are addressed in the report and not scoped out. The ombudsman has total discretion on which aspects to investigate. In 2015/16 only 38% of complainants felt that the ombudsman had dealt with the most important aspects of their complaint. (p42, 2015-16-Annual-Complainant-Feedback-Report)

- There is no obligation to ensure that ombudsman decisions are evidenced based and that public body assurances are substantiated or rejected. In 2015/16 only 34% of complainants reported that the final report provided evidence to support the decisions made. (p42, 2015-16-Annual-Complainant-Feedback-Report)

- Total discretion means that the ombudsman cannot be held to account under judicial review as she/he has been given the legal right to 'act as she/he sees fit'. Unaccountable bodies are able to act with impunity.

The investigation process:

(2.c) it is made to the Ombudsman before the end of the 12-month period beginning with the day on which the affected person first became aware of the matter alleged in the complaint. (p9)

- This is a serious loophole which needs to be closed. People do not always know 'the day' on which they first became aware. Sometimes it can come after a period of reflection or as further information comes to light. This clause has been used to the detriment of the public when the ombudsman refuses to accept the time of first knowledge given by the complainant. For clarity it should be within 12 months of receiving the final closure letter from the public body as this does have a specific date.

- In relation to time it should also be the case that the public can approach the ombudsman earlier in the process to request intervention and alternative dispute resolution (ADR) options. The learning is more effective if it occurs closer to the time of the incident. In Scotland it is possible to approach the ombudsman after 20 days.

(5) The Ombudsman may begin or continue an investigation into a complaint even if the complaint is withdrawn. (p9)

- It should be for the complainant to decide if they wish the investigation to continue. When people lose confidence in the Ombudsman service and wish to take court action they should not have to dispute a flawed ombudsman report where they have not agreed the findings.

7 (4)   The Ombudsman may investigate a complaint only if satisfied that—

(4.b) the designated authority has been given a reasonable opportunity to investigate and respond to it. (p11)

- 'Reasonable opportunity' should be time-bonded to prevent authorities from delaying the process past the 12-month time limit or beyond opportunity for court action.

9 (1) The Ombudsman may not question the merits of a decision taken without maladministration by a designated authority in the exercise of a discretion. (p12)

- Many discretionary decisions lead to action or inaction which causes untold harm. What mechanism is there to evaluate discretionary decisions? When first established, private ombudsman services such as the Pensions Ombudsman and Insurance Ombudsman had powers to examine discretionary decisions which made these bodies powerful champions for the consumer.

10 (4) The investigation must be carried out in private. (p12)

- The 'privacy' rule has been used to deny the complainant access to information during the investigation process before a decision is made. The public have been unable to put the record straight until it is too late. Privacy negates transparency.

- The privacy rule, coupled with the evidence in proceedings rule has been used by the Metropolitan Police to deny investigation into Misconduct in Public Office offences referred to them by members of the public, effectively putting ombudsman staff, who are Crown Servants, above the law. This is in direct opposition to the rule of law which states that no-one is above the law.

11 (7) person may not be required or authorised by virtue of this section to provide information or to answer any question relating to proceedings of the Cabinet or of any Cabinet committee. (p13)

- The Cabinet Office provide themselves with immunity to investigation also protecting the chief decision makers – the Cabinet Ministers.

(8) designated authority must have regard to any recommendations contained in a statement under subsection (1)(c) in respect of the authority (but is not required by virtue of anything in this Act to give effect to any such recommendations). (p16)

- To 'have regard' is permission to ignore and the whole investigation process will have been a futile waste of money. There must be some compulsion on public bodies to comply with the findings or to put in writing to the select committee the reasons for decline. **This clause makes the ombudsman totally powerless if faced with non-compliance**. The Welsh Ombudsman by contrast can issue a certificate to the High Court for wilful disregard of his report without lawful excuse. (p11)[57]

---

[57]

http://www.legislation.gov.uk/ukpga/2005/10/pdfs/ukpga_2005001
0_en.pdf

Persons within scope of Ombudsman's jurisdiction

(1.c) person (other than a local authority) who exercises public functions, or provides services in the exercise of such functions, in relation to a particular local area; (p20)

- This is ambiguous and it needs to be made clear that <u>all</u> those delivering public services using taxpayer funds are within the jurisdiction of the ombudsman, i.e. following the public pound. Currently, it has been determined by PHSO that NHS staff, working within an NHS facility and being paid for by the NHS are working in a 'private' capacity and therefore cannot be investigated. This loophole must be closed, particularly in view of the increasing privatisation of public services.

The Ombudsman as complaint Champion:

(1) The Ombudsman must provide information, advice and training to designated authorities with a view to promoting best practice in the handling by such authorities of relevant complaints. (p23)

- Due to its own inadequate investigation procedures the Ombudsman is currently not in any position to give advice on promoting best practice complaint handling and this may be better delivered by the new Healthcare Safety Investigation Branch (HSIB) when it becomes active later this year.

- The Scottish Ombudsman has been given powers to enforce good complaint handling and operate as a Complaint Standard Authority in their 2010 legislation. Acting as a 'Champion' will not give PSO any powers of enforcement.

- Government needs to unify the Health Service so that good practice is automatically shared and not allow each area to apply its own complaint handling procedures, which is currently the case.

- Data is needed in a standardised and accessible format so that the authorities and the public have access to real time information on complaint handling. A data revolution was promised by **Oliver Letwin** whereby all authorities would be required to put complaint handling data into the public domain. This important aspect seems to be missing from the new proposals. On the subject of data, the current policy of the ombudsman is to destroy evidence 12 months after closure of the case. This short retention span makes it impossible to spot recurring patterns or failure hot spots. In order to gain an overview, this policy should at least be brought in line with statutory archive procedures which are six years retention. This important issue must be addressed in the legislation which has so far remained silent on the matter.

Accountability of the ombudsman:

The ombudsman is required to lay an annual report before the House and essentially a review of this report is both the start and end of scrutiny by parliament. The proposal states the following;

Schedule 1

6 (3) The information referred to in sub-paragraph (2)(a) may in particular include information about—

1. *how many complaints were received by the Ombudsman during the financial year,*

2. *how many of those complaints were properly made or referred to the Ombudsman (see sections 4 and 18),*

3. *how many of the complaints mentioned in paragraph (b) were investigated by the Ombudsman during the financial year,*

4. *how designated authorities have responded to reports made under section 14(1)(c) in respect of them, and 20*

5. *any other matters the Ombudsman considers appropriate. (p30)*

- Absent from this list is a record of the total number of complaints made about the Ombudsman service itself. The total number of review requests, how many were provided with review and how many were upheld. The number of complaints fully upheld as a separate distinction to those partially upheld. Also, clear guidance as to the difference between 'enquiries' received and 'complaints' received. The continual blurring of these distinctions makes it difficult to determine the percentage of actual complaints investigated.

- All complaints about the Ombudsman and reviews are handled internally and there is no provision within these proposals to provide proper independent scrutiny of the investigation process.

This again is a significant oversight, if indeed the intention is to 'better serve the public'.

There is a proposal to set up a 'modern governance structure' to give greater accountability to the ombudsman service.

Membership – Schedule 2

1. *(1) The Board is to consist of—*

    a. *persons who are not employees of the Board ("non-executive members") (see Part 2),*

    b. *the Ombudsman (see paragraph 10), and*

    c. *persons who are employees of the Board ("employee members") (see paragraphs 11 to 13).*

1. *The number of members of the Board is to be determined by the person appointed under paragraph 2(2) to chair the Board ("the chair") with the agreement of the Public Accounts Commission.*

2. *The majority of members of the Board must be non-executive members.*

3. *The following are executive members of the Board—*

    a. *the Ombudsman;*

    b. *the chief executive (if different from the Ombudsman);*

    c. *the employee members. (p31)*

Her Majesty via the Public Accounts Commission determines the selection of the non-executive chair. The chair then 'recommends' individuals to the Commission for places on the board. The CEO of the board is automatically the Ombudsman who is also the Accounting Officer.

- This looks very much like a closed shop. One safe pair of hands recommending another. Boards such as this have consistently failed to hold bodies to account and instead become the first line of defence, using their position to limit reputational damage.

- There can be no public confidence that such a board would make any significant difference to the accountability of the ombudsman, despite the following statement regarding monitoring.

Monitoring service provided by Ombudsman Schedule 2 (23)
(1) The Board must monitor the carrying out of the Ombudsman's functions under this Act, with particular reference to the quality and efficiency of the service provided by the Ombudsman and the desirability of securing improvements in that service.

- *The Board must perform the duty under sub-paragraph (1) in accordance with a scheme prepared by the Board.*

- *The Board—*

   a. *must submit a scheme under sub-paragraph (2) to the Public Accounts Commission, and*

344

b. *must revise the scheme in accordance with any*
    representations made by the Commission.

(4) The Board must inform the Commission about any
findings the Board makes in performing its duty under
sub-paragraph (1).

(5) Nothing in this paragraph entitles the
Commission to question the merits of action taken
by the Ombudsman in a particular case. (p37)

Effectively, a parliamentary selected board, who have
the Ombudsman on their panel, will hold the
Ombudsman to account by assessing the quality of
the Ombudsman's work, much of which is carried out
'in private' and report their findings to a
parliamentary commission who can take no action as
a consequence. And this is what they call
'strengthening accountability'.

Absent from the proposals:

- Any reference to staff training needs and levels of expertise required to manage rising numbers of complex medical complaints.

- Any suggestion that Health Service Complaints should be allocated their own service within the umbrella of PSO with a designated lead Ombudsman equipped with suitable expertise.

- Mention of Alternative Dispute Resolution (ADR) models and how to incorporate these into the new PSO service. Need for standardisation of ADR providers. Specific training required for Ombudsman staff in selecting or delivering mediation.

- Increasing privatisation of public services and the issue of access to information from bodies not covered by the Data Protection Act.

- A proposal to make it a requirement for public bodies to disprove allegations rather than place the burden of proof on the individual citizen with limited access to the evidence. (Presumption of honesty)

- Any duty to identify and notify patterns of failure (presently hampered by 12 month Ombudsman retention policy).

- Power/duty to initiate or direct others such as CQC to investigate systemic failures.

Editor's note: Delay by the Cabinet Office served to take the heat out the debate. The release of the draft legislation, nearly a year behind schedule, and placing it after the EU referendum, resulted in dire consequences for time allocation for subsequent parliamentary debate. Reform fell once more from the political agenda and the doors to Westminster quietly closed to campaign groups such as ours.

Chapter 6. Holding the Ombudsman to Account.
Part II - Court Scrutiny

Editor's note: We have seen that select committees such as the Public Administration and Constitutional Affairs Committee (PACAC) and the Health Select Committee now renamed the Health and Social Care Committee (HSCC) scrutinise the work of the Ombudsman on behalf of parliament. Though PACAC hold an annual scrutiny meeting of senior PHSO staff, they decided at some indeterminate time to no longer review individual cases, which means they have very little insight into the actual investigation process. Every year they receive many complaints from dissatisfied citizens but are able to dismiss them as 'not in our remit'. Before each scrutiny meeting they publish written evidence provided by the public and other interested parties. Every year there is a catalogue of damning criticism from each and every one of these contributions (apart from that provided by PHSO themselves) with most stating that this body is 'not fit for purpose'. These written submissions are held under copyright to the committee so cannot be reproduced here but they are available on the PACAC website [58] so feel free to check them out.

Given that no parliamentary committee will champion the individual complainant, the only means of challenge for the citizen is to take the Ombudsman to judicial review. But just how independent and accessible is that route?

This is what PHSO have to say about judicial review from their 2018/19 Annual Report.

Judicial review

If a person or organisation feels that we have not followed lawful procedures in reaching a decision about their complaint, they can apply to the High Court for that decision to be reviewed by the courts. If their application is granted permission to proceed, then there is a full court hearing.

We received and responded to 24 pre-action letters in 2018-19. Twelve did not convert into legal proceedings. There were twelve new applications for judicial review of our decisions. This is an increase of four applications from the

58 https://committees.parliament.uk/work/69/parliamentary-and-health-service-ombudsman-scrutiny-201819/publications/written-evidence/

previous year. Eight claims were refused permission to go forward to a full hearing. Three of those decisions are being appealed. Four claims have been recently issued and are pending.

The case of Morris vs PHSO, continued from 2017-18, was heard in February 2019, but judgement was reserved and then handed down on 26 June 2019. The claimant's challenge was to the extent of matters covered in our investigation and our approach to recommendations

in relation to legal costs. The claimant was unsuccessful on all counts and PHSO was awarded its reasonable costs, to be assessed if not agreed. Leave to appeal was refused by the judge although it is possible the claimant will seek leave from the Court of Appeal. [59]

Editor's note: Why do so many people take this difficult route to justice? In order to submit a pre-action letter, most citizens would require expensive legal advice to set out

---

[59]

ombudsman.org.uk/PHSO_Annual_Report_and_Accounts_2 018-2019.pdf p.41

their case with the optimum chance of success as the parameters for judicial review are very narrow. From there the money keeps racking up as PHSO will submit a £3,000 cost charge just for replying to your pre-action letter. If you manage to get your case into court you would be looking at a bill of at least £40,000 for yourself and a similar amount to pay the Ombudsman's fees. Not many citizens can risk £80,000 in order to achieve justice. In the majority of cases the High Court judge will refuse permission to go forward on whatever grounds the High Court judge feels are applicable and you are then required to settle up your costs.

I can recall my first meeting with **Rob Behrens** as part of his 'meet and greet' rounds following his appointment as Ombudsman. He had come to this role after his time as CEO at the **Office of the Independent Adjudicator for Higher Education (OIA)** dealing with complaints made by students. By chance my complaint to PHSO had concerned higher education, so I was hoping for an understanding ear. He told me that whilst at the OIA he had successfully won all the judicial review cases taken against the organisation. With some scorn he informed me that the students were all 'on legal aid' giving the suggestion that this made it easy for them. He confidently informed me that OIA always won because the court recognised that their decisions were sound and they were doing the right thing. This conversation was most revealing. There was no consideration given to the fact that the OIA have the best legal aid of all, with access to unlimited funds. Or that the narrow legal remit for judicial review does not look at whether the decision was sound but whether the body followed its own, possibly flawed, procedures. Most significantly, it demonstrated the view held by so many in authority, that citizens who attempt to hold public bodies to account are merely vexatious, trouble makers.

A recent academic article by **David Hockey** entitled '*The Ombudsman Complaint System; a Lack of Transparency and Impartiality*[60] looked specifically at the work of the OIA. On the subject of accountability Hockey states;

The unfettered and unlimited range of discretion available to the OIA and the aim of the scheme make it almost impossible

---

[60] Link.springer.com A Global Journal ISSN 1566-7170

to successfully challenge OIA decisions. Although a principle can be stated (i.e., a fair, open and transparent means of redress), its application, proper or otherwise, will vary on the shifting sands of a case-handler's unfettered discretion.

Hockey's work confirms that 'closed-circuit' complaint systems such as the OIA (and PHSO) use a lack of transparency and total discretion to avoid accountability.

As if it isn't difficult enough, there is also something of a catch-22 when applying for judicial review at PHSO. The law states that your pre-action protocol letter must be received by the Ombudsman within three months of the final decision, i.e. the decision you wish to challenge. However, before you can submit court papers you have to follow the appeal process and request an internal review of the decision. PHSO regularly take more than three months to decide whether to grant a review, let alone actually carry it out and this pushes you over the time limit to apply to court. **M.Boyce**[61] has been trying for well over a year to achieve clarity on the legality of the review process and the

---

61

https://www.whatdotheyknow.com/request/the_legal_minefield_of_the_phso#comment-91177

'transparent' Ombudsman's office has blocked him at every turn. He is now waiting for an ICO (Information Commissioner's Office) tribunal.

Public bodies often deem their services to be 'independent' but effectively they are all working for the same government pay master. It is interesting to note that PHSO investigate complaints about ICO and in turn ICO investigate complaints about PHSO, who both resided in the same building at Millbank Tower. Between 2016 and 2019 PHSO upheld zero cases against ICO and no doubt the favour was returned.

RE: Your information request: R0000390

I write in response to your email regarding your request to the Parliamentary and Health Service Ombudsman (PHSO) for information which has been handled under the Freedom of Information Act 2000.

Please find a table below providing the number of ICO complaints received and investigations concluded from January 2016 to present. Please note there were no upheld/partly upheld complaints regarding the ICO for this period.

Information Commissioner	Complaints Received	Investigations concluded	Upheld	Partly upheld	Not upheld	Discontinued
January-March 2016	33	2	0	0	2	0
2016/17	128	5	0	0	5	0
2017/18	167	6	0	0	5	1
2018/19 year to date	116	3	0	0	1	2

Public bodies can also submit court papers for judicial review. In my case against Ofqual, their solicitor 'reserved the right' to take legal action if the Ombudsman upheld my complaint and also stated that regardless of the outcome, Ofqual would take no action. The problem is then one of managing risk. The citizen must fund their own legal challenge and painstakingly gather the evidence. The public body, on the other hand, have their own legal team with unlimited public funds. It is therefore in the interest of the Ombudsman to negotiate a finding which would mitigate against a public body challenge. No wonder so few complaints are ever upheld against Ofqual.

This next blog post is from an information page made available on the phsothetruestory.com website.

Judicial Review

What happens if I take PHSO to judicial review?

You lose, they win, and it costs you loads of money.

*Judicial review is essentially PHSO's 'get out of jail free' card. It makes them 'accountable' by law but in reality, an individual citizen never wins, so it doesn't bother them one little bit if you threaten to take them to court. Similar to the **review** process a judicial review does not look at the validity of decision itself, but at the process employed when coming to that decision. As the Ombudsman has total 'discretion' concerning the way he handles cases, the Judge will inevitably decide that the Ombudsman's actions are 'reasonable'. This evidence from an oral hearing between **Miss Monica Dyer V PAC 1993** explains how 'discretion', built into the 1967 Act, will effectively deny the chance of any successful court action. (PCA = Ombudsman)*

...it does not follow that this Court will readily be persuaded to interfere with the exercise of the PCA's discretion. Quite the contrary. The intended width of these discretions is made strikingly clear by the legislature: under section 5(5), when determining whether to initiate, continue or discontinue an investigation, the Commissioner shall "act in accordance with his own discretion"; under section 7(2), "the procedure for conducting an investigation shall be such as the Commissioner considers appropriate in the circumstances of the case". Bearing in mind too that the exercise of these particular discretions inevitably involves a high degree of subjective judgment, it follows that it will always be difficult to mount an effective challenge on what may be called the conventional ground of Wednesbury unreasonableness.[62]

---

[62] https://www.bailii.org/cgi-bin/markup.cgi?doc=%2Few%2Fcases%2FEWHC%2FAdmin%2F1993%2F3.html

Officially PHSO has very little to say about the judicial review process, preferring to leave it as a mysterious process which requires solicitors, barristers and deep pockets.

'Once you have received our response, that is the end of our internal complaints procedure. If you disagree with our response you can challenge it through the courts using judicial review. We are unable to give you advice about this and you might need to get your own independent or legal advice on how to do this.' (PHSO)

They do not inform you that you have **three months from the date of their final report** to file your papers. If you make a complaint to PHSO and transfer to their RAFT team (customer care) then the clock is already ticking. If they take longer than three months to deal with your complaint then you may be 'out of time' for putting papers to court.[63]

What is a Judicial Review?

All government bodies are subject to judicial review as in theory this allows members of the public to redress the balance of power through court action. It can be very daunting for an individual to enter the world of legal mumbo-jumbo where participants use the obscure language of Dickens to cloud the proceedings with smoke and mirrors. It costs a lot of money as you have to pay the costs of the other party as well as your own and the legal remit is so narrow that most do not get accepted by the judge and fail to proceed to court at all.

You are extremely unlikely to win if you take PHSO to judicial review and neither will you get any publicity for trying, so putting in legal papers won't cause them much concern.   If they think you have a really strong

---

[63]

https://www.whatdotheyknow.com/request/customer_care_appeal s?nocache=incoming-1086258#incoming-1086258 case, they usually agree to re-investigate in order to quash the action. There is no guarantee, however, that the result of a new investigation will be any different to the first. If you decide to go ahead and your case is accepted for a judicial review you can ask the judge to consider it a case of **'public interest'** which will mean that you are not liable for PHSO costs if you lose. If the judge is not willing to do this (and they rarely are) you will have to be prepared to sign a blank cheque to cover both your legal costs and those of the defendant. (Could be up to £40,000 in total) If you win, (which you won't) but if you did, for all your trouble the judge would simply order PHSO to review your case again and possibly pay you a small sum of money in compensation.

If you want to present your own pre-action protocol letter, and there is nothing to stop you doing so, you will find much useful information in this training pack which also has proforma letters. **How to carry out a JR**

If you are looking to find a good Solicitor then use the **Chambers guide** or the **Legal 500** to identify firms that specialise in JR and public law. Look at those firms who have won awards or been nominated for legal aid work/pro bono work by the **Legal Action Group**, the **Lawyer** and the like. Ask how many JRs the solicitor has done personally and how many they have on the go at the moment. Solicitors are obliged to give you a quote on fees and to set out clearly how much a case or each stage of a case will cost. This should be set out in a very clear letter. If they can't do this and want to put you 'on the clock', and charge you by the hour forget it. Solicitors tend to waste more time on things when they're not specialists so avoid anyone who isn't a public law solicitor in the first place.

You may be able to pay for your legal advice from your house insurance policy.

The relevant code of conduct link for solicitors is here **sra.org.uk/solicitors/handbook** and it has a section on costs. Clients should ask for quotes and ask the solicitor to tell them when they have reached a certain level of costs – e.g. £500 or £1000. If anyone tells you that it is hard for them to quote for the whole case, fine, ask them to quote stage by stage e.g. how much to apply for legal aid, read the file, instruct counsel etc. Solicitors really should be able to do this.

If the Judge rejects your initial JR claim then you can appeal this decision via an oral hearing and put your case directly to the Court. In some cases, people have applied for Judicial Review simply to have this one day in court, knowing that the case will go no further. The present government are clamping down on judicial review applications and if the Judge decides that the case has 'no merit' then he can also deny access to an oral hearing.

Most applications do not get past the first stage, so all the money you paid to your legal team has produced nothing more than a tidy pile of paper. If you do get a hearing then jolly good luck to you. Only one case has ever been found in favour of a citizen claimant against

PHSO and it took the **Balchins** over twenty years to achieve justice, so if you have the stamina then give it a go.

Editor's note: Some people are driven by a burning sense of injustice which gives them no option but to push forward with legal action. Others are compelled to seek justice on behalf of a loved one who was harmed at the hands of the state as eloquently described below.

"I can only echo your mention that it is torturous, every letter received led me to anger, anxiety, and I often attached my failings to receive justice as my failing of my grandfather - however irrational it was, it was felt."

If you don't have deep pockets you must represent yourself as a litigant in person (LIP). This means that without full understanding of your rights under the law, you must try to obtain the evidence which supports your case, when those holding the evidence are the ones defending the action. You must scrutinise this evidence, (if you can get hold of it) much of which is written in jargon or heavily redacted and then compile your case in an acceptable manner to the court. Many hours are required for such a detailed analysis on top of your other commitments to work, family and possibly a caring role. It is a full-time job, which will exhaust you both mentally and physically and no amount of compensation will ever restore you to the person you were before. The following correspondence is from a LIP who took PHSO to judicial review. He describes how the judge denigrated him rather than examining the actions of the Ombudsman.

This is the judgment from 18 Dec 2018 vs PHSO at the High Court. I only received it on 16 Dec 2019, a full one year since the hearing.

The Court of Appeal tried to shut my case down in Feb 2019 with costs threat for missing deadlines, when I hadn't. My compliant was upheld by the Master.

It then twice tried to get me to submit my full grounds and skeleton argument BEFORE I'd received the written judgment. I pointed out the obvious flaw in that approach and cced my MP and the CEO of WBUK into the email. They then accepted that I couldn't submit grounds until the judgment was received.

I then received the judgment only on 16 Dec and was given a deadline of 10 Jan to submit the grounds. I pointed out the undue delay meant I had to start from scratch, again ccing my MP & WBUK into the email. They then extended it until 4 Feb.

So, you literally have to fight the courts to adopt a fair and reasonable process.

You can see from the judgment the authority bias of the judge who agrees I have grounds for failure of process by PHSO, but it made no difference to the outcome apparently because I could never be satisfied with the result of any investigation.

So maladminister the complaint so completely that the complainant can't be happy and then use that dissatisfaction to close the case and any PHSO errors or grounds then become irrelevant to the judge because the complainant could never be happy anyway!!

I forgot to say, that the judge fails to refer to any of the documentary evidence which supports my case in his judgment.

He stated orally that he was striking out from the evidence the two consultant witness emails, but that exclusion is not mentioned in the transcript so I have no idea what's going on, alas!

Would be interesting to note how many times the Judge stated in his judgment that I couldn't be satisfied, and compare it to the number of times he brought up PHSO's behaviour which led to that dissatisfaction. His bias was so outstandingly obvious that he failed to account for the documented lies or inconsistencies in the evidence I presented about both NHSE and PHSO and stated the NHS had investigated matters. He even stated I would have a case against PHSO for its failings, if in essence, I had kept my mouth shut. This will be a point of attack in

365

my submission because clearly it's PHSO's behaviour which should be the issue rather than a complainant's reaction to that behaviour.

Editor's note: knowing how difficult it is to take legal action via the judicial review route, **David Czarnetzki** decided to use the small claims court to examine the legality of the Ombudsman's conduct, rather than the Ombudsman's decision. He acted as a LIP and this open letter to his **MP Philip Dunne** gives a good account of his experience.

David Czarnetzki, open letter to Philip Dunne MP, is PHSO fit for purpose?

5th September 2019

My name is David Czarnetzki and my issues concerning the conduct of the Parliamentary and Health Service Ombudsman have now been ongoing for over four years. The following letter was handed to my Member of Parliament, Philip Dunne at his constituency surgery on 30thAugust 2019.

The detail should impart on the reader a need for extreme caution in pursuing a health service complaint via this particular body. In 2015, the Patients Association described this organisation as "unfit for purpose". Read my story. You may well conclude it still is.

30th August 2019

Open letter regarding the conduct of the Parliamentary and Health Service Ombudsman (PHSO)

Dear Mr Dunne,

You will now recall the issues first raised with you in July 2015 following the publication of a final report, by PHSO on 22ndJune 2015, concerning my earlier treatment at Telford Hospital during 2013 and 2014. You corresponded with PHSO on three occasions in

2015 and, on each occasion, received no response from them. I have since been forced to embark on a determined, tenacious and sustained process to uncover the extent of the failings encountered at Shrewsbury and Telford NHS Trust and also those at PHSO. The PHSO failings are the focus of this letter and fall into three main categories.

1. **Refusal to quash the June 2015 final report**

You will see from the core documents on the file that Mr Behrens the Ombudsman admitted, in a letter dated 9th April 2018, his June 2015 final report came to the wrong conclusion. Since then I have been requesting the report be quashed. In his letter to Sir Bernard Jenkin, dated 1st February 2018, Mr. Behrens confirms he has powers to quash a final report yet has failed to do so in this case. He has refused to explain why or enter into correspondence on this matter. His refusal to quash a report recognized as 'flawed' needs to be questioned at a parliamentary level.

His decision not to quash the final report has the following consequences:

1. Mr Behrens has portrayed me as an individual who made an unsubstantiated complaint in the eyes of Shrewsbury and Telford NHS Trust. I have strong objections to, and resent, being left in this position.

2. The Trust has not been contacted by the Ombudsman and therefore never had an opportunity to learn from the issues raised since the flawed June 2015 report was published. You will be aware this particular NHS Trust is subject of various enquiries into the standard of some of its services and I must confess some sympathy for the relatively new Acting Chief Executive who may well be doing her best to improve things. Incorrect reports absolving the Trust, published by PHSO, can only hamper any genuine effort the Trust CEO makes to create better outcomes.

3. If the Ombudsman is prepared to leave this incorrect report in the public domain, it then

becomes legitimate for complainants, NHS management, clinicians and politicians to suspect and question the level of thoroughness and accuracy in every report he issues including, may I say, his Annual Report which is subject to scrutiny by the Public Administration and Constitutional Affairs Committee (PACAC). It is now fair to say that, if the Ombudsman is prepared to conduct himself in this way in one case, he is prepared to behave in the same way in other cases to users of his service whether they are a complainant or respondent. The very credibility of the Ombudsman is at stake and Mr. Behrens remains at the head of a discredited organisation as previously identified in the Patients Association report issued in 2015.

2.Failure to comply with procedures for resolution

PHSO, on its website, issues guidance on principles of good complaint handling. The outset of this document clearly states; *"We will also apply the*

Principles to any complaints made to us about our own service". Section 5 covers points to consider when deciding an appropriate level of compensation. These are:

- The nature of the complaint

- The impact on the complainant

- How long it took to resolve the complaint

- The trouble the complainant was put to in pursuing it.

PHSO guidance goes on to say; *"Remedies may also need to take account of any injustice or hardship that has resulted from pursuing the complaint as well as from the original dispute".*

The PHSO letter of 9th April 2018 offered me £1000. There was acknowledgement I have suffered injustice and PHSO would have awarded this sum against the NHS Trust had his final report of 15th June 2015 accurately reflected the treatment I received. The letter also offered, in addition, a token sum of £500 to cover PHSO's own poor complaint handling, but this part of the offer failed to demonstrate how his own guidelines on compensation levels were taken into account. My reply dated 11th April 2018, to the PHSO letter of 9th April, was ignored and after a further six weeks I felt compelled to issue proceedings in the County Court. The proceedings were to be primarily concerned with the conduct of the Ombudsman and not his decision regarding the belated award he made against the NHS Trust which, due to the passage of time and the fact that the original report had not been withdrawn, made legal action against the NHS Trust impossible. Subsequent to the issue of legal proceedings, there was an arbitrary improved offer by PHSO to settle the matter for a total sum of £2000. Bearing in mind I had by now spent £205 on Court fees, this represented a real increase of £295 over the offer in the letter of 9th April and still failed to show any compliance with his stated policy on points to consider in calculating financial remedy.

3. The Court Action

My claim against PHSO, amounting to £4537, consisted of £3800 damages, £532 interest in line with Court rules and £205 costs. PHSO filed an acknowledgement of service with the Court on 12thJune indicating an intention to defend the claim. There then followed an astonishing sequence of events.

Despite the in-house legal expertise at their disposal, PHSO failed to properly comply with Court procedure and, on 31stJuly 2018, the Court issued a Judgment in Default against PHSO ordering them to pay me the total sum of £4537. Feeling vindicated, I awaited settlement in accordance with the Court judgment but unaware this appalling organisation had yet to finish compounding my misery.

One must ask how PHSO allowed the Judgment in Default to occur. Their next step was to apply to the Court to have it set aside and my original application struck out.

The first hearing was set for Telford County Court (small claims process) on 31stDecember 2018. PHSO engaged a barrister from 39 Essex Chambers. The Judge agreed the Judgment in Default should be set aside but gave leave for me to re-submit my original application with additional supporting evidence. There was no direction by the Judge at this hearing that the small claims route was not open to me to pursue my claim.

The second hearing took place at Telford County Court on 30thJuly 2019 with a different barrister from the same chambers representing PHSO in front of a different Judge. This time, the Judge ruled he had no jurisdiction to hear the case and the application by PHSO to have the matter struck out was successful. However, no costs were awarded.

The evening before the second hearing, an email timed at 1859 hours 29thJuly (just 15 hours before the appointed hearing) was sent to me by an in-house lawyer of PHSO. The email reads; *"On reviewing the documents in your case we note you have referred to a statement dated 10 November but we are unable to trace this. Could you please send a copy of that statement by email before the hearing tomorrow".*

I complied with the request. However, it raised further issues. 153 pages of evidence PHSO should have been considering before the first hearing accompanied my statement of 10thNovember 2018. I was also concerned that significant personal data had now gone missing. PHSO have since provided proof to my satisfaction they have the data and issued yet another of their insincere apologies, the total number of which now runs into three figures, each becoming less meaningful than the last.

Action required

I seek your re-involvement and have two requests:

1. That you write to the Acting Chief Executive of Shrewsbury and Telford NHS Trust, enclosing this letter and the letter of 9thApril 2018 signed personally by the Ombudsman, Mr Behrens. Your letter should invite her to return the PHSO final

report dated 22ndJune 2015 to him. That action alone will at least demonstrate some integrity exists within the Trust and that the new Acting CEO is not prepared to be part of what can only be described as a PHSO cover up which has taken me over four years to expose. I can confirm the Trust is at no risk of legal action from me. My reason for initially going to PHSO was to avoid having the issue of my treatment dealt with at Court.

2. That you personally meet with Sir Bernard Jenkin, Chair of PACAC, and discuss the ramifications of this case with him. You should also hand him the complete file of case papers in order to demonstrate that, despite the scrutiny of PACAC, nothing has yet changed for the better within the PHSO framework. The fact that Mr Behrens is quite prepared to leave in circulation a final report he has identified as inaccurate should be enough for Sir Bernard and Mr Behrens to consider whether his position as Ombudsman and also the position of his Chief Executive remains tenable. I am quite prepared to accompany you at such a meeting. I do not expect

this matter to be side-lined citing previous comments of Committee Clerks in correspondence that PACAC does not look at individual cases. PACAC has done so in the past and has taken oral evidence in some. The public might have a better Ombudsman Service if PACAC takes a greater interest in individual cases in the future.

I do have to say that, having personally attended the last scrutiny hearing of PHSO by PACAC in January 2019, I was disappointed to see the session lacked understanding, depth and incisiveness, particularly as so many people had made written submissions and also took the trouble to attend. It is worthy of note that, despite Mr Behrens refusing to engage with the co-ordinator of the support group PHSO-The Facts, at least fifteen new people have joined this group in recent months as a result of their experiences at the hands of PHSO. I have seen that PHSO seeks greater own initiative powers and yet resists greater oversight of its work, stating this would undermine the authority of the Ombudsman. This must be resisted if a PHSO "mini dictatorship" within our democracy is to be avoided. It is clear the process of peer review and PACAC scrutiny is not bringing improvement and a wider, independent public enquiry into PHSO must now be carried out.

There is one final comment I wish to make and that is in relation to the offence of Misconduct in Public Office (MIPO). If in the event Mr Behrens or any other person makes a suggestion the Police have found no evidence of misconduct in public office within his organisation, I have to point out that would not be an accurate statement. Letters in my possession from the Metropolitan Police indicate that, according to legal advice they have received, they are **prohibited** from conducting investigations into PHSO of MIPO by virtue of the legislation controlling the operation of PHSO. That is not the same as saying MIPO dhas not taken place. This is also something for PACAC to consider and address as it leaves all employees at PHSO immune from prosecution in the event of any wilful or deliberate misconduct on their part.

PACAC should be asking the question as to whether it should be necessary for the sledgehammer of a Judicial Review to be sought to crack what was, in this case, a miniscule peanut of two parties being £1800 apart in their positions regarding compensation.

I see no point in your writing to PHSO again as they ignored your correspondence in 2015 and much of mine in the intervening period. I await your response, asking you to send me a copy of any letter you write to the Acting Chief Executive at Shrewsbury and Telford NHS Trust. Bearing in mind this is an open letter I intend to circulate widely, I will be pleased to also circulate your response to it. It is clear from this case PHSO maintains its ability to fail at every level be it investigative, administrative, legal or executive.

Yours sincerely,

David Czarnetzki

Editor's note: Mr Dunne did indeed forward the correspondence and case file to PACAC and request that the flawed report from 2015 is returned from the Trust. To date they have refused to do so and no response has been received from PACAC.

I attended the first county court heard with Mr Czarnetzki and spent the previous evening going through the very thick file which he had meticulously constructed to lay out his legal argument. This detailed file was pushed to one side at court as the purpose of the hearing was not to investigate the case against PHSO, but to decide on whether there were grounds for the matter to be struck out. As we waited outside the court room a well-dressed barrister from London breezed in and introduced himself as 'the hired gun' for PHSO. He would have put in significant fees to the Ombudsman's office for his time given that he was defending them on New Year's Eve. Once we went into courtroom the barrister took the lead by introducing all the people present in the chamber. There followed some discussion between the barrister and the judge which was difficult to understand as it consisted mainly of references to legal clauses by their numbers. The judge then addressed Mr Czarnetzki to explain that although he was a litigant in person it was beholden of the judge to treat him in the same manner as if he were legally represented and continued to address both parties using legal jargon. The judge could have taken the time to explain in layman's terms, but chose not to. As in Mr Czarnetzki's letter, the judgement was set aside and we soon found ourselves back out in the lobby, no further forward. I was not able to attend the next hearing but believe it to be of similar short duration and essentially the problem was not that there was no case to answer but that there was no legislation with which to challenge the conduct of the Ombudsman.

The convolutions of the law are repeatedly used to avoid the examination of the evidence.

(The reference made by Mr Czarnetzki to 'misconduct in public office' and the MET police, will be explored in the next section as we look at the attempts of PHSOtheFACTS members to hold the Ombudsman to account using criminal rather than civil law).

In February 2018, two GP's, had their judicial review against the Ombudsman upheld at the Court of Appeal. This was a landmark ruling[64] in recognition of the normal legal deference to the Ombudsman in such cases. See the following summary by Bevan Brittan LLP.

The Court of Appeal has handed down judgment in *Miller v Health Service Commissioner for England* [2018] EWCA Civ 144 in an important decision concerning the scope of the Health Service Ombudsman's power to investigate complaints about clinical judgement.

The appeal was brought by two GPs against a decision of Lewis J in the Administrative Court dismissing their claim for judicial review of a decision by the PHSO. The Court of Appeal granted the appeal and quashed the Ombudsman's decision.

It has already been established by the court that it is for the Ombudsman to decide and explain what standard he/she will apply in determining whether there has been maladministration. In *Miller*, the Court reaffirmed that it would only interfere with the standard adopted if it is *Wednesbury* unreasonable.

---

[64] http://www.bevanbrittan.com/insights/articles/2018/court-of-appeal-overturns-health-ombudsmans-decision-on-gp-medical-care/

In this particular case the court felt that the Ombudsman's standard (which was to *'assess the service provided against the Ombudsman's Principles, and relevant standards for the service at the time of the matters under investigation (such as GMC, NICE and/or local policies)'*) was unreasonable and irrational. The court felt that it did not permit of nuances in clinical opinion or practice and there was no yardstick of reasonable or responsible practice but rather a 'counsel of perfection that can be arbitrary'. However, it is at least comforting to nevertheless see the Court of Appeal recognise the wide scope of the Ombudsman's discretion and that there will generally be only exceptional circumstances where the court interferes (**Wednesbury** unreasonableness being a high threshold to meet).

Editor's note: We saw from the **Miss Monica Dyer** case (Monica Dyer being a citizen not backed by medical insurance) that the Wednesbury 'unreasonable' ruling was near impossible to meet in relation to the Ombudsman, but not for so two GPs who managed to overturn a decision which over time could cost the medical insurance body many thousands of pounds in financial awards to the public.

The result of this ruling against the Ombudsman led to shockwaves which culminated in an independent review into the way in which the Ombudsman uses clinical advice. It is much more difficult for a citizen to fight their case through to the Appeal Court as they would likely be bankrupted by the earlier stage proceedings given that a failed judicial review would set them back approximately £80,000. Public bodies however benefit from an array of legal support teams who specialise in such cases as explained in this blog from December 2018.

When the Ombudsman gets it wrong – who defends the complainant?

3rd December 2018

In June 2018, in an interview with **Dac Beachcroft LLP** [65] **Rob Behrens,** made it clear that the Ombudsman is not the people's champion in a dispute with government departments or the NHS.

> *"I have a responsibility to promote the role of the Ombudsman, explaining very carefully to people that we are not there to be their champions ..."*

---

[65] https://www.dacbeachcroft.com/en/gb/articles/2018/june/how-the-parliamentary-and-health-service-ombudsman-is-revamping-the-complaints-process/

In the same article, he has much sympathy for the bodies who must handle an increasing number of complaints from the public.

> *"We will work with bodies in jurisdiction to help them resolve complaints more effectively. It's very difficult for them [complaint handlers] in a culture that gives primacy to professional clinicians. Challenging clinicians in a*
> *constructive way is a skill and they need support and advice about how to do that."*

So, the bodies in jurisdiction are helped by the Ombudsman to resolve complaints whereas the complainant has no help in navigating a quasi-judicial system for the first time unless they are fortunate enough to receive support from an advocacy group. With the **Patients Association** no longer representing patients in dispute with the PHSO, most will have to battle alone if the Ombudsman has got it wrong.

Public bodies under investigation have not only the assistance of the Ombudsman in resolving the complaint they also have the legal assistance of specialist law firms, paid for with public funds.

Under the heading **'When the Ombudsman gets it wrong'** legal firm **Hill Dickinson** [66] gave the following advice to NHS bodies on what to do if the Ombudsman has made the wrong decision on their case.

'When the Ombudsman gets it wrong'

The Parliamentary and Health Service Ombudsman (PHSO) is the last resort for unresolved complaints in the health sector. If the PHSO believes that an organisation has got something wrong, they can make recommendations for it to put them right. This can include explanations, apologies or recommendations for the service to learn and

---

[66] https://www.hilldickinson.com/insights/articles/when-ombudsman-gets-it-wrong

improve. However, many PHSO investigations will be based on information provided by the complainant alone which may not include all of the facts. For complex investigations, the PHSO may also instruct independent experts to assist them in their investigations. So, what happens if the PHSO gets it wrong? Can they be challenged?

Thankfully, the PHSO will usually share a draft of their report with the complainant and the organisation involved before it is finalised. Both have the opportunity to voice their opinion or challenge the findings and recommendations of the PHSO before publication. There are two options available for challenging a draft PHSO report:

- Judicial Review – where the PHSO's reasoning was fundamentally flawed – factually or legally.

- PHSO to review their draft report in the light of further evidence

Additionally, if a complainant has already brought a civil claim against your organisation in relation to the same issue that they are asking the PHSO to investigate, then the PHSO cannot as a matter of law continue with their investigation into that aspect. It may then be possible to prevent the PHSO from publishing any aspects of the report that has already been explored as part of the civil claim. If this argument is not accepted by the PHSO, then a claim for Judicial Review would be required, however this can be costly.

An alternative option is to provide a written response to the PHSO clearly setting out what findings and recommendations your organisation agrees with and where these are not agreed, provide supporting evidence for the PHSO to consider. You can then ask the PHSO to revise their findings and recommendations. Not only will this help your organisation in 'getting the story straight', but the PHSO will appreciate having any relevant information they have missed brought to their attention so to complete a thorough and fair report, after all, it would be inappropriate for the PHSO to report on the basis of the complainant's evidence alone.

It may be the case that your organisation has obtained statements and expert reports from an earlier internal investigation and/or inquest that are relevant, that the PHSO has not seen. If time allows, you could also seek your own independent expert review of an incident.

Although the PHSO report is confidential up to the point that it is published, from then on there is a strong likelihood of press interest, whether the report is accepted or not. It will therefore be important to be quick off the mark to draft a press statement ready to go in the event that this is needed to prevent any backlash.

Top tips

1. Obtain a copy of the draft PHSO report and ask for details with regards to what information they have reviewed in order to complete their draft report

2. Request copies of any expert reports the PHSO have obtained and the experts CVs. Request confirmation as to what information the experts have reviewed in order to complete their reports

3. Review the draft PHSO report in detail

4. If there has been a civil claim in the past that has settled, consider whether the PHSO has been asked to report on the same issue as the claim. If they have, consider whether you wish to challenge this

5. If any findings or recommendations are not agreed, establish why these are not agreed – do you have evidence to support this? If not,

is it worth obtaining your own independent expert report to try and support this view?

6. Has the PHSO draft report highlighted any lesson learning? If so, create an action plan in order to address this within a set timeframe, highlighting to the PHSO what lesson learning has already taken place

7. Write to the PHSO explaining clearly what findings and recommendations are accepted and which are not. Those which are not accepted should have supportive evidence. Provide the PHSO with a copy of the lesson learning action plan so to demonstrate that you are already addressing those PHSO recommendations which are agreed. Request the PHSO reconsider their findings and recommendations in light of your letter and evidence provided

8. Anticipate press interest and have a media strategy

The most important point is to take action early if you want to challenge a PHSO report. We can provide helpful advice in this regard.

"With a team of over 100 lawyers and national coverage, we are one of the leading firms providing legal advice and support to the NHS and independent healthcare organisations. We act for more than 100 NHS bodies and are on all of the national framework agreements – NHS SBS, NHS CPC, HealthTrust Europe, NHS Resolution and NHS Commercial Alliance. Our expertise and experience mean that we understand the issues you face and the clear and practical advice that you require, especially as services and systems become more integrated."

While the complainant must struggle alone to understand the legal and clinical terms used in the reports, the systems and policies in place, how these have been breached and gather all their own evidence by a series of repeated data requests; the body being investigated can simply put any matter not resolved to their satisfaction in the hands of 'over 100 **lawyers with expertise and experience'** all paid for by the public purse.

Some of the top tips, such as asking for the evidence relied upon at the draft report stage, are useful advice to all parties when attempting to challenge the Ombudsman's decision but the complainant will not be advised to follow these steps by PHSO who, as we know, is not the complainant's champion. You will have to work it out for yourself and quickly. Once the final report lands on your doormat, complete with flaws, unsubstantiated assumptions and perversions of the facts, it will be too late. The complainant is not usually in a position to obtain an **independent expert report** and even if they were there is no guarantee that the Ombudsman would regard it as valid evidence when reviewing their decision.

Complainants are even less likely to be able to take the Ombudsman to **Judicial Review** following a flawed decision-making process as they do not have the financial backing of clinical insurance companies to take cases through the court system, possibly up to the court of appeal. They are also not in a position to release a statement to the media, drawing negative public opinion on the Ombudsman's' work.

When the Ombudsman 'gets it wrong' the complainant is shouting in the wind trying to get their voice heard above the roar of the clinical body legal team who have the resources, experience and expertise to challenge upheld decisions and threaten negative media coverage or damaging court action. And this is what Rob Behrens, calls an 'impartial process'.

Editor's note: It can be concluded that judicial review or alternative court action is not a route by which the citizen can hold the Ombudsman to account. It is yet another dead end.

Chapter 6. Holding the Ombudsman to Account
Part III – Police Scrutiny

Editor's note: By late 2015 members of PHSOtheFACTS realised that we were unlikely to hold the Ombudsman to account via judicial review or by appeal to Parliament. By sharing our case stories, we could see repeated instances of caseworkers distorting the evidence in order to find no maladministration. Key documents were often overlooked, key aspects ignored and, in some instances, events were even fabricated; always in favour of the public body. PHSO reports were illogical, with findings based on unsubstantiated conjecture. Caseworkers were compiling official documents in a fraudulent manner for the benefit of their own organisation and that of the body under investigation. This constituted the criminal offence of **'Misconduct in Public Office'(MIPO).** Collectively, we had evidence of repeated incidents, leading us to conclude that this behaviour was wilful and systemic across the organisation.

From late 2015 through to mid 2016 we supplied files to the **Metropolitan Police Service (MPS).** We collated our evidence to demonstrate breaches in the **Ombudsman's Principles**. As noted in the successful **Miller** case, it was for the Ombudsman to determine which standards to apply and these standards were represented by the Ombudsman's Principles.

> "It has already been established by the court that it is for the Ombudsman to decide and explain what standard he/she will apply in determining whether there has been maladministration. In **Miller**, the Court reaffirmed that it would only interfere with the standard adopted if it is **Wednesbury unreasonable.**
>
> In this particular case the court felt that the Ombudsman's standard (which was to *'assess the service provided against the* **Ombudsman's Principles,** *and relevant standards for the service at the time of the matters under investigation (such as GMC, NICE and/or local policies)* was unreasonable and irrational."[67]

Although this approach was considered appropriate for the Court of Appeal in the Miller case, the police took the view

---

[67] http://www.bevanbrittan.com/insights/articles/2018/court-of-appeal-overturns-health-ombudsmans-decision-on-gp-medical-care/

that repeated breaches in the Ombudsman's Principles were of no concern to them. Once we crossed the 30 mark the MPS put a stop to new submissions. Here is a summary of our legal case:

The legal case against PHSO:

In this year (2015) celebrating the 800th anniversary of Magna Carta, we, the undersigned, request a meeting with you to present a dossier of evidence supporting the Allegation set out below that the Parliamentary and Health Service Ombudsman ("Ombudsman"), namely Dame Julie Mellor and her predecessor, Ann Abraham, have or may have committed the Common Law offence of Misconduct in a Public Office as a result of the respective holders of the Office acting, or omitting to act, in a way contrary to their duty and contrary to the Nolan Principles. We have carefully considered the Authorities and understand the key elements of the offence to be:

> *A public officer acting as such wilfully neglects to perform his duty and/or wilfully misconducts himself to such a degree as to amount to an abuse of the public's trust in the office holder without reasonable excuse or justification.*

As a Crown appointment we are fully aware of the seriousness of the Allegation and the political sensitivities and ramifications attaching thereto. In advice given by **David Lock QC** regarding holding the Ombudsman to account under the law, he quotes Mrs

Justice Andrews DBE who presided over the case of Rapp v The Parliamentary and Health Service Ombudsman & Anor [2015]. Given the discretion of the Ombudsman enshrined in the 1967 act Andrews concluded that; *"It is for the Ombudsman to decide and explain what standard he or she is going to apply in determining whether there was maladministration, whether there was a failure to adhere to that standard, and what the consequences are; that standard will not be interfered with by a court unless it reflects an unreasonable approach. However, the court will interfere if the Ombudsman fails to apply the standard that they say they are applying;"*

In 2009 the Ombudsman introduced the **'Principles of Good Administration/Complaint Handling'** as a guide for public bodies and a means of monitoring its own service. These are the standards formally adopted by PHSO and confirmed by advocacy groups.

It would therefore be logical for a court to hold the Ombudsman to account by the standards they have set themselves, namely the **6 Principles of Good Complaint Handling.**

Our evidence demonstrates widespread breaches in the appointed principles which are repeated and systemic, leading us to conclude that these actions have been taken wilfully by members of PHSO staff, in lieu of the Ombudsman, in order to unfairly close down valid cases and avoid holding public bodies to account.

These actions are in breach of **Article 6 of the Human Rights Act 1998** and cause significant harm to the

398

public. We are therefore submitting evidence which demonstrates that Ombudsman personnel, acting as public officers, have wilfully neglected to perform their duty to apply the Principles of Good Administration to such a degree as to amount to an abuse of the public's trust in the office holders, without reasonable excuse or justification. This is a criminal offence and our evidence demonstrates that the decisions made are 'irrational' when measured against the Principles of Good Complaint Handling.

Our evidence represents that from a group of citizens who have come together to form the **PHSO Pressure Group**, as we have been failed by all those in authority to date. Our evidence is complemented and reinforced by that contained in the Patients Association Report, 'The people's Ombudsman - How it failed us' released in November and 'PHSO, Labyrinth of Bureaucracy released in March 2015.

Editor's note: There was a flurry of correspondence with the MPS, which is summarised in the following review of their response.

The Metropolitan Police response

The various responses to our criminal allegations by the Metropolitan Police have strikingly similar hallmarks to the issues G raised with them outlined in his letter of 8th March. These include:

- *Assessment before gathering evidence*
- *Decisions of no case to answer or no offence committed without seeking evidence*
- *Refusing to interview witnesses or suspects*
- *Not taking CPS advice at an early stage despite the 'uniqueness' of the allegations*
- *No adequate explanation of what the Police consider 'reasonable grounds' to suspect an offence has been committed.*

We refer to the letter from Detective Inspector Howard Holt dated 15th March 2016, page 2, paragraph 3 which includes:

"...it is for the individual officer to decide if there are sufficient grounds to support those allegations...Police officers are responsible in law for the decisions they make and are subject to the consequences if they get it wrong. It will be my decision as to whether there is sufficient evidence in any of your referrals to submit them to the Crown Prosecution Service".

Detective Inspector Holt's letter acknowledges if the Police have come to the wrong decision, they are themselves accountable under the law.

The next key letter is from Chief Superintendent Michael Duthie of the Metropolitan Police dated 7th July 2016. Here Mr. Duthie focuses on the premise that Section 15 of the

Health Service Commissioners Act 1993 (HSC) and the Parliamentary Commissioner Act 1967 (PCA) privacy restrictions prohibits disclosure by PHSO to the Special Enquiry Team (SET) of information/documentation obtained by PHSO in the course of an investigation. His letter goes on to say on page 2, paragraph 2:

"The legislation also states that no officers of the PHSO can be called upon to give evidence in any proceedings...of matters coming to their knowledge in the course of their investigations. The MPS cannot therefore obtain any witness evidence from officers of the PHSO in relation to any of the submitted allegations of crime.

...The MPS is unable to conduct any criminal investigations into allegations of misconduct in public office by the PHSO."

Mr Duthie advised he had passed the allegations to Bernard Jenkin MP, Chair of the Public Administration and Constitutional Affairs Committee who have scrutiny oversight of PHSO, but no ability to investigate the reported criminal actions.

Mr Duthie missed two important points:

1. Evidence was and is readily available from complainants if the Police had cared to examine it, much of it obtained by Freedom of Information requests
2. PHSO staff are potential suspects, not witnesses.

He did, in his letter, offer a meeting to enable further discussion. The offered meeting took place on 11th October 2016.

Representing the Police were:

Chief Superintendent Michael Duthie and Detective Inspector Gail Granville.

Representing PHSOtheFACTS were:

Della Reynolds, D.H and David Czarnetzki.

The meeting was recorded by PHSOtheFACTS with the consent of the Police Officers and lasted approximately 90 minutes. A transcript is available. The Metropolitan Police were also presented with a three-page document, plus a file consisting of the wording of the **Misconduct in Public Office** offence, CPS guidelines, the Patients Association reports and our casefile report "Off the Hook".

During the meeting it became very clear that the Police Officers had no knowledge of the impact of a Tribunal decision in the case of **Miguel Cubells v Information Commissioner and Wrightington, Wigan and Leigh NHS Foundation Trusts (Case EA/2011/0183)** and its relevance to their decision that due to privacy restrictions they were unable to interview PHSO staff.

In para 29 and 31 of that decision, Judge Chris Ryan declared:

402

"There is no logical reason for the prohibition (in section 15 of the Act) to be imposed on those holding information that has been shared with the Ombudsman. The profoundly unattractive consequences outlined demonstrate the absurdity of such an outcome".

"Once a report has been issued, the <u>privacy of the investigation falls away</u>".

The position of the Police as at 11th October 2016 seemed to be they made an assessment they had no power to interview staff at PHSO, therefore collecting evidence from complainants would serve no useful purpose. In essence, despite PHSO staff being in Public Office, they were **immune from prosecution.** No other reasonable conclusion can be drawn from Mr Duthie's letter of 7th July 2016. He did agree to look again at the issue in light of the Cubells decision.

Subsequently, Mr Duthie wrote on 10th January 2017, stating the Police had taken advice from Queens Counsel on **their behalf**. They have refused to give details of the QC advising them which could be an issue should another party seek an opinion. There is no mention in this letter as to why PHSO staff cannot be interviewed in light of the Cubells case and the Police retain the position that there needs to be 'gateway offences' for them to investigate.

They do not include **Misconduct in Public Office** as a 'gateway offence'. Therefore, the position, according to the

Police as at 11th October 2016 and 10th January 2017 is constitutionally, PHSO employees and commissioned clinical advisors are above the law of misconduct, despite the principle of English Law that no-one is above the law.

Further clarification has been sought and a reply received from Acting Detective Chief Superintendent Stuart Wratten dated 8th March. There is now inconsistency in the Police position as in paragraph 4 he states:

"The Parliamentary and Health Service Ombudsman and her staff are neither above the law nor immune from prosecution for criminal offences..... A reasonable ground to believe or suspect is the threshold for the exercise of almost all the coercive powers available under the Police and Criminal Evidence Act 1984 and other relevant legislation In the absence of reasonable grounds to believe or suspect, the exercise of those powers is not permitted"

Here we have similarities to those so eloquently presented by G in his letter of 8th March. The Metropolitan Police make assessments without reviewing the evidence and then use the excuse not to proceed because there is an 'absence of evidence'. A classic 'chicken and egg' situation used to avoid investigating allegations of serious wrongdoing within PHSO. Only 4 of the 32 individuals who submitted cases were even contacted by the MPS Special Enquiry Team.

It should be noted from the transcript of the meeting of 11th October that Detective Inspector Gail Granville indicated if the group presented a strong individual case for investigation, it would be looked at. Della Reynolds responded to say that because the criminal activity within the PHSO is on-going and not a single act, it would be possible to send cases to the SET until the 'reasonable grounds' threshold is reached.

Subsequent developments

The police officer who currently has the SET in his portfolio of responsibility is Commander Stuart Cundy. He attended, and gave evidence to, a hearing of the London Assembly Police and Crime Committee on 9th February 2017, accompanied by Detective Inspector Gail Granville, who also gave evidence. The hearing was recorded and can be reviewed, but the important comment from Commander Cundy was that:

"The SET seek to involve the CPS at an early stage"

This comment can be contrasted with the final two paragraphs of Chief Superintendent Wratten's letter:

"In the absence of evidence to justify a reasonable suspicion or belief that PHSO staff have been involved in criminal wrongdoing we have not sought assistance or advice from the Crown Prosecution Service and nor is it appropriate or necessary for us to do so.

Finally, we have no intention of commissioning the witness statements requested by you…. We are unwilling to engage with you in protracted correspondence about the same".

These last comments add to concerns about police accountability. In a letter sent to G dated 8th March 2017, Commander Cundy states:

"The MPS is currently assessing how best to provide information in the public interest. The review may conclude that individual correspondence will no longer be undertaken in some circumstances".

Such action would allow the Police to consign legitimate issues to the dustbin and take us one step closer to a Police State. It is astounding that a Police Officer of such high rank can make the comment in the last paragraph on page 1 of the letter:

"If an individual is not charged they are, by law innocent of those criminal offences".

The reality is that, if a person is suspected of an offence and not charged, it is likely due to the fact that the Police have not pursued the evidence, precisely the issue we and G separately raise with regard to the activities of the Metropolitan Police Special Enquiry Team.

Further correspondence has been sent to Acting Detective Chief Superintendent Wratten and copied to Commander Cundy challenging the Police response. To date, no reply has been received and we are drawn to the conclusion the MPS have already decided not to undertake individual correspondence on this issue.

We understand Commander Cundy is now occupied with investigating the tragic events at Grenfell Tower which resulted in a large loss of life. We argue that continued **Misconduct in Public Office** committed by PHSO should also be investigated with the same rigour as lives are also being put at risk by the failure of the Ombudsman to hold NHS bodies to account for poor safety standards.

Editor's note: Essentially, the MPS used the fact that the Ombudsman legislation states that investigations are carried out in 'private' to prevent them from interviewing staff or gathering evidence. This is despite the fact that we supplied a court ruling that the 'privacy rules' fall away once the investigation is complete and we suggested that the MPS could interview staff members who had since left the Ombudsman service. It was also the case that we already had in our possession much incriminating evidence, none of which was requested for examination.

When MPS state there is 'insufficient evidence' it is simply due to the fact that no evidence was requested or reviewed; not that it didn't exist.

The actions of the MPS made these public servants effectively above the law. We must ask the question why Chief Superintendent Duthie sought advice from the Queens Council and not the Crown Prosecution Service as ultimately, any prosecution decision would rest there. As the MPS ceased all further correspondence we decided to inform the **Home Secretary, Ms Amber Rudd** of this legal ambiguity. We attempted a number of times to alert Ms Rudd but none of our correspondence ever reached her desk. They were fended off by a variety of civil servants who made helpful suggestions that we should write to somebody else. Our September 2017 response to **Mr Foley** at the Home Office gives a good account of this correspondence.

Reference: T6791/17

PHSOtheFACTS letter to Amber Rudd

Dear Mr Foley,

Thank you for your response of 10 August concerning our correspondence with the Home Secretary, Amber Rudd. Whilst we appreciate the time you have taken we are anxious that our concerns have not been brought to the attention of Amber Rudd, the Home Secretary. Our correspondence raises a serious constitutional issue due to the **legal ambiguity** created by the response of the MPS Special Enquiry Team (SET) to our cases of Misconduct in Public Office against PHSO staff.

To ensure that Ms Rudd has full understanding of the issue we are requesting a personal response from the Home Secretary to this correspondence.

To recap - in 2016 PHSOtheFACTS supplied the MPS with 32 cases of Misconduct in Public office against PHSO staff. These were all handled by the SET and after taking external legal advice it was confirmed that due to PHSO legislation the MPS were unable to investigate Ombudsman staff in order to verify our claims.

> *"The legislation ... states that no officer of the PHSO can be called upon to give evidence in any proceedings ... of matters coming to their*

knowledge in the course of their investigation. Therefore MPS could not obtain any witness evidence from officers of the PHSO in relation to your allegations. In conclusion, because of the provision of the Parliamentary Commissioner Act 1967, the MPS is unable to conduct any criminal investigation into allegations of misconduct in public office by the PHSO."

DI Gail Granville SET, July 2016

We challenged this legal position on the basis that this would put **Crown Servants above the law** creating a serious constitutional anomaly. We found it difficult to believe that this was ever the intention of the legislation. On 10 January 2017, DCS Duthie informed us that following our meeting with MPS in October 2016 the Metropolitan Police Service Department of Legal Services instructed Queens Counsel who confirmed that, *"...the position remains unaltered."* This correspondence also included for the first time that none of our 32 cases would be taken forward to investigation due to 'lack of evidence'.

"Having obtained further legal advice I am satisfied that no evidence is available to the enquiry team sufficient to justify a reasonable suspicion or belief that PHSO staff have been involved in criminal wrongdoing."

410

"The effect of the legislative regime, taken together with the absence of any evidence of relevant wrongdoing, bars the police from obtaining PHSO material obtained by them during the relevant investigations."

DCS Duthie January 2017

We had made it clear in our meeting with MPS that we had more cases pending and could supply further evidence in order to cross the threshold of 'reasonable suspicion' which we would present once it was confirmed that legislative restrictions did not prevent the MPS from investigating the Ombudsman. On 6 February we asked DCS Duthie for specific responses to questions we raised at the meeting. On 8 March Acting DCS Wratten replied but failed to address any of the specific questions raised. He confirmed the position that MPS were prevented from investigating Ombudsman staff stating;

"This situation is the creature of statute. It is a counter balance to the considerable powers vested in the Ombudsman. It is not in the gift of the MPS to go behind legislative restrictions. Only Parliament may remove a person's statutory rights."

DCS Wratten March 2017

He also confirmed that there was insufficient evidence to exercise the coercive powers available under the Police and

Criminal Evidence Act 1984 and consequently MPS had not sought advice from the Crown Prosecution Service resulting in the SET making the decision without external advice.

It would therefore appear that according to the MPS and their legal advisors the Crown Servants of the Ombudsman are above the law in regard to prosecution for Misconduct in Public Office. This it is suggested is a 'counter balance to the considerable powers vested in the Ombudsman'. Is it appropriate that the Ombudsman should have both considerable powers and at the same time be unaccountable under the law? In what respect does this act as a 'counter balance'? This legal ambiguity is compounded by DCS Wratten's statement that, *"The Parliamentary and Health Service Ombudsman and her staff are neither above the law nor immune from prosecution for criminal offences."*

In order to seek clarity on this matter we are calling upon Amber Rudd in her role has Home Secretary to confirm that PHSO staff cannot be investigated by MPS due to the legislation governing their role. We are aware that G and others have written to the Home Secretary with concerns that the SET are systematically closing down high profile cases by refusing to acknowledge the weight of evidence presented. Of the 32 cases presented to the MPS the SET contacted only 4 individuals and did not call in complete files of evidence for any of the cases, as their legal advice forbade them from taking further action.

If Ms Rudd is satisfied with the legal position of the MPS and feels that they have handled our cases appropriately can she outline her position regarding the fact that Crown Servants are above the law? In your correspondence Mr Foley you state at the last line; *"Ministers cannot instruct the police on which cases to investigate."* We are not requesting such instruction from Ms Rudd but confirmation that the legal position of the MPS is correct.

You have suggested a number of routes for us to obtain clarification of this matter but each would take us back to the MPS, so that they can investigate themselves, via either the PSD or the IPCC route. We have no confidence in such self-evaluation and our concerns are fully justified by the case of the **Skeltons** which was recently published in the Guardian. Between 2012 to 2014 the Skeltons appealed to the IPCC over the mishandling of the death of their daughter Susan Nicholson. The IPCC instructed Sussex Police to reinvestigate three times over this period and three times Sussex Police found that their initial investigation had been handled appropriately. Yet when the Skeltons appointed their own legal team there was sufficient evidence to convict the killer of their daughter, **Robert**

Trigg, in just six hours. The determination of this elderly couple took a dangerous man off the streets, a job which should have been done by the police who had evidence of Trigg's violent past from the outset. This comment from Mr Skelton sums up their experience of the police investigation.

> *Peter Skelton is determined to see someone within Sussex police held to account. "I think the officers should be charged with something," he says. "What they did is more than incompetence. They fobbed us off for six years."*[68]

It is clear from this case that Sussex Police were incapable of holding themselves to account and the same would be true of the MPS, given their refusal to even enter into dialogue with us on this matter.

> *Finally, we have no intention of commissioning the witness statements requested by you…. We are unwilling to engage with you in protracted*

---

[68] theguardian.com/uk-news/2017/aug/28/the-police-knew-another-girl-had-died-in-his-bed-robert-trigg-susan-nicholson

*correspondence about the same". DCS Wratten
March 2017*

Mr Foley, you suggest that should we be unhappy with the
PSD or IPCC then we can raise our concerns with the
Mayor of London *'who is responsible for supervising the
Metropolitan Police Service and is directly accountable for
policing performance in London'.* Whilst this option does
indeed provide more independence and therefore more
confidence in the process, unfortunately MOPAC have
already informed us that they are unable to assist us with
our concerns.

> *Thank you for your letter of 10 August regarding the
> Metropolitan Special Enquiry Team (SET) and your
> allegations of Misconduct in Public Office against the
> Parliamentary Health and Service Ombudsman
> (PHSO).*
>
> *I appreciate that the conclusion of the investigation is
> not what you had hoped and that members of
> PHSOThefacts will be disappointed. MOPAC does not
> typically become involved in individual cases.
> Operational investigations are, quite rightly, the
> responsibility of the Metropolitan Police Service (MPS).*
>
> *Judith Mullett
> Strategic Advisor*

You then helpfully suggest we contact the **Public
Administration and Constitutional Affairs Committee**

who has oversight of the PHSO. Unfortunately, this oversight does not extend to the examination of individual cases and would certainly not clarify the legal position of the PHSO regarding Misconduct in Public Office.

We sent a copy of our previous correspondence to Ms Rudd on this subject to **Sir Thomas Winsor**, HM Chief Inspector of Constabulary and **Steve O'Connell**, Chair of London Assembly Police and Crime Committee. Neither has responded.

We appear to be caught in a **'not in our remit'** situation. A constitutional dilemma where Crown Servants are, according to the MPS, immune from prosecution; this should surely be dealt with at the highest level - the **Home Secretary, Ms Rudd**.

Mr Foley it would appear that no-one holds the police to account except for the police themselves. Given the trials soon to take place over Hillsborough we are all aware that the police do not have an unblemished record. Indeed, recent payments to **Lord Bramall** and **Lady Brittan** regarding the mishandling of **operation Midland**[69] give graphic depiction of just how wrong the MPS can be.

Former Conservative MP **Harvey Proctor** was also caught up in this bungled investigation and in 2016 (whilst a sitting MP) **Sir Gerald Howarth** contacted Amber Rudd, in her capacity as Home Secretary.

> Mr Proctor's former Conservative colleague, Sir Gerald Howarth has written to Amber Rudd, the Home Secretary, to demand that the Metropolitan Police compensate him for his financial losses.
>
> In his letter to Mrs Rudd, Mr Howarth, who has been friends with Mr Proctor since the 1960s, said:
>
> *"I believe that given the extent of the failure by the Police, as Home Secretary you should move swiftly to ensure that the "unreserved apology" is followed by a substantial payment to go some way towards compensating Harvey for his loss."*[70]

---

[69] telegraph.co.uk/news/2017/09/01/met-police-pays-compensation-lord-bramall-lady-brittan-disastrous/

[70] telegraph.co.uk/news/2016/11/09/operation-midland-police-helped-nick-claim-compensation-for-fals/

In your letter you state that, *"...Ministers are unable to intervene in individual cases or in operational decisions made by the police. To do so would undermine the principle that the police are entirely independent of Government."* Yet it would appear that in certain instances the Home Secretary is called upon to 'move swiftly' when the police have misinterpreted their remit. Perhaps this is one of those occasions?

To clarify; we are requesting confirmation from Ms Rudd herself that she is satisfied with the legal position of the MPS which puts Crown Servants above the law in regard to the criminal offence of Misconduct in Public Office. This clarification will become important when this matter is tested in court.

We await Ms Rudd's response.

Yours sincerely,

PHSOtheFACTS

Editor's note: this matter has never been tested in court, nor is it likely to be. For some reason, possibly the turning of every stone, we did make a complaint about the MPS, who investigated themselves and found no case to answer.

Police Scrutiny: Fraud

Editor's note: In April 2018 PHSOtheFACTS received correspondence from whistle blowers at PHSO that there had been a misappropriation of funds leading up to the end of the financial year. They had tried to report their concerns to senior management but to no avail as senior management were the alleged instigators of the act. Misappropriation of public funds is 'fraud' and an issue to be taken seriously. Consequently, we did our best to report the offence to the Police, the National Audit Office (NAO), the Public Administration and Constitutional Affairs Committee (PACAC) and Action Fraud. The following article provides a summary.

Who cares about fraud at Parliament's Ombudsman?

I turned on radio 4 the other day to hear that *'corruption has permeated every part of civic society'*. Wow I didn't expect to hear that confession on the BBC but it turned out that they were talking about Africa, a continent synonymous with corruption; while here in the UK we are known for our 'British fair play'. Public money pays for a large number of organisations in order to ensure that the UK is not rife with corruption. But are they effective?

The Parliamentary and Health Service Ombudsman (PHSO) is one such body and acts as the final arbiter for complaints about government and the NHS. It sits at the apex of the complaint handling process, a position which requires impeccable integrity. Yet, in April 2018, as the coordinator of an Ombudsman watch group, I was contacted by whistle-blowers [71] who were concerned that managers were encouraging staff to use up funding at the end of the financial year by claiming overtime that had not been worked.

A summary of key points:

- *The overtime rate paid to operational staff and managers was higher than can be justified by any public sector organisation.*
- *Staff were told by managers to fraudulently claim for overtime even though they did not work. This can clearly be seen by scanning the IT system to see who actually claimed but was not logged on*
- *Staff and managers openly talk about this. All the people in the quality team were asked to fill in overtime; many operational teams were asked to do the same - even though they did not work*
- *Senior Managers promoted the behaviour.*

Given that this fraudulent behaviour was driven from the top, the staff had been unable to raise concerns, so as a

---

[71] phsothetruestory.com/2019/02/21/fraud-what-fraud-part-1/

'last resort' blew the whistle in the hope that I could bring this to the attention of the authorities. I did my best.

On 9th April 2018, I filed a freedom of information request [72] asking PHSO to reveal a monthly record of overtime and bonus payments. If the claims were true, there would be a spike in payments for March/April. On the 31st March, just days before my request, PHSO had taken a 'snapshot'[73] of all staff payments in order to calculate gender pay difference. They were required to consider;

- the difference between the average hourly rate of pay paid to male and female employees
- the difference between the average bonus paid to male and female employees;

Which meant they must have reviewed the pay data quite recently yet, PHSO told me that it held no monthly payments records for overtime or bonuses. The PHSO argued that the data was held by **CGI** a private company which handles staff payments. PHSO only had a record of the total hours worked (which included overtime) but not broken down on a monthly basis, despite the fact that staff are paid monthly. Public body outsourcing is a growing trend. It converts public money into private shareholder profit, in this instance, £32,741 p.a. In addition to that it allows data to be hidden - because private companies are not subject to FOI laws. The 'snapshot' data had simply

---

[72] whatdotheyknow.com/request/phso_pay_gap#comment-84699
[73] ombudsresearch.org.uk/2018/04/06/gender-pay-gap-how-do-ombuds-services-fare/

disappeared. How could PHSO defend themselves against accusations of fraud with no records of payments?

I approached The National Audit Office (NAO) whose motto is, **'Helping the nation spend wisely'**, and whose remit is to

"audit the financial statements of all central government departments, agencies and other public bodies, and report the results to Parliament. Our other work comprises value-for-money studies, local audit, **investigations,** support to Parliament and international activities."

The NAO replied [74] that PHSO was audited under a 'mutual agreement' – so they were unable to hold an investigation as requested. The NAO recommended I should provide evidence to **Action Fraud**, run by the City of London Police instead. Why would NAO have such a clause in their remit, as it was obvious that a public body carrying out fraud would **not** agree to an audit and the crime would go undetected. It's almost like they don't want to know.

Before contacting Action Fraud, I had the opportunity to give my evidence to the **Public Administration and Constitutional Affairs Committee (PACAC)**, which was set up specifically to monitor the Ombudsman. Fortunately, its focus for 2019 was **'value for money'** perfect, so ahead

---

[74] phsothetruestory.com/2019/02/22/fraud-what-fraud-part-2-national-audit-office/

of the scrutiny meeting I shared my concerns via written evidence.[75]

> *Whistleblowers reported to PHSOtheFACTS discrepancies in bonus and overtime payments made by PHSO at the end of the 2017 financial year. A FOI request confirmed that PHSO do not hold data on individual payments made to staff for bonus or overtime due to contracting out to a third party. Without the data it is difficult to know how PHSO will defend against such accusations which are presently being reported to Action Fraud.*

I attended the scrutiny meeting of Rob Behrens (the Ombudsman) and Amanda Campbell (the CEO), but the members of PACAC were apparently not concerned about the whistle blowing which demonstrated that all internal procedures had broken down, nor the claim of fraudulent payments condoned by management, nor the fact that PHSO held no records of monies spent, as not a single question was asked on any of these issues.

With no further options I tried to report the matter to Action Fraud. **Action Fraud** have a website and a twitter

---

[75] phsothetruestory.com/2019/02/23/fraud-what-fraud-part-3-pacac/

feed but have neither an email or a postal address. I called them twice but was kept hanging on the phone endlessly, then I spotted this on their website:[76]

*Action Fraud **does not investigate** the cases and cannot advise you on the progress of a case.*

Apparently, they just record the information to form a 'picture'.

The reality is that due to the legislation governing the Ombudsman the police can only investigate perjury or a breach of the official secrets act. So were the police to get involved, they would only search out and prosecute the whistle blowers who had done the right thing and reported a crime. Crazy world eh?

What is to stop PHSO committing further fraud at the end of this tax year? Absolutely nothing. Government bodies charged with holding others to account are, by design, lacking in the powers needed to do so. Including the Ombudsman himself who has no powers of compliance resulting in a 'flaccid' Ombudsman who is unable to ensure that public bodies comply with his findings.[77]

---

[76] phsothetruestory.com/2019/02/25/fraud-what-fraud-part-4-action-fraud/
[77] APPG Consumer Protection – January 2019 Report from Ombudsman Inquiry.

Here in the UK there is show of accountability, which costs us all a lot of money, but the cosy club support each other and play the 'not in our remit' card at every opportunity.

Editor's note: We can see that all the organisations you would expect to hold a public body to account either have no jurisdiction, insufficient powers or no appetite to take on the task. It is not possible for members of the public to hold the Ombudsman to account and this is not by chance but by design. A quick word on the media. Apart from exceptional circumstances[78] the media generally portray the Ombudsman as a chastising nanny, extolling public bodies to 'do better' but they consistently fail to question the fact that yet another scandal has been allowed to fester unnoticed. Rogue breast surgeon, Paterson submitted over 1,000 patients to unnecessary operations over 14 years. The Ombudsman didn't spot a thing. [79]

Patients treated in the NHS have the right to refer their complaint to the Parliamentary and Health Service Ombudsman to investigate and make a final decision if it has not been resolved by the NHS Trust and it is within the Ombudsman's time limit. The Ombudsman looked at four cases, but none of the cases went beyond an assessment of the issues.

---

[78] See chapter one – dark days for PHSO
[79] Paterson Independent Inquiry Report

Chapter 7.   The role of academics

Editor's note: The work of academics should help shape public opinion. In an ideal world, their impartial research would feed directly into government policy. At the present time, parliamentarians are more likely to be influenced by 'thinktanks' of dubious financial origins and agendas. But even when politicians fail to take notice, rigorous, independent research can be used by campaigners to amplify and validate their call for action. On this basis we approached academics concerned with **Administrative Justice,** an area which covers aspects of social justice, including the role of the Ombudsman. This definition is from the UK Administrative Justice Institute (UKAJI) website.[80]

> Administrative justice concerns how we interact as individuals when the government, or those working on its behalf, act in ways that appear wrong, unfair or unjust. It encompasses matters of everyday importance to all of us, such as housing, education, health care, immigration, planning, social security and taxation.

---

[80] ukaji.org/what-is-administrative-justice/

At some point, most citizens will tangle with administrative justice issues given that there are numerous ways in which a citizen is reliant upon the state; yet there is little public discourse on this subject with academics working in silos.

Initially, the academics were delighted to hear from us. We were raw data on legs and they invited us to a workshop in London. Two from our group attended and we listened with interest to their research project ideas, contributing where we could. It soon became obvious that our lived experience did not match the version we were hearing. Essentially, the academics recognised that administrative justice often failed the public but they put this down to bureaucratic inefficiency, lack of training or funds. They agreed that it was a system which had long been neglected by the political agenda; but overall it was better than nothing and we should be grateful for what we had. Our talk of deliberate denial of evidence, deliberate manipulation of the facts and deliberate bias towards the public bodies was not well received. The academics were unable to process the information we were giving them. It jarred so completely with their theoretical knowledge that we had to be wrong. (Cognitive dissonance?) Given the lengths we had gone to, perhaps we were just perpetual whingers, only happy when we were unhappy, and this is the fly-paper on which all persistent complainers get caught.

By 2019 we were no longer welcome at academic events. Unable to weave our narrative into their understanding they simply closed the doors on us. By now we were getting used to being dismissed as 'delusional' or 'vexatious'. After all, where was the evidence to back up our story? Then we uncovered a research paper written by **Paul Burgess** in 1983, which totally vindicated our account. This document was tracked down at the British Library, so limited was its publication. The academics we sent it to had not previously known of its existence. The article, first published in New Society, 13th January 1983 was entitled, **'Whose side is the Ombudsman really on?'** Sharing this account enabled us to open up a new dialogue with the academics as you will see in this blog from March 2019.

Whose side is the Ombudsman on?

20th March 2019

This is a question that only complainants seem to ask. Those in authority collude with the proposition that the Ombudsman is impartial. Rigorous academic research could provide the answer, as data would have to be gathered from both sides. I wanted to present such an opportunity to the recent Administrative Justice Council pop up event (12th February 2019) where academics met to agree new research objectives. Unfortunately, after securing a ticket I was informed by **Naomi Creutzfeldt,** one of the organisers, that it would be inappropriate for a 'hostile campaigner' to attend as it might frighten off new researchers. When telling the truth about your own lived experience becomes 'hostile' you know things aren't right in the academic world.

The 'pop up' was essentially a 'pimping service' where representatives from government bodies such as the **Ministry of Justice (MOJ), Parliamentary and**

Health Service Ombudsman (PHSO) and **Her Majesty's Courts and Tribunals Service (HMCTS)** could connect with researchers who were prepared to take payment for services rendered. Admittedly, that does sound rather hostile but they themselves accept there is a risk that their autonomy is jeopardised by the lure of government grants. Quote from their roundup session:

> *There is a risk that research will focus on what organisations or government want done, what data are available, or what funders are interested in, rather than on a consensus view of what is needed in the way of administrative justice research. Both Ministry of Justice and HMCTS are interested in working collaboratively with researchers and to have input on what data should be collected in evaluation work.*

More than just a risk when other voices are actively kept out of the room. You can bet that both the **MoJ** and **HMCTS** will be interested in working collaboratively with researchers on data collection as by controlling the data you can control the outcome.

On this point, it is interesting to note that academic **Dr Chis Gill, lecturer in Public Law at the University of Glasgow** informed PACAC that he was particularly impressed with the consumer feedback data gathered by PHSO and presented to him as part of a peer review into 'value for money'. It gave him 'great confidence' in the progress of the reform. [81]

> *We were particularly impressed with the consumer data. That compares very favourably with consumer data collected by other public service ombudsmen. As to the scope of it and how it is collected, it is independently collected, and it is done in tandem with an internal QA process; all of that, to our mind, was very good-quality evidence that helped put in context some of the more acute issues that have maybe occurred in the past, with particular complainants being*

[81] Q9 oral evidence to PACAC - 2017/18

dissatisfied. That was one of the things that we built our level of confidence on in terms of this report.

This confidence overlooks the fact that PHSO act as the primary gatekeeper for this data by controlling access to the consumer survey in the first place. Or that the customer satisfaction levels for the new PHSO administration were actually lower than those for the previous Ombudsman, **Dame Julie Mellor** who had supposedly, 'lost her way'.[82] Equally, no consideration was given to the feedback recorded on more independent consumer sites such as **Trust Pilot** where 96% gave PHSO the lowest score available, similarly with **Google Reviews.**[83] Dr Chris Gill used just one source of data, that supplied by the Ombudsman themselves to judge the Ombudsman service. This was selective use of data at its worst.

---

[82] See Fig.4 PHSO Customer Satisfaction data 2014/15 to 2018/19 p9
[83] See Fig.3 Reviews from independent consumer platforms p8

Way back in 2015, before they considered us 'hostile' we were asked by UKAJI to write a complainant's eye view of the Ombudsman experience.[84] Here are the key points:

No victim empowerment here; instead you become a victim all over again, a victim of the complaint process. Many regret that they ever took a case to the ombudsman, as it served only to compound their emotional stress; others wish that the body didn't exist at all rather than raise false expectations.

Key obstacles

Some of the key obstacles faced by complainants are:

- o delay

---

[84] ukaji.org/2015/10/26/a-complainants-eye-view-of-restorative-justice/

- lack of communication – you have to drive the case forward

- secrecy – no knowledge of statements made by public body, though they are given access to your evidence

- manipulation of the facts

- factual error

- staff away on leave regularly or case passed between staff so you start again with new case worker

- blanket statements from staff which do not address key points raised

- acceptance of statements made by public body at face value

- refusal to release details of clinical advisor used – report written by clinical advisor – questions asked of clinical advisor or evidence supplied to clinical advisor

- no action taken if a service delivery complaint made

- any complaint made about the decision will be met with suggestion to go to judicial review

Since then we have been rather side-lined by the academic establishment and by those in authority. Notably, the Ombudsman himself, **Mr Rob Behrens,** who describes us as a 'small group of dissatisfied complainants' who are unable to engage in 'constructive dialogue'. Our negative experience just doesn't sit well with the 'open, transparent, impartial, remedy' rhetoric regularly trotted out by PHSO, but now we find we are not alone. Concerns about the Ombudsman are as old as the Ombudsman office itself and way back in 1983 an academic/journalist named **Paul Burgess** actually talked to complainants in order to answer the question 'Whose side is the Ombudsman really on?' The feedback from those complainants is an exact echo of our own concerns some 35 years later.

Published in **New Society V55 on 13.1.1983** Burgess opens with the following paragraph:

> *Whose side is the Parliamentary Ombudsman on? Is he the people's champion against red tape and officialdom? Or is he an arbitrator seeking the middle way, the acceptable compromise between the aggrieved citizens and state bureaucracy? There is rising disquiet about the Parliamentary Commissioner for Administration, to give the Ombudsman his official title, and about his effectiveness in checking administrative abuse. Close scrutiny of some of his recent investigations suggests the disquiet is well-founded.*

Openly criticising the Ombudsman was the first of many mistakes for **Paul Burgess** who was roundly slated for his article which must have bucked the trend for the time. He compounded his crime by including data to support his concerns and witness statements from complainants, a Mrs Ward and a Mrs Wilson breaking a number of unwritten rules.

rule no 1. – use only selective data to show how the Ombudsman service is improving

rule no 2. – never listen to complainants as they are unreliable narrators.

He foolishly pointed out that the Ombudsman has total discretion to cherry pick the cases to investigate in the first place and in 1983 just a third of the 1,031 complaints received an investigation. **Burgess** was appalled to learn that in 1981 it was even worse with fewer than one if four of the 917 complaints being taken up for investigation. He was clearly concerned about the many dissatisfied citizens who were simply turned away from the only arbiter who could assist them. Heaven knows how he would feel to learn that in 2017/18 the Ombudsman investigated just 8% of the 32,389 complaints which came his way and upheld just 3% of all those complaints. This is a shocking statistic of failure to deliver justice and remedy to the public, but one which gets little attention. **Burgess** revealed that customer satisfaction was low.

> *The eventual outcome, after investigation of the cases he accepts, is apparently satisfaction for less than one in eight of all complainants. What has gone wrong?*

With only a 3% uphold rate, satisfaction in the Ombudsman has gone from bad to worse. Perhaps if the **Burgess** article had opened up an honest debate at the time, things would have improved but unfortunately, his article must have been stifled.

There has always been some confusion about the role of the Ombudsman and **Rob Behrens** uses this to good effect with claims that *'the public do not understand'* and *'they expect us to deal with their issues'* and when disappointed with the results the public are unable to *'manage their expectations'*. Back in 1983 **Paul Burgess** understood the role to be;

> *Constitutionally, his job is to protect the citizen from maladministration and to pursue officialdom for unjust treatment.*

If protecting the citizen is the primary role, then the Ombudsman is failing 97% of the citizens. By default, the actual role must be to protect the government as the Ombudsman has consistently achieved low uphold rates for the last 50 years. **Burgess** goes into some detail of **Mrs Ward's** case, a woman who actually received an upheld verdict on her complaint about the DHSS but was distressed by the failings of the investigation process. This is an interesting example for analysis as the well-rehearsed line on disgruntled complainants is that they are dissatisfied because they *'didn't get the decision they were looking for.'* Well, Mrs

Ward did get the decision she was looking for but the process was long-winded, opaque, riddled with error and failed to take note of anything she had to say. That sounds familiar. Here are a few snippets from **Burgess** analysis which chillingly chime so accurately with our own experiences:

> ... in an investigation which took a year, he [the Ombudsman] made no contact at all with the complainant. Consequently, relying upon the DHSS version of events, he got his facts wrong. As it happens, Mrs Ward is a diary-keeper and could have given him a detailed record at least as reliable as that of the DHSS local office.

> When pressed by George Morton her MP to explain this interpretation of an impartial investigation, Clothier [Ombudsman] replied that the DHSS files had provided 'ample' information. He was not, of course, to know that the local office involved had acquired some notoriety among welfare rights workers, and was

indeed found by an independent appeal tribunal, within a year of his report, to have fabricated evidence against a claimant.

You don't have to be an academic to spot that if the Ombudsman relies on evidence from only one side, fabricated evidence would not come to light. An easy thing to put right, but this still happens at PHSO, who allow government departments to tell their own story without probing or correlation to the facts. Some would call this bias, in fact, most reasonable people would call it bias for bias it is.

Burgess also notes an aspect of the Ombudsman's reports as **'accommodating observations'** aimed to give balance where none is deserved. Bending over backwards could be another apt description.

Scattered through the report are accommodating observations about the DHSS. This is a common feature of his reports in general and contributes significantly to the overall 'tone'. Legal obligations fulfilled by the DHSS are presented as concessions – the back-dating of the invalidity pension for Philip, when in fact good cause had been legally established; and the writing-off of an over-payment which was caused by yet another mistake at the local office and was therefore not recoverable.

Many who receive long-awaited PHSO reports are surprised to find that despite acknowledging damning evidence of failure resulting in harm to the citizen, the Ombudsman is prepared to reserve negative judgement on the basis that the organisation has informed them that it has since improved or that even if procedures had been followed the same harm would most likely have occurred. The Ombudsman in full limbo dancing mode whilst holding aloft a crystal ball.

Burgess also used the case of **Mrs Wilson** to demonstrate how the Ombudsman manipulated the facts to show the government body in the best light. Mrs Wilson received uphold in two of her three complaints but was dissatisfied with the service stating that *'the system to which he belongs does not understand what ordinary people want from the Ombudsman.'* How very true.

> *The report says, "The local social security office were not to know that the rules governing Family Income Supplement were about to be changed." But two months previously, the DHSS had announced the forthcoming change. It seems reasonable to expect the Ombudsman to establish that the local office should have known; Mrs Wilson did!*

Burgess throws caution to the wind when he goes on to criticise parliament's **select committee** which is the only body charged with holding the Ombudsman to account.

The Ombudsman is responsible to MPs and to parliament through a select committee. Unfortunately, apart from the occasional splutterings, the committee appears to be singularly docile. Its reports have a complacent, self-congratulatory air. Most disturbing of all is its failure to prevent the Ombudsman from being taken to the bosom of the Establishment.

If you are snuggled inside the bosom of the Establishment, as the Ombudsman most surely is, protected on all sides from proper scrutiny, then it is impossible to call yourself 'impartial'. The figures alone tell the story as year after year the Ombudsman dismisses, without uphold, well over 90% of the complaints it receives. But try telling that to the academics or the media and you will be met with a roll of the eyes as they encounter yet another hostile citizen hell-bent on revenge. Let us leave the last word to **Paul Burgess** who reveals the truth having spoken to complainants themselves and studied first-hand the

Ombudsman reports, something which is unheard of today. He also sets a challenge for those now working in the field of administrative justice in his final conclusion.

> *At grassroots level, I believe the ombudsman scheme has been a failure. It does not offer the ordinary citizen a satisfactory remedy against administrative abuses; indeed, it has become a part of the oppressive network of official institutions which, though purporting to offer public service, have effectively acquired purposes and justifications of their own. This failure was anticipated by some people from the beginning. The late J.D.B. Mitchell, former Professor of Constitutional Law at the University of Edinburgh, argued; "Public authorities have moral responsibilities and these moral responsibilities can never be translated into legal responsibilities without a specific system of public law."*

So, who is going to fund the academics to put out papers on the moral v legal responsibilities of the Ombudsman? Any offers?

Editor's note: It mostly comes down to funding of course. The public bodies are able to use taxpayer money to requisition research which supports them on the adoption of a chosen path. No one seems concerned that the body under examination provides both the funds and the data for the research. Encouraged by the academic's response to the Burgess article, we put together our own academic proposal, listing the evidence which supported our argument. To make the project manageable, we narrowed the focus to the key issue of 'bias' within the system. As a citizen campaign group, we were not able to write this in the format of a proper academic proposal and neither were we able to offer any funding. It was put out as a blog post in May 2019 and to date we have received no responses from the academic community, apart from the inclusion of our proposal on the UKAJI website.

Why campaigners need academics

6th May 2019

It's not difficult for **Rob Behrens, the Ombudsman** to stimulate academic debate. The following is from the June 2018 meeting minutes;

12.5 Rob Behrens said that, through the Ombudsman Association, he had raised concerns that academics had not used their unique position to comment on a possible PSO Bill. In response, a group of academics had agreed to set up a project to explore this further, and were holding a conference in January to discuss what a PSO Bill could contain.

In January 2019 the academics held a 'roundtable' event' which produced a **'Manifesto for Ombudsman Reform'** – as reported by UKAJI in March 2019.[85]

"...this post outlines a Manifesto for Ombudsman Reform based upon a roundtable discussion at the University of Sheffield in January 2019. A cross-section

---

[85] ukaji.org/2019/03/28/a-manifesto-for-legislative-reform-of-the-ombudsman-sector/

*of stakeholders to the ombudsman community
participated in the event…"*

It was refreshing to see reference to the service user viewpoint but PHSOtheFACTS, the only citizen group working for Ombudsman reform, were not part of the cross-section of stakeholders invited to the event. There is a certain irony in the final recommendation considering that the academics themselves failed to directly 'incorporate the views of users' though they stated afterwards that some service users were present.

*7. The office [PHSO]should be challenged to evidence
its capacity to assist all sections of society and
incorporate the views of users and investigated bodies
into the design of its decision-making processes and
setting of standards.*

The reality is that the views of the service user are rarely sought, yet when they are, these views give a consistent narrative and central to that narrative is the claim that **the Ombudsman is biased against them.**

From 1983

In an article in the **New Society in 1983** 'Whose side is the Ombudsman really on?' **Paul Burgess** cites examples of bias such as relying on the information provided by the public body without cross-referencing with the complainant; information which turned out to be flawed. Also, the repeated use of 'accommodating observations' to put the public body in the best light. He concluded that;

At grassroots level, I believe the ombudsman scheme has been a failure. It does not offer the ordinary citizen a satisfactory remedy against administrative abuses; indeed, it has become a part of the oppressive network of official institutions which, though purporting to offer public service, have effectively acquired purposes and justifications of their own.

2014 – 2016

The **Patients Association** released three damning reports into the Ombudsman service. Recording the views of over 200 service users, 66% stated that there was 'weak justification' for the PHSO decision and 62% reported that PHSO ignored or overlooked the evidence, apparently siding with the Trust.

2015 – 2017

Lack of impartiality was a key issue in research carried out by **Gill and Creutzfeldt**[86] in 2015 and reported in 2017 which looked at the views of **on-line critics** of Ombuds services.

Lack of impartiality (the ombud siding with the public body), lack of transparency (private deliberations) and lack of robust inquiry are the key criticisms identified. Watchers refer to lack of opportunities for face-to-face

---

[86] ukaji.org/2017/09/01/new-research-kafkaesque-and-demoralising-how-online-critics-perceive-the-uks-public-service-ombuds/

interaction, interviews, fieldwork; they suggest that the paper-based approach is inevitably weighted against the citizen, as control of official records are in the hands of the public body. Ombuds are experienced as emotionally and professionally attached to public bodies and their staff rather than to citizens. The form of expectations management used by ombuds is seen as patronising and concerned more with KPI issues (speed, cost, politeness) than with questions of justice. The ombud is seen as a 'pseudo-system of administrative justice'.

2017

In 2017 **Martin Lewis from Money Saving Expert** carried out a consumer review of Ombudsman services and released a report called **Sharper Teeth** [87] Approximately 100 citizens supplied data concerning PHSO and 75% claimed that the Ombudsman appeared biased towards the other

---

[87] moneysavingexpert.com/images/documents/MSE-Sharper_teeth_interactive.pdf

party. 82% said their experience with PHSO had been 'poor'. [88]

2018 – 2019

Completed in December 2018 but released without fanfare in March 2019 the **clinical advice review**[89] gives a rare insight into the investigation process at PHSO. **Sir Liam Donaldson** was able to internally assess how PHSO gathered and utilised expert clinical advice when making decisions on clinical care complaints. He spoke with caseworkers, clinical advisors, management and importantly, talked directly to service users with access to written contributions from complainants. His report revealed a number of unpalatable facts which exposed the ways in which error is allowed to permeate the process without proper check and balance.

---

[88] See Fig. 5 Satisfaction Table from 'Sharper Teeth' p.10

[89] ombudsman.org.uk/sites/default/files/PHSO_Clinical_Advice_Review _Report_of_Independent_Adviser.pdf

Given that the Ombudsman has been able to investigate health complaints since 1973 and was empowered to investigate clinical judgment from 1996 the opening statistics given by Sir Liam are a shocking indictment of the value of this service.

Just one example illustrates the ineffectiveness in system level learning and improvement. Recently, the government's Health and Social Care Secretary commissioned a major academic study of the prevalence of medication error in the health service in England (6). This showed that an estimated 237 million errors occur at some point in the medication process each year. Yet, most categories of medication-related harm that happen today were delineated in a study in 1961 (9). No other major high-risk industry has such a poor record of safety improvement. (p4)

There were around 208,000 written complaints made to the NHS in England in 2017/18 (10). This equated to about 572 per day. There is no information available to show how these complaints align with each of the six sources of poor quality or unsafe care. There is little information to show how complaints are used to systematically improve in these areas of quality and safety. (p4)

Just what has the Ombudsman been doing all this time? By casting an external eye over the procedures, Sir Liam was able to identify the ways in which the prescribed 'process' failed to meet the core objectives of protecting the citizen.

The handling of complaints by the PHSO service is very procedurally driven. In part, this is because of legislation governing the PHSO role in NHS complaints, in part because of internal procedures, both written and unwritten. Both are underpinned and reinforced by the induction, training and supervision of the organisation's staff. Generally, close adherence to these procedures is important and a good thing but not when they do not serve a necessary wider purpose (e.g. of safeguarding future patients from harm) or when they discourage thinking and common-sense reasoning (e.g. not taking up a serious concern about care because it is not one of the strands of the complaint) or when they confuse and upset too many complainants. Some staff are very protective of the current procedures and seem to hold the belief that, because of the statutory role of the PHSO, little can be changed. (p9)

PHSO has no external scrutiny of its investigation procedure and is, therefore, able to operate in 'a self-confirmatory bubble'. The dangers of this were immediately apparent to Sir Liam.

On reading the judgement, [Miller & Anor V Health Service Commissioner] it is a perfect example where the internal world and the external world see things differently. Those handling the complaint believed themselves to be following the normal rules, customs and practices. Yet, the account of the Appeal Court Justices on the handling of the complaint brings an entirely reasonable expectation from the external world that decisions and actions should be appropriate and fair. The PHSO's team in this case believed that their

work was procedurally sound. Impartial scrutiny found
that they were not. P10

'...an entirely reasonable expectation from the external
world that decisions and actions should be appropriate
and fair' is a very telling phrase as is the fact that the
PHSO team believed their work to be procedurally
sound when it was found to be **'irrational to the**
point of illegality' by the court of appeal.

When Sir Liam met with service users, the issue
of **bias** once more topped the league table of
complaint.

It is striking, that in the Clinical Advice Review
Team's meeting with complainants, there was a
widespread view that the PHSO would take sides with,
or protect, the NHS organisation complained against,
or fail to challenge the provider of care robustly
enough. (p11)
Accusations of bias, secrecy, insensitivity, error and
failure to listen, occurring as they did, in the period

before this Clinical Advice Review was commissioned
are extremely important in considering what changes
now need to be made. One way or another, the process
of clinical evaluation of complaints is interwoven with
such criticisms and concerns. (p12)

Sir Liam cites a number of ways in which 'error' permeates the process such as the lay caseworker making assumptions which then affect the quality of the evidence provided by the clinical advisor. Or the caseworker failing to provide key evidence to the clinical advisor, failing to take heed of warnings given by the clinical advisor or failing to include harmful acts by scoping them out of the investigation altogether. He concludes;

Overall, based on my review of cases, together with my
discussions with staff and complainants, I judge that
the current process of commissioning and use of
clinical advice is prone to three types of error: errors of

fact, errors of interpretation, and errors of omission.
(p18)

The current procedures have clear problems with a real
risk of drawing the wrong conclusions. (p20)

Sir Liam stresses the importance of listening to public
criticisms of PHSO which include those made prior to
the appointment of Rob Behrens.

These may be thought of as past events of no direct
relevance to the current Clinical Advice Review. This
would be a mistake. Addressing their underlying causes
and dysfunctions is essential to the new PHSO
continuing to implement his reforms whilst retaining
the confidence of patients and the public. These past
criticisms echo many of the risks that are quite clear in
the present handling procedures for complaints. Also,
the negativity from these events is swirling around the
present service, even though it has made a fresh start
under the new PHSO. Moreover, the complainants,
with whom the Clinical Advice Review Team met,

*brought serious concerns about their cases to the meeting. **Their experience was consistent with the previous criticisms.** Although information is available on people who were satisfied with the PHSO's work, the complainants who responded to the consultation should not be regarded as an unrepresentative minority. Changes to the current way of working should be such as to restore confidence in the PHSO's ability to get right the assessment and investigation of complaints. Errors should be rare. **There should be no hint of bias** towards NHS bodies. Complainants should feel fully engaged in the process. (p19)*

*'**These past criticisms echo many of the risks that are quite clear in the present handling procedures for complaints.** Many of the 'past criticisms' emanate from members of **PHSOtheFACTS** who have repeatedly tried to alert both PHSO and PACAC to the failures now identified in Sir Liam Donaldson's report. It will come as no surprise to learn that no members of our group were offered the chance to*

meet with Sir Liam as part of his review into the use of clinical evidence.

Our calls for review of our cases have been repeatedly denied by Rob Behrens on the basis that the decisions were 'sound' despite the fact that in the recent Value for Money report [90] the staff stated that

"previously, performance management had been too driven by artificial targets and process, rather than a concern with the quality of decisions being reached" (6.4 p21)

and despite the fact that the **Miller & Anor case** demonstrated the inability of PHSO to accurately evaluate its own performance. Following this judgement against PHSO it was reported that the use of clinical expertise had been dysfunctional for at least 8 years, hence the call for Sir Liam's clinical advice review.

90

www.ombudsman.org.uk/sites/default/files/Value_for_Money_repo rt_final.pdf

The following correspondence between Rob Behrens and **Sir Bernard Jenkin chair of PACAC** sent on 23rd February 2019 ⁹¹ refers to a meeting held in October 2017 with members of **PHSOtheFACTS**. This correspondence demonstrates that according to Behrens it is impossible to have an independent review of Ombudsman decisions or process.

Dear Sir Bernard,

I cannot let the email to you from [REDACTED] pass without comment. Leaving aside his accusations of corruption and 'abusive' letters, I draw your attention to the basic issues in this case:

1. [REDACTED] was one of more than 30 families I agreed to meet in October 2017;

91

https://www.whatdotheyknow.com/request/564954/response/1354352/attach/5/email.html?cookie_passthrough=1

461

2. I listened to their stories and agreed to look again at their historic cases with an assurance process involving a senior colleague who had no previous involvement. This involved a significant amount of work;

3. As I reported to PACAC in January a very small number of those cases were found to have unreliable decisions and were/ are being looked at again;

4. [REDACTED] case was not. You have the letter I wrote to him at the time.

5. Along with others, [REDACTED] then called for an 'external independent review' but as I have always maintained, the Ombudsman is the external independent review and anything else – leaving aside unprecedented, very rare circumstances – undermines my authority and my relationship with Parliament.

Yours sincerely,

Mr Behrens reviewed the case files presented to him and informed us that he was 'horrified' by the contents but later found that just a few cases needed closer review. Most of these cases remain in the PHSO system without resolution, despite on-going reviews which have lasted over 18 months. It is clear that without independent scrutiny of these cases, inherent, institutional bias will not be identified.

Sir Liam stressed the validity of the claims made by the service users to confirm they were a **'representative group'**. He also found that the views he heard at the roundtable meeting reflected the same views he had seen in the written evidence. This demonstrates a consistent narrative despite the fact that no PHSOtheFACTS members were present at the meeting to influence the debate. Members of PHSOtheFACTS directly handed case files to Sir Liam at a prior public event, having lost confidence that PHSO would share our correspondence.

*It would be wrong to simply note the critical comments
and conclude that they were an unrepresentative
minority. The sources of information on complainants'
experience provide rich and important insights into the
functioning of the PHSO service. It was particularly
striking that the group of complainants, with whom I,
and the Clinical Advice Review Team, met, was not
made up of vexatious or unreasonable people. They
expressed frustration and, anger, but the problems that
they described with the handling of their complaints
should be a vital source of learning. Many of their
criticisms of the PHSO's processes, and those in the
documented accounts and submissions, were consistent
with what I had already observed, having read a
sample of records provided to me. (p13)*

PHSOtheFACTS Proposal for academic research:

It can be seen that in its role as Health Service
Ombudsman, PHSO have failed to deliver

improvements in patient safety. There is also evidence from **Sir Liam Donaldson's clinical review** that the internal processes of investigation are subject to error of fact, error of interpretation and error of omission. The consistent narrative of service users is that such errors lead to bias and the failure to deliver justice. The evidence gathered for the recent clinical review provides significant new data about the current practice which could be explored further by academics. The twelve service users who attended the roundtable meeting with Sir Liam have been confirmed as 'representative' voices. Sir Liam also confirmed that their criticisms echoed those made previously, which remain unresolved. He stressed the importance of listening and learning from these criticisms in order to restore public confidence and effectively move forward. It can be seen that PHSO are culturally unable to carry out a meaningful review into their own practice. As part of the **Manifesto for Ombudsman reform**, the academics could learn much by examining in detail the case files of the twelve participants in the round table event and could widen their research to include the written evidence provided and source the case files from members of PHSOtheFACTS who contributed to the review directly through contact with Sir Liam Donaldson. Independent academic research is needed to identify the areas where bias enters the process and to propose new quality control measures to ensure that final reports are totally free from bias as recommended by Sir Liam. Our collective lived experience has been repeatedly denied by those in a position of authority. Independent academic research is, therefore, essential and would contribute to the important debate surrounding the proposal for a new People's Ombudsman.

Editor's note: This blog post presents quite a body of damning evidence from a variety of sources. The 12 case files from the 'Roundtable' event would have provided the perfect source of data for further academic research. These files were chosen as representative by PHSO themselves and the citizens concerned had previously given their consent to the examination and publication of aspects of their content.

Although we have not received an offer of independent research into the issue of 'bias', we have possibly been influential in triggering a similar research project by **Elisabeth Davies,** a non-exec board member at PHSO, as seen in the October 2019 Minutes[92]

8.   Declarations of Interest

8.1   Elisabeth Davies informed the Board that as part of her MSc course in Dispute Resolution at Queen Mary University (QMU) she would be carrying out research looking at complainants' understanding of impartiality. She had agreed with the Ombudsman that she could carry out her research with PHSO complainants. Her role would be as an independent academic researcher and not as a PHSO Board member. It was essential to be transparent about this and to manage the risks. She had obtained the required ethical approval from QMU. An information sheet setting out her role will be sent to all participants. The research will be conducted using a QMU email address.

interviews. She is looking at whether complainants have an accurate perception of impartiality and by default an accurate perception of bias. Dealing only in perception and not in hard evidence suggests an opportunity for batting away public criticisms with a little more gaslighting. It is notable that the public body 'stakeholders' will not be asked for their understanding of impartiality as a check and

---

[92] October 1st 2019 Board Meeting Minutes

balance. There has been a recent update to the **'Manifesto for Ombudsman Reform'** on the UKAJI website. [93] On the back of the global Coronavirus pandemic the academics start by saying that 'institutional reform is rightly very low on the agenda'. If reform is low on the agenda when a crisis reveals gaping flaws in the system, it rather begs the question as to when it would be high. Further into the article **Rob Behrens** claims the problem is insufficient hard evidence to support the need for reform. He clearly needs to read this book. Finally, the 'impartial' academics discourage investigation into the core roles of the Ombudsman, namely uncovering systemic problems in public services and resolving complaints, on the basis that such questions would be 'cynical'.

> If future inquiries into the public sector's handling of the coronavirus uncover systemic problems, the question may be asked why the ombud sector had not formerly raised the alarm. Others may question whether the focus on complaint handling of recent decades has been misplaced, and costly. Such cynicism needs to be resisted.

---

[93] https://ukaji.org/2020/04/29/a-manifesto-for-ombudsman-reform/

Any reform which does not address these core roles will be just more window dressing, or as one concerned citizen commented on the UKAJI site; 'old guard, new uniform'.

A state captured regulator is worse than no regulator at all. The flawed PHSO process gives an illusion of accountability for public bodies where none exists. It validates poor performance, condoning the harm caused to citizens. It allows politicians to absolve their responsibility to the public as they knowingly refer cases into oblivion. With unforgivable cruelty it sets up false hope, resulting in victims of injustice wasting many hours, months and years repeatedly putting the facts before an organisation which is institutionally deaf and blind to them.

At best the academics have been muted, at worst they have been used to validate poor research. Easily done as their careers are dependent upon government funding and peer approval. There is no incentive for hard-hitting or critical research, particularly as the media are unlikely to lift it from behind the paywall of academic journals into the public domain where it might have some impact. Those ivory towers have never been more remote.

Editor's note: The Ombudsman is on a perpetual journey of self-improvement where they set their own targets and measure their own progress. All public criticism of the Ombudsman can be met with, 'we are on to it - just give us time'. PHSO announced their new 3-year strategy in April 2018, one year after the arrival of Rob Behrens. The following blog post places the PHSO rhetoric alongside the reality to reveal an organisation largely in denial.

Back to the future for PHSO – or is it ever decreasing circles?

17th April 2018

Just as we come to the end of the 5-year strategy of restructuring under **Dame Julie Mellor** the new Ombudsman, **Rob Behrens**, announced this week the launch of a 3-year **'back to basics'** strategy for the **Parliamentary and Health Service Ombudsman (PHSO).** Before we explore the new package of promises, bear in mind that PHSO is 50 years old. Enough time for 16 previous 3-year strategies to iron out any wrinkles in procedures. Also, take into account that **Rob Behrens** has to pull off some kind of miracle to deliver any beneficial change given that PHSO will suffer a 24% cut in funding, they have lost 70 experienced staff in the move to Manchester and taken on at least 25 new (untrained) recruits to fill the gaps. To top it all they are presently working with a significant backlog of cases waiting for assessment, investigation and review. Against this backdrop, **Mr Behrens** is promising to make PHSO an **'exemplary ombudsman service'.** Will this new strategy[94] help to 'manage our expectations' or just promise more than it can deliver?

Our strategy 2018-21

Delivering an exemplary ombudsman service

---

[94] Our strategy 2018 – 21 PHSO website.

We want to be an exemplary ombudsman
service – one that continually learns from
the best of what others are doing, while
contributing to improvements elsewhere
across the public sector and the wider
ombudsman sector. We also want to
continue building public confidence and
trust in our service. While the PHSO Service
Charter tells us that a significant majority
of people who come to us say they get a
good service, we know that too many
think this is not the case and there is more
we must do to address this.

Objective 1

To improve the quality of our service,
while remaining independent,
impartial and fair

We will introduce new ways of working that
resolve cases more quickly, improving both

the quality and timeliness of our decisions and the overall experience of people making complaints.

We will invest in our staff so they are equipped to deliver a professional casework service that remains sensitive to the complex, often tragic, issues that are brought to us.

Objective 2

To increase the transparency and impact of our casework

We will publish more information about our casework online to help improve public services, while enabling complainants, the public and organisations we investigate to have confidence in what we do. We will target our insight reports so that important lessons from our casework and systemic *reviews contribute to raising standards in public services.*

Objective 3

To work in partnership to improve public services, especially frontline complaint handling

We will strengthen our relationships with other ombudsman services, and collaborate with others to improve how the public sector responds when things go wrong, from sharing good practice to offering training to complaint handlers.

Drawing insights from our casework, we will work with those best placed to apply the lessons learned to improve public services.

Well, he did say to the Health Service Journal that he wanted to **'get back to basics'** and these three objectives represent nothing more than the core function of any Ombudsman service. Did the management at PHSO consider the outcomes of the previous strategy before they started 'going backwards'?　　Here is a summary of the 2013/18 **5-year strategy** with the ambitious title of **'More impact for more people'**.[95]

To help make our vision real, our aims for the next five years are to:

1. Make it easier for people to find and use our service

This includes raising awareness of our work for everyone and helping people who find it hard to complain to contact us.

2. Help more people by investigating more complaints and to provide an excellent service for our customers

This includes using different ways to investigate and resolve different types of complaint and setting high standards for the service we provide.

3. Work with others to use what we learn from complaints to help them make public services better

This includes sharing information about what went wrong with different organisations so that mistakes can be avoided in the future. We will help Parliament find out the reasons for mistakes and how services can be improved.

4. Lead the way to make the complaints system better

This includes working with Parliament to help make it easier for people to complain. We will also share information about the way in which public services respond to complaints to help them do it better.

5. Develop our organisation so that it delivers these aims efficiently and effectively

This includes helping our staff develop new skills and developing new ways to handle complaints and to manage knowledge and information. We will also look hard at how we spend our money to make sure we are delivering the best value.

---

[95] Our strategic plan 2013 – 18 PHSO website.

So, there we have it. PHSO has only just completed overhauling its investigation model, setting high standards and improving productivity. Working with stakeholders and parliament to 'shine a light' improve complaint handling and save money along the way. So confident were they back in 2013 they gave the following prediction of success. This must be a great starting place for **Mr Behrens,** lucky man.

The impact we will have	
In 2011-12	By 2018
We investigated 421 individual complaints and, where mistakes had been made, we found out what went wrong.	We will investigate thousands of complaints each year and, where things have gone wrong, we will find out the reasons why.
We aimed to finish 90% of investigations within 12 months. We achieved 79%.	We will conclude 95% of enquiries and investigations within six months and 99% within 12 months.

If more evidence of success were needed, we can see from the much valued **'Service Charter' data** that using these improved investigation models, PHSO was able to make an impartial decision 100% of the time. Hard to improve on perfection.

10. We will evaluate the information we've gathered and make an impartial decision on your complaint	100%	-	+3%	-

Certainly, some of the staff at PHSO feel that the **continual** imposition of new strategies is the very thing which prevents them getting on with their work.

5 Jul 2017

"Suffering through change"

▼ Former Employee - Anonymous Employee

◼ Doesn't Recommend   ◼ Negative Outlook

I worked at Parliamentary and Health Service Ombudsman full-time

Pros

The core staff there are generally dedicated and believe in what the office does. Salary and the supporting package - leave, flexible working etc. is good.

Cons

An ongoing, chaotic, sometimes directionless and apparently never-ending change programme since 2013. Large amounts of senior managers in and out in a short period, many of whom did not seem to understand the core business or value the experience of existing staff. Experienced staff have continued to be lost throughout the change programme.

Advice to Management

Communicate properly. Get some stability. Let your people get back to doing the job they are there to do.

There are of course some advantages to having 'a never-ending change programme', it means that when criticism comes your way, you can promise that improvement is just around the corner and ask for patience as you put in place the glowing rhetoric of your current plan. This 'jam tomorrow' message has worn pretty thin with those of us who have been following the ups and downs, well mainly the downs of PHSO since 2012.

But perhaps we are being unfair to **Rob Behrens**. He has introduced some radical new ideas. If we can just wait until 2020/21 we can all benefit from the new **'mediation'** service for early intervention and know that staff working on our complaints are fully **'accredited'**.

In 2020-21 we will:

- Begin accreditation of caseworkers.

- Evaluate mediation and other dispute resolution pilots, implementing the most successful as part of our new 'Ombudsman toolbox'.

- Build the approach from our pilots into our training and accreditation programme, so staff are fully equipped to use these methods.

These new tools require pilot studies and new measures to be created to assess success. This could take a lot longer than 2021 to be up and running, particularly as PHSO has still to find a body willing to provide the accreditation. Still fifty years of muddling through without the core functions in place (apparently) what harm in taking the time to get things right?

Dame Julie Mellor, despite her grand 5-year strategy, failed to deliver in pretty much all respects. She presided over a huge backlog in casework performance, a dramatic fall in employee satisfaction, financial scandals and resigned early from her post having acted inappropriately when informed that her Deputy Ombudsman **Mick Martin** had been named in court proceedings and was found to have colluded with a colleague to cover up a valid complaint whilst working in the NHS. She simply lurched from one crisis to another.

Consequently, both the Ombudsman and Deputy Ombudsman left the service before seeing the fruits of their labour. But what exactly was the legacy left for **Rob Behrens** to inherit at the end of her five-year change programme? A look at the last published **Board Minutes for PHSO** gives us some idea of what was going on behind the scenes and it doesn't look good.

From **September 2017** (latest published)

On the staffing issue, **Amanda Campbell CEO** confirmed the loss of 70 staff from the London office.

9.6 **Amanda Campbell** acknowledged that staff had felt let down by the slow pace of consultation and change. However some difficult decisions had been made and only eight compulsory redundancies had been necessary, from a reduction in staffing of over 70 posts.

Having survived the 'cull' there were issues with staff engagement.

9.10 The Board discussed the contents of the report. **Ruth Sawtell** said that it had been disappointing to see the fall in staff engagement reported in the June 2017 pulse survey. **Amanda Campbell** said that the survey had been taken in the middle of the collective consultation period at a time of maximum uncertainty. However a significant change was not expected in the October 2017 survey, as transition was still underway.

Always look on the bright side **Amanda** but you need to take the staff with you when sharing your vision of an exemplary Ombudsman service.

> 9.3 **Amanda Campbell** advised that there were now many changes happening simultaneously and quickly. She said she wished to assure the Board that PHSO recognised and were managing the volume of activity across the organisation.

> 9.8 **Amanda Campbell** recognised that communications with staff about the change programme had been poor. As a result of this a weekly cascade was now in place that had received positive feedback from staff.

Not managing change well was the same complaint from staff under the previous Ombudsman. Referring to the **'training programme'** which is essentially the key to all the improvements put forward by **Rob Behrens** there was this comment:

9.12 **Jon Shortridge** commended the training programme but said that it must go beyond a 'sheep dip' approach. **Amanda Campbell** reported that, following the training, experienced staff should continue to support new staff. Staff were integral to the design and delivery of training, which was modular and was aimed at meeting the range of different needs. The training would eventually lead to accreditation.

No mention here that PHSO had just lost 70 experienced staff and taken on at least 25 new recruits in Manchester as their replacement. So, the experienced staff must meet their targets to get the backlog down whilst supporting new arrivals who had received their 'sheep dip' training. However, it was recognised by **Ms Campbell** that the training of new recruits and the re-training of all current staff would have an impact on the backlog.

11.4 Unallocated assessments and investigations had both risen significantly since the end of Q1 and were likely to increase further as caseworkers were taken offline for training. **Amanda Campbell** tabled a chart showing projections that by the end of the business year there would be **788 unallocated assessments and 567 unallocated investigations.** The numbers would then reduce gradually with assessments projected to be at or close to zero by August 2018, and investigations to be at or close to zero by December 2018. These projections were based on a mitigation agreed by the Executive Board on 27 September 2017, to recruit 25 caseworkers above establishment.

One minute it all relies on staff who are professional to accredited standards and the next it is deemed by the Board perfectly acceptable to take 25 people with no experience and with minimum training and have them manage complex cases where the complainant has already had a significant wait. Perhaps the following statement reveals how PHSO management ensure that staff (new and old) caught in the trauma of reallocation and restructure perform to a given target.

9.13 **Julia Tabreham** expressed concern about the reported rise in bullying in the pulse survey. **Amanda Campbell** replied that there was no increase in staff saying that they had personally experienced bullying. Rather there was a **perception of bullying** through performance targets and the way the consultation had been managed. The trade union side had been asked to provide evidence of incidents of bullying, but no direct evidence had been received. There was perhaps a need to be more clear about what was meant by bullying and harassment.

Ah, just a 'perception' of bullying. Well if you feel bullied I guess you would call it bullying but management know best and seem to have the only dictionary that matters. The title of their policy on casework does suggest rather a heavy hand.

11.2 **Amanda Campbell** tabled before the Board an extract from a presentation first made by **Rebecca Marsh** to the Quality Committee on 14 September 2017 on **'Driving the Quality of Casework at PHSO'.** The presentation set out a list of areas where it was perceived that there were quality issues, and identified actions planned for dealing with three of these areas:

Thoroughness, Communications and Clinical Advice. **Elisabeth Davies** said that this paper had been discussed by the Quality Committee, who had focussed on the potential quality impacts of the Target Operating Model.

'Driving the Quality of Casework' does sound pretty hostile, particularly when you bear in mind that there is a major problem at PHSO with the technology available to do the job.

> 13.14 ICT was now a RED risk. A number of issues had arisen which had the potential to impact on service delivery in future. Mitigations had been agreed and were outlined in the risk register. It was recognised that PHSO now needed to carry out a full review of the ICT structure, looking at the robustness of service provision and how the systems delivered the Corporate Strategy.

Poor things, they have yet to receive all their new training and benefit from the wisdom brought to PHSO by having a 'real Ombudsman' take the helm, but already they are being 'driven' to perform without the IT systems to support their work. And what of **Mr Behrens**, how did he share his vision with the Executive Board in order to lead the way to an exemplary service. Only one statement in the entire meeting was assigned to the man himself and you can see it below.

> 10.5 **Rob Behrens** highlighted his series of engagement meetings with staff. These had been very productive and the output from the meetings would be fed into the strategic plan for 2018-21.

Now that sounds familiar. **Mr Behrens** regularly has 'productive meetings' even if no-one else agrees with him. Can't possibly be his fault then that the sickness levels at PHSO have gone through the roof.

> 13.2 The Board were concerned that PHSO were very close to the sickness absence target. **Gill Kilpatrick** said that PHSO were looking at this very closely to understand the trend.

So, the Board has no idea why the staff are going off sick. Could it possibly be linked to rapid and repeated change, loss of experienced staff, lack of essential IT resources and a hostile working environment?

Given this is the current state of affairs at PHSO it is difficult to have any confidence that the new 3-year strategy will be any more successful than the previous 5-year strategy. But the real benefit of a change programme is that it stops critics in their tracks by saying 'we are working on it'.

Editor's note: Under Dame Julie Mellor the staff had been 'driven' to increase the number of investigations 10-fold without additional resources. We learnt on her departure that this led to a 'toxic culture' as staff struggled to meet performance targets regardless of the quality. As PHSO moved into their new 3-year strategy there was a 'drive' to reduce the backlog of cases. The easiest way was to close more complaints without assessment or investigation. In 2016/17 (under Dame Julie Mellor) 25.8% of complaints were assessed and 13.4% investigated. This fell to 20.8% assessed and 8.2% investigated in 2017/18 and a further fall to 18.9% assessed and 5.4% investigated by 2018/19. Cutting your investigation workload by more than half and failing to carry out assessments will reduce the backlog for sure, but it goes without saying that valid complaints will be rejected along the way. But this is just business as usual for PHSO who investigated none of the cases which concerned the **Mid Staffs** scandal where 1,200 people died as a result of unacceptable neglect and maltreatment. It investigated just 5 of the 43 complaints made about the dysfunctional **Liverpool Community Health NHS Trust** but failed to uphold a single case. A panel led by **Dr Bill Kirkup** later recorded a damning review of the Liverpool

Trust. How did PHSO fail to spot 'significant harm due to multiple, serious failings?'

> Patients suffered "significant harm" because of multiple serious failings by a dysfunctional NHS trust... Liverpool Community Health NHS trust (LCH) provided poor, unsafe and ineffective care to patients, including inmates at HMP Liverpool, the scathing report concluded.[96]

If there is any point to the Ombudsman it must surely be to protect the public from such scandalous behaviour. Yet independent reports continually inform us that such behaviours are carried out with impunity, over long periods of time. All under the nose of the Ombudsman, who has repeatedly failed to sound the alarm over a single scandal.

Certainly, doing more to protect the public is high on the list of rhetoric, yet the very low investigation and uphold rate tells a different story.

---

[96] /www.theguardian.com/society/2018/feb/08/liverpool-nhs-trust-dysfunctional-and-unsafe-report-finds

Rob Behrens power struggle.

11th February 2019

It's not easy for **Rob Behrens,** the Ombudsman to ask for additional powers. When you are paid the salary of a **High Court Judge** people tend to assume that you have all the powers you need. To draw attention to the fact that you don't, could damage the veil of **'public confidence'**. But Rob Behrens is a man on a mission – to make PHSO into an 'exemplary' Ombudsman and time is running out.

Mr Behrens has been using every opportunity to ask Parliament to grant more legislative powers in order to

'...increase our capacity to improve public services and make it easier for people to access justice when things go wrong.'

Good to know that his heart is in the right place

with protecting the public uppermost in his argument for legislative reform. He is asking for **'own initiative'** powers so that the Ombudsman can open an investigation even when no official complaint has been made. And he is asking for PHSO to become a **'Complaints Standard Authority'** with the power to set standards on good complaint handling across public bodies, as is the case in Scotland.

Given that the Ombudsman has been carefully chosen by Parliament to be a person of high integrity, why would Parliament not grant such powers at the earliest opportunity, in fact why were they not granted in the first place if they can, as Mr Behrens states, provide justice and improve public services?

There was always a fundamental flaw in parliamentarians being the ones who designed the **'Parliamentary Commissioner'** who would ultimately hold them all to account. Through a series of amendments, lasting some years of debate, they decided not to give this body either teeth or claws by which some damage may be done. The following paraphrased quotes from **Hansard** [97] give a flavour of the 1967 debates

"The Bill was always drafted to be a swiz, and now it is spelt into the Bill............Anyone who contemplates an office of this kind is faced with the dilemma of making it either a Frankenstein or a nonentity—a Frankenstein if it has effective powers and a nonentity if it has not. The Government, quite rightly, has opted for its being a nonentity, and in that sense it is a fraud......... I congratulate the Government on its being a nonentity. A Frankenstein would, I think, have undermined the power of Ministers...... it is a noble facade without anything behind it." "I see the Amendment as an admission on the right hon. Gentleman's part that the powers in the Bill as it stands would scarcely suffice to pull the skin off a rice pudding."

---

[97] JAN 1967 VOL 739 CC1375-400 AND JAN 1967 VOL 739 CC1419-53

There was concern that the Commissioner (renamed Ombudsman) would become overworked and consequently stretched beyond his resources if too many options were made available to him.

"I was somewhat amazed to find the Leader of the House suggesting that Schedule 3 was designed to assist the ombudsman in limiting the work he would do. [Laughter.] I gather from the laughter that the House shares the absurdity of that which I had seen.

Given that the stated purpose of the Ombudsman was to provide justice for aggrieved members of the public (plus the added bonus of providing a route for backbenchers to hold the executive to account) there was, quite rightly, concern that the powers granted would not be sufficient to meet expectations.

"But if we are to have an ombudsman, then it is absurd so to limit his powers by exclusion that one turns him not only into the swiz he started off as but into a double swiz upon swiz. Our objective throughout has been that, if we are to have an ombudsman, it is wrong for the purposes

of the public that they should be led to believe that they are going to get opportunities or rights through his powers which were not the case."

And this most telling prophecy should the Ombudsman fail to deliver a fair outcome.

"The people affected live with their bitterness for the rest of their lives."

But times change and in our modern, 'transparent' government there can be no reason not to extend the powers of the Ombudsman beyond 'servant to the House' (hence the MP filter). Yet, **Sir Bernard Jenkin, Chair of PACAC** suggests that the request for more powers could be deemed '**Empire building**' on the part of Mr Behrens. (i.e. an attempt to obtain power as an act of self-aggrandisement). There could be some mileage in this argument given that last year only 20% of the complaints received by the Ombudsman made it through to assessment and just 8% received a full investigation.[98] If Mr Behrens genuinely wished to *increase capacity to improve public services and provide access to justice for more people* he could simply investigate more complaints. But the role of the Ombudsman (according to Mr Behrens) is wider than merely delivering justice to members of the public. Mr Behrens meets often with his international counterparts who take own initiative powers as standard. Perhaps it is something of an embarrassment for Monsieur Rosbif to hold his own in these international talking shops?

Equally, he is in competition with the Scottish Ombudsman (SPSO) who became a **Complaints Standard Authority** in 2010 giving them the power to ensure that public bodies follow an agreed complaint procedure which allows just 20 working days to provide the final decision.

- A shared definition of what is and what is not a complaint
- A two stage process where complaints are resolved as close to the frontline as possible
- Frontline resolution of complaints within five working days
- An investigation stage of 20 working days, which provides the organisation's final decision
- Recording of **all** complaints
- Active learning from complaints through reporting and publicising complaints information.

---

[98] 2017/18 Annual Report data

The wee Sassenach can only look on with envy at such powers. Could you imagine Parliament allowing the English Ombudsman to publicise the complaint handling stats of the DWP or the Home Office, not to mention the NHS. Or heaven forbid hold them to account within 20 days. Effective redaction is a time-consuming process.

Shame Mr Behrens didn't include **the powers of compliance** in his wish list. **Martin Lewis, Money Saving Expert** put that high on his priorities for Ombudsman reform stating that legal powers of compliance were essential to an effective Ombudsman.[99] *'As a minimum – to be called an ombudsman – ombudsmen should have statutory powers to require firms within their sectors to be members, to cooperate with investigations, to comply with decisions, and they should also have the power to enforce their decisions in court if necessary."*

---

[99] Report to **APPG on Consumer Protection** Pub. Jan 2019

Martin Lewis went so far as to say that without powers of compliance the term Ombudsman was **'flaccid'.** Ouch! Not easy being the mighty Ombudsman when you know that the powers you need lie elsewhere.

Editor's note: Essentially the Ombudsman was never designed to hold public bodies to account. It is a 'nonentity' but one which creates an illusion of accountability while deflecting public anger away from Parliament. No amount of 3-year strategies will make any difference to the fundamental issue that the Ombudsman was set up to investigate a mere smattering of the 30,000+ complaints it receives each year. It uses its 'wide discretion' to cherry-pick the cases it wishes to investigate and rejects those which may open up a can of worms. It has no powers of compliance, so must bend over backwards to reach an agreement with the body under investigation to accept the Ombudsman's findings. The degree of careful negotiation required between the 'watchdog' and those supposedly under his watchful eye, adds considerably to the delay experienced by complainants.

The truth is we have for some lived for many decades in a society of 'light-touch' regulation where the Ombudsman has the lightest touch of all. We allow public bodies to investigate themselves with no concern that their publicly funded legal teams are the first to sift through the evidence. Too often the person named in the complaint is also involved in the investigation on the basis that they are best placed to say what happened. Those in authority apparently trust these internal processes to be unbiased but when the

Russians suggested they helped with the **Skripal nerve agent inquiry** it was met with much justified indignation.

If the Skripal incident were an NHS complaint ...

6th April 2018

A UK official said that Russia asking to be involved in the investigation of the Salisbury nerve agent attack is akin to an arsonist "investigating his own fire".

If the Skripal incident were handled like an NHS complaint by PHSO it would go something like this:

UK: Hi Russia, sorry to bother you but we have had a complaint that your chaps have used a highly toxic nerve agent to assassinate a citizen on UK soil. This is in breach of the Geneva protocol and in direct contradiction to the UN Convention on the storage and distribution of toxic chemicals. What do you have to say?

Russia: As you know our legal team have already been through all the evidence regarding this complaint as part of the first-tier complaint handling process. We can confirm that this accusation is entirely without merit. Also, both the Geneva protocol and the UN Convention are only guidelines so I can assure you that there have been no breaches on our part.

UK: Thanks for the confirmation Russia. Are we able to see the evidence you relied upon to make your decision that no breaches occurred?

Russia: Unfortunately, we are just in the process of updating our IT systems causing a loss of data for the official record. We would be happy to provide you with our expert witness statement but this is personal information which belongs to the individual and we must protect his confidentiality. We take complaints of this nature very seriously and I give you my word that our investigation has been both robust and thorough.

UK: That's fine. You will be in receipt of our draft report in the next few days and the final report the day after that and we are happy to confirm no uphold. See you at the next UN conference in Geneva?

Russia: Absolutely, I owe you a coffee. Cheers.

Chapter 9. The Accidental Campaigners

Editor's note: None of us wake up one morning and decide to put our lives on hold for a decade or more while we fight for truth and justice for our fellow citizens. Campaigning starts with a personal trauma. At our most vulnerable we reach out to those in authority only to find that instead of investigating our concern, WE become the subject of the investigation. Our evidence is refuted, no matter how substantial and gaslighting techniques are used to discredit our version of events. It is all in your head.

> *"I was also labelled anxious in the medical notes as if I was part of the problem to be dealt with. It's not surprising to be anxious when your loved one is being treated incompetently. It's another example of labelling to discredit genuine concerns."*

If you become persistent, desperate to find the truth, they cease all contact on the basis that you have become 'vexatious' and unreasonable. When you point out their often-glaring errors, they simply state that your matter has been 'dealt with', no further comment and no specific answers to your carefully crafted questions. Once your eyes are opened to this systemic betrayal of human rights you can never return to being the person you were before. You lose trust in authority, there is no closure, no moving-on, you are forever scarred by the experience. Some suffer from life-changing mental health issues such as PTSD, others withdraw to lick their wounds, and some fight back.

Complainants inform those in authority of the harmful dysfunctions of the system through a genuine belief that they do not already know. As you move through the years and see the different talking heads delivering the same rhetoric you come to realise that they knew all the time. It is not by chance that the inefficiency always works in their favour. Those in authority don't work to protect the citizen, they work to protect the system and maintain the status quo.

This blog records the early days of **PHSOtheFACTS,** a citizen pressure group who have been calling for reform of the **Parliamentary and Health Service Ombudsman. (PHSO)** since 2013.

Fiona Watts interviews Della Reynolds – coordinator for phsothefacts

30th October 2014

Q1. Where and when was the Pressure Group formed?

A. We first met as a group when twelve persistent complainants were invited to give evidence to the Public Administration Select Committee (PASC) on 26th November 2013. This was part of the PASC inquiry 'Complaints – do they make a difference?' After we gave our evidence most of us met up again in the House of Commons cafe and it was there among the coffee cups that the Pressure Group was born.

Q2. Who suggested the formation of the group?

A. While we were exchanging stories and email addresses, Lindsay Roy an MP from PASC, came down to see us. He congratulated us on our calm presentation and suggested that we formed a Pressure Group. As I already had the website phsothefacts.com I agreed to act as the coordinator.

506

Q3. How many are in the group as of October 2014?

A. The group consists of about 40 people right now. New people join and others leave so it has stayed at this level for some time now. [We have had over 60+ members and people regularly contact the group seeking advice and support]

Q4. What have been the highlights so far?

A. When PHSO agreed to hold a seminar for Pressure Group members this was a major breakthrough. We had all been through the system and our files were stamped 'do not acknowledge'. It didn't matter how many times we tried to tell them that they had got the facts wrong, the door was firmly shut. Attending the seminar on 26th June 2014 was very emotional. The raw pain of injustice soon surfaced and for once the Ombudsman staff could see the suffering of the people behind the data.

Q5. Which Ministers or public servants are in a position to progress genuine improvements to the PHSO remit?

A. It seems to me there is no political will to reform the Ombudsman. The issues and flaws have been known in political circles for many years. Every now and again there is an inquiry which blows a lot of hot air around, then it all settles down again, much like before. In theory Oliver Letwin, Minister for Policy at the Cabinet Office is in a position to progress genuine improvements when he reports back on his inquiry into complaint handling and the Ombudsman landscape. Will he bite the bullet and deliver a radically reformed service which actually protects citizens from the abuse of power? We will have to wait and see.

Q6. What are the shared issues that all members of the Pressure Group have in common?

A. Injustice and a determination to fight it. Most of the group members went to PHSO with NHS complaints. It matters not whether your complaint was NHS or Parliamentary we have all been through the same system in much the same way. Our stories are so similar that it has to be deliberate policy to close cases down in this way. Firstly, when PHSO look at the evidence there will be unresolved discrepancies and contradictions in the accounts of the two parties. Despite evidence to the contrary, PHSO will always accept the version supplied by the public body and decide that their account is 'beyond question'. They will simply skirt around or totally ignore any evidence which doesn't match up to this version of events. They will reword the account given by the public body in order to make their draft report, without asking to see any evidence of their claims. Accepting on face value without any probing cannot be termed an 'investigation'. The draft report is often full of factual errors and assumptions accepted as truths. The complainant may spend painstaking hours correcting this draft report only to find that the final report is virtually the same. After the final draft is agreed the decision is set in stone. You can ask for a review, but this is just an internal rubber stamp of the PHSO assessment. Your case is now closed, 'no acknowledgement' is placed on your file and your only option is to go for Judicial Review. Job done – next.

Q7. Which issues could PHSO easily improve by this time next year?

A. They could provide proper investigations, remedy and closure for historic cases. People have waited a long time for the facts of their case to be fully investigated. They want answers to questions and accountability for failings. They want to identify where things went wrong for their loved ones so that it never happens again to another family. Closure requires acknowledgement and remedy and PHSO have the power to provide this. They have started assessing historic cases and hopefully by this time next year all members of the group will have the answers they have been seeking for such a very long time.

Q8. What do you believe to be the greatest challenge for the future of PHSO?

A. Political interference has always prevented PHSO from acting to protect the citizen rather than protect the government. They may be called 'independent' but they work hand in glove with the Cabinet Office the Department of Health and the Treasury. The Ombudsman herself, Dame Julie Mellor, is an establishment figure and all the real decisions are made behind these particular closed doors. PHSO is just another part of the cover-up culture used at will by the government of the day.

Q9. You receive lots of positive feedback from the group, on average, how many hours do you tend to do behind the scenes?

A. Not sure if the two parts of this question are related. Firstly, on the subject of positive feedback, I think it has been of tremendous value to everyone, myself included, to be part of this group. To realise that it is not your fault and that the system has conspired against you to shut out your complaint. There is a great strength in sharing our stories and knowing we are not alone. Also, since we have come together we have had a louder voice. Doors at PHSO and Parliament have started opening to us. We are being heard and hopefully, in the fullness of time, our words will trigger appropriate actions from those in authority. How many hours? Impossible to say. I don't do too much in the evening as I need to switch off, but other than that if I have the time there is always something which needs my attention.

Q10. Why do you do it?

A. I guess I have a strong sense of injustice. I also think that the people are the guardians of democracy. Once we stop being vigilant then the elite rule with impunity. It is easy to look the other way, to say, as so many do, that you can't do anything to change the system. I believe that collectively we have more power than we could ever imagine. If enough of us stood together on a single issue we would frighten the life

511

out of them. We need to continually challenge acceptance of the status quo.

Editor's note: Oliver Letwin did not become the complainant's champion. To give him an iota of credit, he may have had good intentions but nothing concrete materialised from his time at the Cabinet Office. In 2016 he become the first **Brexit Minister**, appointed by **David Cameron**. That didn't turn out too well either. Our historic cases are still closed and very few of us have achieved any personal justice for the harm caused to us. In 2016 my husband left, citing my campaigning as the chief culprit. When you devote yourself to a cause it is difficult to balance the other demands on your time. I have no regrets. I could either fight back or be complicit in my silence. Together we formed a strong and supportive group and have used our voice to speak truth to power. **This book is a testament to our campaign. They can never say they didn't know. They knew, because we told them and they did nothing.**

The next blog post is from **Dr Sara Ryan** who lost her 18-year-old autistic son **Connor Sparrowhawk**, (known as

LB for Laughing Boy) in an avoidable death whilst under the care of Southern Health. Some background from her blog 'My Daft Life'.

> *"LB died in a local NHS run short term treatment and assessment unit on July 4th 2013. He was found dead in the bath. There were five patients and a minimum of four members of staff on duty 24 hours a day. Investigations are continuing (seemingly forever) into how this could have happened."*

This recent account of the ordeal she endured as she sought answers and justice for her son, tells so sharply of the impact on the individual and those closest to them when you challenge the system.

Stolen time, mother blame and writing back

5th March 2020

Gawd. Not written a blog post for what seems like yonks. I think this is a good thing. I've also been on strike for what feels about a decade which is generating unusual space to think and reflect about stuff.

This morning crafting vintage crochet squares my eyes/thoughts drifted to beautiful, beautiful photos of our kids. And reflections about stolen time. Time spent enduring accountability processes, on fighting, meeting, demanding, researching, reading, raging, reading, raising, howling, meeting, missing, fighting, raging, howling and missing. Missing so bloody much.

I totted up one strand of this stolen time.

It is unnecessary. These processes shouldn't take years. Or force families to become almost vigilantes in pursuit of justice.

I also thought about the tenacity and strength of the tentacles of mother blame that continue to try to drag me/us down. Me/us flagging here how the 'mother blame' stain works to circulate a narrative of 'unbalanced woman' disconnected and distinct from a loving family and friends.

Undertones, hints and hammers

The still busy blame work continues across diverse settings and spaces. Examples from the last few weeks:

A comment in a Hampshire newspaper. *Mazars a tool to discredit one trust or just to appease a certain someone?*

A Facebook discussion. *What worries me is her being in this position of power over very vulnerable people and seemingly completely unaware of what's she's saying.*

Disproportionate indignation and the personalising of a wider, independent work outcome.

An extract from a draft manuscript in which a senior exec is portrayed as victim in contrast to an obstructive mother who *really* should have been offered grief counselling early on.

Writing back

A form of writing back, to borrow from post-colonial literature, is part of my/our personal, academic and activist life. Rich and I talk about it. Katherine Runswick-Cole and I have published about it. #JusticeforLB ran with it and, with George Julian's clear vision, generated new ways of being, doing and acting.

Writing back is about trying to redress oppressive and enduring imbalances. Of re-appropriating and resisting harmful discourses. Shades of refrigerator mothers, accusations of hysteria, irrationality and, ironically, imbalance.

The techniques available to public sector bodies wanting to silence people include discrediting, crushing and co-opting. In this order. I was never big on titles or throwing about my business so early attempts to discredit were short lived. Hints of a generic single mother on benefits are hard to sustain when you are married with a senior academic post. From being invisible, the Dr ('Dr') title assumed almost comedic proportions as events unfolded.

Attempts to crush are woven into the fabric of accountability processes as well as the everyday actions of senior health and social care figures. No funding for legal representation at inquests without punitive and intrusive scrutiny. Interview transcripts with NHS staff with sub-sections titled 'My Relationship with Dr Ryan'. The secret review by Oxfordshire County Council in which the author spoke to everyone but us spinning a teeth achingly biased yarn. The commissioner's letter about the terrible harm 'my' campaign was causing. Countless crushing examples.

Co-opting can be an effective tool in terms of maintaining the status quo. Selfie slide shows of families with ministers, politicians, big charities... People sign up to working with different strands of health and social care to generate change, working with and influencing from the inside. Rich and I dipped our toes into the co-opting pool. Both were short lived experiences as futility shone through. Outrage and incredulity this week from long term National Autistic Society supporters as the penny finally dropped. This is a corporate, self-serving beast.

And what if the silencing techniques don't work?

Mmm. This has been a ponder and a half. The following points all overlap...

If the techniques don't work you are not playing the game. You are at fault.

If you remain uncrushed you are clearly not assuming the appropriate, culturally ascribed role of grieving mother. You are stripped of feelings, your bereavement stolen.

People you've never met develop a strong and irrational (again heavy on the irony) dislike of you. A disproportionate monstering. A danger to others...

If you resist co-opting there is no resolution. And there is no resolution if you don't. Superficiality of 'improvement' efforts continue with an ever-ready queue of co-optees while necessary structural and cultural changes remain untouched. From the outside we don't have the distraction of insider tinkering and remain a nuisance.

Finally, and what gets lost in all of this, is bereaved families are the only interested parties, to use coronial language, who are typically not directly connected to or part of what happened. This makes the attempted silencing and subsequent monstering all the more monstrous.

Editor's note: Sara Ryan powerfully describes the tools of 'discrediting, crushing and co-opting'. Every persistent complainant would have experienced the first two but only those with breakthrough cases, those which hit the headlines and delivered something of a successful outcome, tend to be offered co-opting. The system, which has just fought you tooth and nail, now asks you to speak to their board or invites you to deliver your insight at a conference or training scheme. Sara Ryan was right to step away from co-opting as although on the surface it appears to be grounded in morality those in authority use such 'trophy' campaigners as symbols of false hope for those still struggling to be heard. They are 'evidence' that the complaint system works, as long as you are resilient, articulate and tenacious. That your truth, once it is accepted, will be embraced by a system which is designed to learn. But as Dr Ryan points out, no matter how many times you tell your story the necessary structural and cultural changes remain untouched and someone else, somewhere else starts on the same journey as you, alone, naïve and trusting.

Other notable NHS complainants are **Julie Bailey** who along with **Cure the NHS** revealed the scandal at **Mid-Staffs**, and **James Titcombe** who raised concerns about maternity care at **Morecambe Bay** following the avoidable death of his son **Joshua** at just nine days old. Through great tenacity and despite concerted personal attacks (Julie Bailey was forced to give up her business and move away from the area) both achieved public inquiries into the events which had led to their complaints. A public inquiry is as good as it gets and in theory, once the report is released (many years after the event) a series of recommendations are made to ensure that 'lessons are learnt'. Julie Bailey still attends the occasional NHS conference and stands at the podium calling for the introduction of safe staffing levels and accountability for NHS managers seven years after these recommendations were made in the **Francis Report**.

Mainstream media moves on, so to the public eye it would appear that things have been put right and confidence has been restored. **Twitter** is the place for real-time updates and this recent post from **Shaun Lintern,** health correspondent for the Independent**,** confirms that the **Kirkup Report**, released after the inquiry into Morecambe Bay maternity care, has been largely ignored a full five years after its release.

Shaun Lintern
@ShaunLintern

Today mark's the 5th anniversary since the Morecambe Bay report was published. @JamesTitcombe rightly concerned that the vast majority of Bill Kirkup's national recommendations have not been implemented:

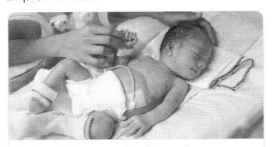

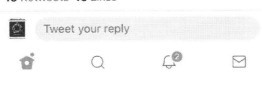

Opinion: The way maternity services are going, another Morecambe Bay...
independent.co.uk

14:09 · 03/03/2020 · Twitter Web App

19 Retweets **15** Likes

Tweet your reply

Will Powell is the most persistent of all complainants. A thirty-year (and counting) battle for justice after the avoidable death of his son **Robbie Powell** aged 10. During that time, he has challenged every authority within the UK and the entire British legal system. This account of **Robbie's Story** from **Nick Davies**[100], (an old-school investigative journalist) gives a harrowing account of the way in which the narrative changes as Powell gathers evidence to prove his case. You should also note the impunity with which fraud and perjury are committed as those in authority protect the reputation of their organisations.

ONE FATHER'S FIGHT FOR THE TRUTH ABOUT HIS SON'S NEEDLESS DEATH

The Guardian, December 24 1994

When people are hit by a really devastating disaster, it often seems to happen that instead of giving in to sadness, they elect to feel angry, to become almost consumed by a furious determination to uncover all of

---

[100] /www.nickdavies.net/1994/12/24/fighting-for-the-truth-about-a-boy-s-needless-death/?catid=124

the causes of the disaster which has struck them and to punish all of those who were responsible.

Sometimes, this is merely an emotional reflex – anger being more tolerable than misery – but there are other times when this kind of rage for justice is a uniquely powerful tool for exposing scandal. Think of some of the relatives from the Lockerbie disaster or the Marchioness or the Herald of Free Enterprise, who simply will not give up their quest for the truth. Will Powell has this kind of anger.

The doctors and Government officials against whom he has aimed it, say he has simply succumbed to the emotion and lost all sight of the truth. He does not accept that. He says he has got his grip on a real scandal and he says that he would have proved his case long ago if the Government had not systematically boarded up the windows which once allowed the public to look in and see how their health system was being managed. He says he will never give up, not while he has the police and the Government investigating his claims of corruption, not while the anger lasts.

Will Powell's journey to disaster began in the weeks before Christmas, [1990] exactly five years ago, when his youngest son, Robbie, who was then ten, fell ill at their home in Ystradgynlais in South Wales. He was throwing up and complaining of stomach pain and he looked so bad that his mother, Diane, phoned the health centre, and Dr Elwyn Hughes came out and called an ambulance to take him to Morriston Hospital 12 miles down the road on the outskirts of Swansea.

Now, Powell was very close to his boy. He loved his two older sons just as much, but Robbie had always clung to his side, full of infant pride about his dad. He was always asking people: "Do you know my dad? Willy Jock they call him. Do you know him?" Powell had thrown in his work as a motor mechanic to become a plasterer, and it was always Robbie who hung around and watched him work. Powell was a keen fly-fisherman in those days – he was in the Welsh national team – and he would come back from a fishing trip and throw himself down on his bed and again it was Robbie who would come and lie down beside him to hear all about how he had got on.

So when Powell saw him lying there in the hospital bed, all groggy with his eyes sunk in his head and his arm wired up to a drip, he simply cried with fear of losing him. And then, four days, later when the doctors said Robbie could go home, it was just a bout of gastroenteritis, probably brought on by a throat infection, Will Powell was a happy man. They had a good Christmas together. And three weeks later, on January 18, Diane took him back to the hospital for a check-up, and the paediatrician said Robbie looked so much better that he hardly recognised him. He agreed that it had probably just been a nasty bout of gastroenteritis.

It was April 1 when Robbie became ill again. He said his jaw hurt and his throat was sore. The next two and a half weeks were a blur of doctors: seven different sessions with five different GPs at the health centre in Ystradgynlais; Robbie repeatedly saying he was weak and unwell, being sent home from school, chucking up his supper, lying limp on the sofa in the front room; the GPs offering different solutions, different suggestions; one saying he would get him back into hospital; another saying he would start him on anti-biotics; another saying he would test his blood sugar except that his kit was out of date; all of them offering reassurance. Then, on April 17, at about 3pm, Robbie collapsed upstairs in the bathroom at home.

His mother, Diane, screamed and ran to cradle his head. Powell sprinted downstairs and called the health centre. The last doctor who had seen Robbie, just the day before, had said Robbie should go straight to hospital if he vomited or deteriorated but 30 minutes later, it was a different GP who arrived, Nicola Flower, and she suggested that he had a throat infection which had gone to his chest. She thought he had probably fainted because he was weak from spending two days in bed.

Powell was now deeply worried. He called the hospital and spoke to one of the nurses on the ward where Robbie had been treated in December, but she said they must trust their GP. By 5.30, Robbie was complaining of stomach pains again and, once more, Powell called the health centre. Dr Nicola Flower arrived again and after a passionate argument from Powell, she agreed that Robbie should go to hospital if only to put Powell's mind at rest. He wanted an ambulance, but Dr Flower believed it was not necessary. Powell and Diane drove their aging Talbot Sunbeam to Morriston Hospital as fast as they could, trying to keep Robbie awake while he sprawled along the back seat with his thumb in his mouth.

It was just before seven when Powell walked through the doors of the hospital, with Robbie lying limp across his arms. His eyes were dilated, rolled up into the back of his head, his lips were blue. When the hospital staff saw him, their alarm was so obvious that Diane collapsed and had to be taken out. Powell tried to tell them that the GPs said there was nothing seriously wrong but, as he watched, he saw Robbie had stopped breathing. He was told to leave the room but he could still hear the crashing and banging of the resus team at work. A doctor came and asked questions. A nurse came and told him Robbie was really very ill. Powell saw some tears in her eyes. It was several hours before a young doctor came and told them that he was sorry but their boy had died.

They went in to see their young son where he was lying still on the bed in the Intensive Care Unit and they held him in their arms and told him how much they loved him and how much they would miss him always. Powell was crying desperately but even then, at the height of his grief, there were questions he had to ask. Couldn't any of these doctors have done more? Why had it taken so long to get him referred to hospital? Did Robbie have to die?

It was three days later, on April 20, when Powell first felt the flame of rage inside him. One of the GPs from the health centre, Keith Hughes, came round to see him to tell him about the post-mortem. He explained that Robbie had been killed by a rare condition called Addison's Disease, which meant basically that his adrenal glands had ceased to function and had stopped pumping vital hormones around his body. Powell hardly understood a word of it.

"All I want to know is – did my Robbie have to die?"

"No," said the doctor.

Powell felt sick with sorrow. He saw the doctor had Robbie's medical notes with him, so he asked if he could have a look, and as he slowly turned the pages, he saw several things which started to make him feel curious. One of them, dated back in December, mentioned Robbie needing a test, an ACTH test.

"What's this then?"

"It's from the hospital," the doctor said. He explained that it was a test for hormones, though the detail passed Powell by.

He had never heard of this ACTH test. No such test had ever been done in December or any other time. It had never even been mentioned. Yet the notes seemed to say that Robbie's parents had been told about this. Then he saw something else, a reference to hormonal imbalance, and to two words he had never heard before this day.

"What's this about Addison's Disease?"

"The hospital should have told you. They suspected Addison's."

"What!" Powell shouted, so loud that Diane in the kitchen was frightened. "They suspected my boy had this fucking Addison's Disease? And they didn't do anything?" That was when the anger came.

Will Powell was about to be transformed. This was a man who had left school a few days before his 15th birthday, who had never passed an exam in his life and who had never even written a letter for 20 years. But he liked to say that though he might not be educated, he was not daft either. He had a tough streak, something to do with growing up in a rough patch of Glasgow before his parents moved to Wales and having to start a milk round when he was only 12 to buy himself clothes, and he had spent long enough as a motor mechanic to have learned to be methodical.

Later that evening, when the doctor had gone, he started to think. It was the beginning of a process which would see the man who did not write letters become a prolific source of letters and briefing papers and legal arguments, all of them clear and concise, all of them tapped out on the keyboard of a cheap computer which he bought for his fight; and which would see the man who had never passed an exam educate himself in all the complexities of the hormonal feedback system that linked the adrenal glands to the pituitary gland and the hypothalmus. To him, it seemed simple. It was just like the inside of an engine: switches came on, switches came off, the fuel went round. His whole life was about to become one long quest for answers.

On that first evening, as he absorbed the implications of the doctor's visit, it occurred to him that if he had been working on a man's car and he had failed to report some kind of deadly fault and then there'd been an accident, well, he might feel a bit nervous about the truth coming out. He had no reason to think that the doctors were dishonest but, just in case anyone got any funny ideas, he decided to make sure of his facts. So he asked Dr Keith Hughes to come back and see him again and, this time, he arranged for a local vicar to be there with him.

So it was that three days later, on April 23, Rev DG Thomas, heard Dr Hughes confirm that Robbie need never have died and, when the vicar took Robbie's medical file, he heard the doctor say: "I don't know if this is a wise thing I am doing. Have to be careful what I say." And, with the file on his knee, Rev Thomas wrote : "Clinical Summary Sheet dated December 1989. Detailed long letter on back page. Headed 'Information: Needs ACTH Test. Parents Informed.' Mentions hormone imbalance – possibility Addisons." He also noted a second letter, the size of a half page, dated January 18, when Robbie had returned to the hospital for his check-up, in which the paediatrician had asked to see the boy again if there was any recurrence of his symptoms.

Now the questions were bigger. If the hospital had suspected this deadly illness, why hadn't they done the ACTH test that would have confirmed its presence? Why hadn't the doctors said anything about the test being needed? And if the hospital had passed all this information to the GPs, why hadn't they sent Robbie straight back to hospital when he became ill again?

Powell recalled that in one of their seven meetings with GPs during April, one doctor – Mike Williams was his name – had told them he was definitely going to send Robbie back to hospital. That had been on April 11, six clear days before Robbie died. So what had happened? Powell contacted Mike Williams who confirmed he had sent off the referral letter. So Powell went to the hospital, where the paediatrician who had dealt with Robbie, Dr Forbes, was equally clear that he had never received any such letter from Mike Williams. Powell was not sure what to make of it.

However, he did find the answer to one mystery. Dr Forbes explained that although he had suspected Addison's Disease back in December, his colleague at the hospital had disagreed with him and thought that Robbie was suffering from nothing more than gastroenteritis. It so happened that Dr Forbes had been away on the day that Diane asked for a diagnosis, and so it was that no one had ever told them that their son might be suffering from a life-threatening condition nor that his paediatrician wanted to check by giving him an ACTH test. And, somehow, this danger had passed the GPs by.

By now, Powell had decided to file an official complaint with the Family Health Service Authority, FHSA. Some months passed before, at the end of July, the various GPs at the health centre replied to his complaint in formal statements. One point leapt from the pages: four of the five GPs who had dealt with Robbie in April said that for one reason or another they had never read his medical notes, so they had never seen any of the warning signals which had been transmitted by the hospital. Powell could hardly believe it. And the one GP who had read the notes – Mike Williams – said he had not been too concerned. He reckoned that the child had shown no signs of Addison's, such as vomiting, and so he had referred him to hospital without any special urgency.

The more he read the GPs' statements, the more puzzled Powell became. Their recollection of events kept clashing with his. For example, he and Diane had a clear memory of Robbie chucking up his food and of himself and Diane taking Robbie to Mike Williams the next day and telling him. Yet Mike Williams not only denied there had been any report of vomiting but also made no mention of the drug which Powell believed he had prescribed to deal with it. Powell even remembered its name: Dioralyte it was called.

Powell recalled that one GP, Paul Boladz, had told him Robbie might have glandular fever while the others had given him no diagnosis at all. But, in their statements, two of the GPs said they had diagnosed a virus and Mike Williams added that Mr and Mrs Powell had told him this. Powell remembered no such thing, nor did he remember being advised to give his boy Calpol and paracetomol to deal with this virus, as the GPs now recalled.

Will Powell decided to do a little digging. He started by trying to prove that Mike Williams, contrary to his recollection, had prescribed Dioralyte for Robbie. He searched the house for the packet, but they had thrown it out. He went to the chemist who had supplied it but he said he had wiped his records when Robbie died. He contacted the Prescription Pricing Authority in Cardiff, but they refused to speak to him because he was not a doctor. Finally, he contacted the FHSA and, disguising his real interest, he asked them for all of the records of all the precriptions which had been supplied to Robbie. And he got them – and there was the Dioralyte, just as he remembered. So Dr Mike Williams' statement was wrong.

He did a little more checking. He confirmed that Dioralyte was often used to stop vomiting. And if the GP had known Robbie was vomiting, Powell reasoned, then surely he should have seen the danger of Addison's and referred him back to hospital urgently. Tying down his facts, Powell now made a series of phone calls to the hospital paediatrician, Dr Forbes, and finally persuaded him to confirm in writing that he had received no referral letter from Dr Williams before Robbie's death.

However, just as he thought he was beginning to win, Powell discovered he had lost his biggest weapon. For seven months, he had been waiting to receive copies of Robbie's medical files so that he could refer to the letters from the hospital which had first sparked his anger. According to the rules, the GPs were supposed to hand over their records within a month. When they finally reached Powell, on November 22, he had a shock. The crucial letter for which he had been waiting – the one which said that the hospital had suspected Addison's Disease – was not there. He was dumb with confusion.

He felt sure that it had been typed on the back of the Clinical Summary Sheet which had been produced when Robbie was discharged from hospital in December. The vicar was equally sure – he had written it down in his notes. Yet, here was the Clinical Summary Sheet, with its back completely blank. And there was something else. Powell and the vicar both recalled seeing a half-page letter from the paediatrician, Dr Forbes, dated January 18, when Robbie had gone to hospital for a check-up. The file did contain a letter with that date, but it was on a full page and, instead of giving the GPs a clear warning to send Robbie back to hospital if he showed any signs of hormone deficiency, as Powell recalled, it contained a weak warning about hormones and added that he was suffering from gastroenteritis.

Even odder, in Powell's eyes, there was an envelope in the file, addressed to the Appointments Officer at Morriston Hospital. Its top was torn open and, inside, there was a referral letter, asking the hospital to look at Robbie Powell. It was signed by Mike Williams and dated April 12, the day after he had seen Robbie.

Alongside it in the file was another, loose copy of the same letter. Powell could now see how the GPs might say that Mike Williams had written his referral letter on April 12, put a copy in the file, and put the top version in an envelope addressed to the hospital, which had then been lost in the surgery until it was found and torn open and placed in the file. But, if that was true, the copy of the letter would have been in the file when he saw it at his home on April 20, three days after Robbie's death, and, again, when he saw it with the vicar. And Will Powell was sure that it had not been there...

Powell went to the health centre, saw Dr Keith Hughes, who had brought the file to him and who had shown it to him again in front of the vicar. With some passion, Powell told him he wanted him to confirm in writing that that letter had not been in the file on either of those visits to his home. Dr Hughes complied. Powell reckoned he now had made a very visible hole in the doctors' version of events. Two weeks later, the hole became even bigger when the GPs produced a new statement, made by one of the secretaries at the health centre.

She explained that she had typed the referral letter for Mike Williams – not on April 12, as it was dated, but on April 19, two days after Robbie's death. She had been away, she said, and so the typing had been delayed , and when she had finally got round to it, Mike Williams had instructed her to back-date the letter 'for the record'. Powell was staggered by the shifting story.

And, for him, it still did not explain why the copy of this letter had not been in the file when Dr Hughes visited him on April 20 and 23, nor why Mike Williams and all of the other GPs had submitted formal statements in July in which they all said that Robbie had been referred back to hospital and in which none of them mentioned that the referral had been delayed until the boy had been dead for 48 hours. And if no-one typed the letter until 48 hours after his death, what on earth was the point of putting it in an envelope and addressing it to the hospital? And why on earth would they then tear it open and put it back in the file with their copy?

Powell could not help thinking that if he had not pursued this, he would simply have accepted the GPs' bland statements that his son had been referred to hospital. Convinced that the doctors had tried to mislead him, Powell now tried to make sense of the other medical notes he had been sent. What had happened to "the Addison's letter"? If he and the vicar had not simply imagined its existence, the only possibility he could think of was that somebody had disposed of it. The more he studied the notes, the more convinced he became that someone somewhere had tampered with them.

The Clinical Summary Sheet, on whose reverse he believed the Addison's Letter had been typed, had no doctor's signature on it and no typist's initials. When he compared it to the hand-written original, it contained half a dozen errors of detail. He trawled through his family's medical records and found no other Clinical Summary Sheet without a doctor's signature, a typist's initials nor any that varied from its hand-written original. He speculated that the original summary sheet had been destroyed along with the Addison's letter on its back and that the surviving document was a forgery. In their present form, the notes contained no reference at all to Addison's Disease. If they were genuine, he reasoned, there was no way that the vicar could have written

"Addison's suspected" when he copied their details into his notebook.

There were other possible signs of tampering. Next to the one surviving reference in the notes to Robbie needing an ACTH test, someone seemed to have added a question mark. Someone had added the word "gastroenteritis" to a hospital document recording Robbie's illness when he was in hospital in December. He could not say that any doctors had done any tampering, but he felt pretty sure that at some level in the Welsh medical establishment, someone had decided to intervene to weaken the evidence that his son had been suffering from Addison's in December 1989.

It was December 1990 by now. The hearing into his official complaint was due to start. Powell believed he could prove that four of the GPs had failed to read his son's medical history; that Mike Williams had prescribed a drug which was commonly used to stop vomiting even though he had failed to mention this in his statement; and that all five GPs had stated formally that his son had been referred to hospital and that none of them had mentioned that he was already dead when this was done.

But against him, the records appeared to show that even if the GPs had read Robbie's medical files, instead of seeing the clear hospital warning of Addison's which Powell believed he had read, they would have seen instead that this boy had had a simple history of gastroenteritis with only the weakest hint of the possibility of hormonal problems. The notes also appeared to confirm that, contrary to Powell's understanding, the GPs had diagnosed a virus in April, advised the Powells to give him Calpol and paracetomol, that Robbie had not vomited or shown any other sign of Addison's Disease, and that Mike Williams had done his best to refer him to hospital.

For Powell, the hearing was a disaster. He felt ill-at-ease from the outset, making his complaint to the very same hierarchy which was responsible for hiring the doctors and which stood to lose face if his complaint was upheld. He felt out of his depth, a layman pitted against medical experts. The GPs had a union to pay for their lawyers; the only advice he had was from his friend, Sid Herbert, who ran an ice cream parlour and who had agreed to come with him to lend him support. Throughout the hearing, he found himself at odds with the chairman, unable to make the points which he considered vital. When the FHSA duly published their report, they entirely exonerated four of the GPs and found that Dr Flower alone had failed to react effectively on her first visit to Robbie on the day that he died. They admonished her, the mildest possible punishment.

But Will Powell was still angry. He took out a mortage on his house, hired lawyers, filed an appeal, won a new hearing in front of the Welsh Office, whose start was repeatedly delayed until March 1992, when it opened and was then adjourned after three days without hearing all the evidence. When it re-opened in September 1992, Powell was fired up and ready to win. Then something odd happened.

Powell's barrister was trying to explain that one suspicious feature of the document which was supposed to have had "the Addison's letter" on its back was that it carried no block stamp to mark its arrival at the health centre. This was consistent with its having been forged at a later date. The barrister had already explained all this at the hearing in March. Now, when he rose to repeat the point, he suddenly discovered that the document, which he had handled repeatedly in the past, had precisely the kind of block stamp which he was describing, firmly stamped on its back. There was uproar.

The documents for the hearing had been in the care of the Welsh Office but when an official was called to the stand, he said that he had had only half of them. He did not know where the others had been. Each side accused the other of tampering with them. Powell and his barrister wanted the police called in. The chairman of the hearing refused. Powell and his lawyers then retired to a local hotel and decided that they no longer had any confidence in the hearing and refused to take any further part in it. It cost Will Powell some £35,000 in legal fees. He had to mortgage his house to pay.

At that point, so far as the system was concerned, the fight was over, but Will Powell refused to accept defeat. He lodged a complaint with the Welsh Health Service Ombudsman about the GPs, but the Ombudsman said that was outside his remit. So he made a complaint about the FHSA hearing, but the Ombudsman said that, too, was outside his remit. Undeterred, Powell complained about the Welsh Office hearing, but the Ombudsman said he could not investigate the Welsh Office unless he was asked to do so by an MP. So, Powell contacted his MP, but the Ombudsman said he could not investigate a complaint from an MP about the Welsh Office if it dealt with personnel who were responsible to a Minister – such as doctors.

Drawing deeper on funds he did not have, Powell decided to sue the FHSA for negligence and, in the meantime, he continued to write to the Ombudsman who now said he could not investigate any complaint which might be the subject of legal action. Powell still did not give up, but the Ombudsman then explained that he could not investigate a complaint which was so old and, in any event, even if he did have the power to investigate, he still had the discretion to decide not to.

This year, Powell went to Dyfed Powys police and provided them with 20 pages of tightly-argued summary. He explained his case to two MPs, Jonathan Evans and Rhodri Morgan, and this summer, the Welsh Office agreed to set up a formal inquiry. Last month the police sent a report on the case to the Crown Prosecution Service, and the doctors announced that they would not give evidence to the Welsh Office's new inquiry.

The GPs have refused to discuss Will Powell's claims, but their lawyer issued a statement on their behalf, declaring that they would answer him in court in the action for negligence. "All Mr Powell's allegations, both relating to Robert's treatment and to the records, are absolutely denied by my clients and the reasons for that denial will become fully apparent from their evidence to the court in due course."

Will Powell is still running on anger. But he has never worked since Robbie's death, he no longer cares to go fly-fishing, he has trouble sleeping and sometimes during the day, he just shuts himself in his bedroom and thinks his way back to that hateful day when Robbie went away from him and then, for all his anger, a horrible sadness still creeps over him.

Editor's note: Will Powell is currently calling for a public inquiry into the handling of his complaint and **Rob Behrens**, the Ombudsman has agreed that this historic review should go ahead. However, the final decision rests with the **Department of Health and Social Care**, who no doubt realise that any inquiry would lift the lid on the entire establishment.

One of the main difficulties Will Powell experienced in holding the doctors to account was the fact that there was no **'duty of candour'** to ensure that doctors were legally required to tell the truth about harmful incidents. This from a blog written by Will Powell for **AvMA** (Action against Medical Accidents) in April 2016 continues the story.[101]

> In 1990 our son Robbie died as a consequence of medical negligence. However, rather than provide the truth about Robbie's death, the doctors involved made a conscious decision to falsify his medical records, allowing them to evade criminal and professional accountability as well as civil liability.
>
> I complained under the then NHS complaint procedures but to date that complaint has not been concluded because of allegations of a conspiracy between Welsh Office officials, the so-called independent tribunal members and the doctors under investigation.
>
> I had no other option but to turn to the civil courts to seek truth and justice. However, the High Court in Cardiff found that there was no legal obligation for

---

[101] www.avma.org.uk/policy-campaigns/the-avma-blog/will-powell-blog/

doctors to tell the truth about the circumstances of Robbie's death, a ruling upheld by the Court of Appeal and the House of Lords.

Robbie's case was then submitted to the European Court of Human Rights but was found inadmissible. However, the Court set out the law as it stood then and stated:

"Whilst it is arguable that doctors had a duty not to falsify medical records under the common law (Sir Donaldson MR's "duty of candour"), before Powell v Boladz there was no binding decision of the courts as to the existence of such a duty. As the law stands now ... doctors have no duty to give parents of a child who died as a result of their negligence a truthful account of the circumstances of the death, nor even to refrain from deliberately falsifying records."

Editor's note: Through heroic tenacity Will Powell forced through a legal 'duty of candour' regulation but in doing so a loophole was created which once again allowed healthcare professionals to deny the truth.

@MedicineGovSte #NHS #MedLearn #TeamPatient 🍃 ... · Feb 26 ⌄
Did you know that the current #dutyofcandour applies to organisations
not individuals?
It was only thanks to the amazing work of #patientsafety expert
@willcpowell that this came to light.

Public sector complaints are taken over by state sponsored legal teams who have no duty of candour and the 'organisation' is only required to reveal the truth if the individual healthcare worker has revealed it to them.

There are two more flies in this particular ointment. Healthcare workers who reveal the truth become accidental 'whistleblowers' suffering the full wrath of the management as a consequence. And, the statutory duty of candour is policed by the **Care Quality Commission (CQC),** an organisation which also has a role in protecting whistleblowers. The effectiveness of any statutory or non-statutory requirement is dependent upon the strength of the regulator who monitors and upholds breaches. Sadly, CQC, much like PHSO have a poor record and lean more towards appeasing government than appeasing the public.

Before publication I contacted Will Powell for his approval and he provided me with the following update:

1. It is difficult to believe that the Guardian article was published more than a quarter of a century ago and that the serious issues that it raised are still not resolved and ongoing.

547

GMC (General Medical Council)

2. The above Guardian article was provided to the General Medical Council [GMC] in January 1995 by the Chief Officer of the Community Health Council [CHC]. Although the GMC took no action regarding the content of the article the Chief Officer of the CHC was informed that there was no time limit. I was also informed by the GMC, in writing, on more than one occasion that there was no time limit. In October 2001 the GMC informed me that they would await the outcome of the independent criminal investigation before considering what action they should take against the doctors. I was also informed that if the situation changed, for any reason, the GMC would write and let me know [GMC letter dated 30th October 2001].

In November 2002 the GMC covertly introduced a 5-year time limit. In March 2003 the Crown Prosecution Service [CPS] made a decision on the 35 criminal charges set out following the independent criminal investigation [Gross Negligence Manslaughter, forgery, attempting to pervert justice and conspiracy to pervert justice]. The charges were set out against 5 GPs and their secretary. It is interesting to note that Dyfed Powys Police, who retained the GPs as police surgeons, claimed after two criminal investigations between 1994 and 2000 that there was no evidence of any crimes.

In 2003 the CPS accepted there was sufficient evidence to prosecute two GPs and the secretary for forgery and perverting the course of justice. However, the CPS refused to prosecute because of the passage of time and the fact that Dyfed Powys Police had given the GPs a letter of immunity when the gift of immunity is with the Director of Public prosecutions and/or the Attorney General. Also, the passage of time was caused as a

548

consequence of the decade of cover ups by the NHS, Welsh Office, police and CPS to mention just a few.

No referral was made to the GMC by the police and/or CPS following a meeting to do so on the 10th March 2003. It was later claimed by the police that the GMC influenced them not to make the referral. I formally complained to the GMC in July 2003. They sat on the complaint for 5 years and then rejected the same by engaging the 5-year time limit, which is something they could not have done had the police and/or CPS made the formal referral. The Senior Investigation Officer [SIO] of the independent police investigation had formally put the GMC on notice of a police referral two years before the introduction of the 5-year time limit. Please note the SIO was excluded from the meeting with the GMC.

During the subsequent Judicial Review (JR) the GMC falsely claimed to the Court that it could not investigate a doctor without first receiving a formal complaint and, in any event, the December 1994 Guardian article above, was too sparse [GMC letter dated 15th August 2012 to First Minister]. A FOI request subsequently confirmed that 575 complaints against doctors were considered by the GMC between 1993 and 2009 [time of JR] as a consequence of newspaper articles alone - 428 were investigated.

In August 2012 the GMC, in response to a letter from the then First Minister, accepted that I should have been informed of the introduction of the 5-year time limit and apologised for the oversight [GMC letter dated 15th August 2012].

AvMA were so outraged by the GMC's 2008 decision that they Judicially Reviewed [JR] the GMC in 2009 as a matter of public interest. At the permission hearing the judge reluctantly granted permission for the JR. However, the same judge, who informed me that anything I said would make no difference to his decision, before I gave evidence under oath, refused AvMA's application for a Protective Cost Order. As a consequence of AvMA's risk of £100,000 in legal costs, had the JR been unsuccessful, they discontinued the proceedings. I raised my serious concerns about the GMC with its regulator, Council for Healthcare Regulatory Excellence and subsequently with the Professional Standards Authority. However, my concerns, set out in 13 questions were not answered by the then Chief Executive, Mr Harry Cayton.

PHSO (Parliamentary and Health Service Ombudsman)

3. Although the current PHSO and Welsh Public Services Ombudsman are currently calling for a public inquiry into Robbie's case their predecessors let Robbie and my family down after being first contacted back in 1991. In 2004 I received a personal and written apology from former PHSO, Ms Ann Abraham. The apology was with regards to the way in which I was treated by the PHSO's office and for unjustified and derogatory comments made about me by the PHSO's staff [Ms Abraham's letter dated 26th October 2004 - extract below]

> *What I can, however, say (in response to the ninth point in your list), is that the comments made about you personally in the files by some of the Ombudsman's officers were highly judgmental, inappropriate and entirely unacceptable. I can only offer you my most sincere apologies for that. In my view they demonstrated a deplorable lack of sensitivity and understanding by those concerned, all the more so given the very difficult and painful circumstances which had led to your complaints.*

You asked in your final point what action could be taken to ensure that other complainants would not be treated in a similar fashion in the future. As I have already indicated above, I will be talking to Adam Peat about your case and the lessons to be learned from your experience of our respective Offices. I can, however, assure you that, having identified the failings demonstrated in our handling of your case, we are using those lessons to inform the changes in our practices that we are currently developing. Those new working practices will, I hope, ensure that we can guarantee that no future complainant should have cause to feel aggrieved that we have failed to involve them fully from the start in our consideration of their complaint, that we have not done everything within our powers to help them resolve matters, or that we have failed to treat them with appropriate respect.

Whilst I appreciate that that does not in any way mitigate our poor handling of your complaints, I hope that you can take some comfort from the fact that your efforts to change things will have had a significant impact on the way this Office treats complainants in the future.

Editor's note: the next extract is from a letter written by Will Powell in March 2002 which details the way in which this man was vilified by the Ombudsman for asking questions about his son.

In the light of the many derogatory comments that you and/or your officers have made about me over the years [e.g. that I do not tell the truth, withhold information, vindictive, an alley cat, caveman, bully, aggressive and loud] it is highly unlikely that I will ever contact you or your office again even if I have grounds to do so. However, you may be hearing from my solicitor in due course.

The thing that deeply concerns me about you and your office is that you are prepared to assassinate my character and criticise me in my approach rather than attempt to put right the obvious injustices that I have endured as a consequence of my son's medically negligent death and the subsequent cover up. My wife and I are proud of what we have achieved in Robbie's memory over the past twelve years but my greatest concern is for the other parents who suffer similar injustices but who do not have the ability, strength, determination and tenacity to challenge a system that purports to be there to serve the public but is really there to exploit the uneducated and the most vulnerable which in turn protects doctors.

I would appreciate any comments you may wish to make. Please acknowledge receipt.

Yours faithfully,

Mr William Cassie Powell

Editor's note: Way back then the Ombudsman was 'learning lessons' yet somehow nothing ever improved. It can be seen that all roads lead back to government. Successive governments, complicit in administering policies which are harmful to the public, then putting every obstacle between themselves and public accountability; allowing the harm to continue. When the heat builds the government 'do something' to distract attention, such as holding an inquiry when they have no intention of implementing the findings or creating a new arm's length body to prevent further scandal. Essentially, there is no intention on the part of government to listen, learn or improve.

The Final Word.

This book is a testament to the truth. We are users of the complaints system and victims of the Ombudsman. It is a record of our collective, lived experience. We have been there, fighting the system, kicking back against the lies and manipulations and we have the evidence to prove it.

We have focused here on the Ombudsman. Just one of the tools used by the state against its citizens. You could tell the same story about any of the others. We have tested the democratic processes available to hold this body to account and all of them have failed. This is essentially a story about power. It is neither of the left nor of the right, and it is not unique to the UK. We are governed by consent, but do we know what we are consenting to?

"When the truth offends, we lie and lie, until we can no longer remember it is ever there. But it is still there. Every lie we tell incurs a debt to the truth. Sooner or later, that debt is paid." **Valery Legasov, Chernobyl**

Please help us to spread the word. Share this book, recommend it to friends, copy it, paste it, use it freely with no fear of copyright breaches. We want people to know and to understand. You will find more blogs on the phsothetruestory.com website as our campaign continues. Thank you for reading. If you have a story to tell then contact us at **phso-thefacts@outlook.com**

I would like to thank all the members of the **PHSOtheFACTS** who came together and stayed together giving hope that eventually the truth would be known. We have provided support for each other and insight into the workings of this state machinery. We are not the ones who are delusional. We are the ones who can see clearly, and hopefully you can see more clearly now.

Special thanks go to **Peggy Banks** for her detailed editing and compilation of the main glossary. Also, to **David Czarnetzki** for editing and compiling of the People glossary and finally to **Ron Chi** for assistance with the graphics.

Illustrations - **Simon Ellinas**.
Cover illustration - **Dissidentdaubs**

Thanks to all those who submitted their case stories. I appreciate that it is painful to re-live your trauma, so I thank you for sharing your personal story for the greater good. Thanks also, to other contributors such as **Will Powell,**

Dr Sara Ryan and **Eileen Chubb**. All greatly admired fighters for the truth. And finally, a word of praise for all those unsung heroes, who continue each day to struggle against the system hoping for a breakthrough.

Della Reynolds
PHSOtheFACTS

Glossary of people:

This glossary indicates some of the key individuals who have had the opportunity and influence to bring about the necessary improvement in complaint handling and patient safety since the publication of the Patients Association 2015 report 'PHSO-Labyrinth of Bureaucracy'.

Prime Ministers

David Cameron	2015-2016
Theresa May	2016-2019
Boris Johnson	2019-

Secretary of State for Health

Jeremy Hunt	2015-2018
Matthew Hancock	2018-

Members of the Public Administration and Constitutional Affairs Committee (PACAC) (From 2015-2019)

Sir Bernard Jenkin (Chair)	2015-2019
Sarah Champion	2018-2018
Oliver Dowden	2015-2016
Paul Flynn	2015-2019
Marcus Fysh	2015-2019
Dame Cheryl Gillan	2015-2019
Kate Hoey	2015-2017

Adam Holloway	2016-2016
Kelvin Hopkins	2015-2019
Dr. Rupa Huq	2017-2019
Gerald Jones	2015-2017
Sandy Martin	2017-2019
David Morris	2017-2019
Dr. Dan Poulter	2016-2017
Tulip Siddiq	2018-2019
Eleanor Smith	2019-2019
Tom Tugendhat	2015-2016
Andrew Turner	2015-2017

Members of the Public Administration and Constitutional Affairs Committee (PACAC) commencing December 2019

William Wragg (Chair)

Ronnie Cowan

Jackie Doyle-Price

Chris Evans

Rachel Hopkins

David Jones

David Mundell

Lloyd Russell-Moyle

Tom Randall

Karin Smith

John Stevenson

Members of the Health and Social Care Committee (HSCC) (From 2015-2019)

Dr. Sarah Wollaston (Chair)	2015-2019
Heidi Alexander	2016-2017
Luciana Berger	2016-2019
Ben Bradshaw	2015-2019
Dr. Lisa Cameron	2017-2019
Jackie Cooper	2015-2016
Angela Crawley	2019-2019
Andrea Jenkyns	2015-2017
Dr. Caroline Johnson	2017-2018
Rachel Maskell	2015-2015
Liz McInnes	2015-2015
Johnny Mercer	2017-2019
Anne Marie Morris	2019-2019
Emma Reynolds	2015-2016
Andrew Selous	2016-2019
Paula Sherriff	2015-2016
Derek Thomas	2018-2019
Emily Thornberry	2015-2015
Maggie Throup	2015-2018
Martin Vickers	2018-2019
Helen Whately	2015-2017
Dr. Philippa Whitford	2015-17/19
Dr. Paul Williams	2017-2019

Members of the Health and Social Care Committee (HSCC) for the parliamentary session commencing December 2019

Jeremy Hunt (Chair)

Paul Bristow

Amy Callaghan

Rosie Cooper

Dr James Davies

Dr Luke Evans

James Murray

Taiwo Owatemi

Sarah Owen

Dean Russell

Laura Trott

Parliamentary and Health Service Ombudsman (PHSO)

Dame Julie Mellor	2012-2016
Rob Behrens	2017-
Amanda Amroliwala (nee Campbell)	2016 -

GLOSSARY

A

Academics – person who holds an advanced degree often working as a researcher or lecturer.

ACTH test, Adrenocorticotropic hormone – a test to assess the adrenocorticotropic hormone is functioning correctly, which is produced in the pituitary gland which stimulates cortisol by the adrenal glands

Action Fraud – deals with scams, and is the responsibility of the City of London Police.

Addison's Disease – caused by the malfunction the adrenocorticotropic hormone which stimulates cortisol.

Administrative Justice – academic approach to how individuals act when things are not working well which includes health care, education, social security and education.

Administrative Justice Council – set up following the abolition of Administrative Justice and consists of leading academics who research to provide recommendations for making decisions.

Assembly of the Police and Crime Committee – examines the work of the Mayor's Office for Policing and Crime (MOPAC) who in turn oversee the Metropolitan Police.

Alternative legal remedy – legal action that can be taken instead of an ombudsman investigation.

Alex Allan Report – an independent review commissioned by the PHSO with regard to the procedures and their accuracy prior to the appointment of Mick Martin as Deputy Ombudsman.

Annual Complaint Feedback Report – issued by the PHSO.

APPG – All Party Parliamentary Group – informal cross-party groups formed with MPs and Members of the House of Lords sharing common interests.

AQA, Assessment and Qualifications Alliance - a registered charity, independent of the Government, an awarding body for GCSC, A level and AS Level.

Asperger Syndrome – A form of autism but sufferers have good language skills.

Attorney General in England – offers legal advice to the government.

Autism – a disorder whose main attributes are lack of social interaction and repetitive behaviour.

AvMA – Action against Medical Accidents, a registered charity offering advice following avoidable medical harm.

B

#Backto60 one voice campaign – a campaigning group whose goal is to restore the state pension age back to 60 for women born in the 1950s.

Better Serve the Public (Robert Gordon) – review carried out by the Cabinet Office dealing with the Ombudsman landscape.

Black Box – used to describe a component in science, computing, or engineering for example and an Institution or government which has inputs and outputs with the internal workings being opaque.

Boilerplate – a term which refers to text that is reused for a standard paragraph, usually employed for a press release.

BREXIT – Britain existing from the UE - the process for the United Kingdom to withdraw from the European Union.

Burden of proof (*Latin – onus probandi*) the law that requires the person or persons who makes a claim or have a dispute to produce evidence in support.

Bureaucratic – complex system devised to keep control and uniformity.

Burn out – emotional, physical and mental exhaustion which leaves the sufferer with feelings of emptiness and powerlessness.

C

Cabinet Office – A Government department which supports Government objectives including the activities of the PHSO and their value for money in terms of the taxpayer.

Cash cow – exploitation of an individual for a reliable source of money.

Cerebellum – area at the base of the brain.

CGI – 'Conseillers en Gestion et Informatique' (consultants in management and information technology) - a payroll company that also handles staff payments for the PHSO.

Chambers Guide – research by Chambers and Company which regularly updates to provide the rank of top lawyers that specialise in Judicial Review and Public Law.

CHC – Community Health Councils - acted as effective, local complaint monitoring panels from 1974 to 2003. They were abolished by Tony Blair who declared 'war' on complainants.

Civil Procedure Rules 1998 – designed to make civil procedures less costly, speedier and easier to comprehend by losing previous archaic language.

Clinical Advice Review Team – established by the PHSO to review how their clinical advice was used with their casework, in particular the advice taken from independent clinical advisors.

Colcutt Report – written in relation to Ombudsman issues, instigated by PASC (Public Administration select Committee),

Commonspace – a news website, based in Scotland.

Complaints Standards Authority – power to set standards on good complaint handling across public bodies..

Complaints and Litigation Report - report released by the Health Select Committee confirming that the legislative remit of the Ombudsman was ineffective in meeting public demand.

Complaints and Raising Concerns (2014) – report issued by PASC focussing on whistle-blowers and service-users and the effect poor complaints handling has on the individual.

Complaints Standard Authority -a power that can be vested via Parliament so standards can set for all the complaint handling public bodies.

Constitutional Law – defines powers and the role of structures within a county relating to Parliament, the Judiciary and its citizens' basic rights.

Court of Appeal – the highest Court within England and Wales that reviews decisions by other Courts.

Corrupt - dishonest handling of cases by the PHSO (systemic Corruption).

CPS – Crown Prosecution Service – the principal public prosecuting service for England and Wales.

CQC – Care Quality Commission – an executive public body of the Department of Health and Social Care who inspect and regulate healthcare services.

Crichel Down Affair (1954) following the resignation of an MP, in order to persuade the British Government to adopt the Ombudsman model. This scandal culminated in the first resignation of a Minister since 1917 and was marked by a very public scrutiny of a Minister carrying out his discretionary duties. It was primarily to safeguard the rights of citizens.

Crown Servants – no positive definition but refers to those employed by the Crown, including civil servants.

CSA – Child Support Agency - now called the Child Maintenance Service, deals with maintenance payments for children, usually with regard to absent fathers.

CT Scan – computed tomography - radiation-based medical imaging which produces cross-sectional images.

Culture of Impunity – inbuilt into the PHSO meaning that it is impossible to hold the Ombudsman to account.

Cure the NHS – an organisation, founded by Julie Bailey OBE which successfully campaigned for a public Inquiry into the failings of Mid Staffs Hospital.

D

Data Protection Act 1998 – is a set eight principles to control how personal data is used with regard to personal information used by organisations including the Government.

DHSS – Department of Health and Society Security - was a Government department which ran for 20 years until 1988 and was then spilt, currently replaced mainly by the Department for Work and Pensions.

Disclosure of Information (aka The Secrecy Schedule – information held or created that should be publicly available from the organisation who holds or creates it. Secrecy is maintained if information is regarded as 'privileged'.

Discretionary powers – held by the Ombudsman ensuring legal challenge by the public is virtually impossible.

DoHSC - Department of Health and Social Care – a Government department which supports Ministers in leading the nations' health including independent living and to live longer, healthier lives. Supported by 29 government agencies and public bodies.

DOLs - Deprivation of Liberty Safeguarding – an official practice when it is considered that someone may lose their liberty for their own safety.

Duty of Candour – a legal statutory obligation for NHS staff to be open and honest with patients and their families when mistakes occur causing significant harm or the potential to do so in future.

DWT – Department of Work and Pensions.

E

ECHR - European Court of Human Rights – hears applications lodged, made by an individual or group when it is alleged that a contracting state has breached civil or political human rights set out in its convention.

End of life Pathway – an often-controversial plan instigated by medical practitioners for end of life care, usually for the elderly.

Egress Secure System – a method of sending encrypted emails to keep the data secure.

Employment Tribunal – deals with unfair dismissal from work, unfair deductions from pay and discrimination.

ESFA – Education and Skills Funding Agency - current Government body responsible for educational funding which incorporates the former Education Funding Agency (EFA) and for former Skills Funding Agency (SFA) to form one single agency.

Establishment (the) – dominant, elite group controlling a nation, the term is sometimes used in the context of an organisation.

Expert Witness Statement – an opinion from an expert in the subject matter in the form of a report.

F

FHSA – Family Health Service Authority, involved with the planning and delivery of primary care.

First-tier complaint process – the idea that a complaint can be reviewed formally or informally with the goal of learning from errors and therefore making improvements for the future.

FOI – Freedom of Information Request - which enables members of the public to ask for information from public bodies, although some information can be withheld.

FPPR – Fit and Proper Persons Requirement - an obligation that providers ensure that they employ persons fit for the role which includes mental and physical fitness and any Disclosure or barring in hand with total employment history.

Francis Report (2014) – this was written due to a call for public inquiry, following avoidable deaths because of the failings of Mid-Staffs Foundation Trust.

G

GMC – General Medical Council – register of Doctors who pay a fee for registration. It is a public body that sets standards and investigates complaints.

Gosport Hospital – infamous avoidable deaths subject to cover up. Families sacrificed years of their lives to being about justice and future safety measures for future patients.

Government targets – for the purposes of the NHS (National Health Service) targets such as waiting times for operations are set, plus a four-hour maximum wait at Accident and Emergency Departments.

Grenfell Tower – infamous for catching fire initially due to a faulty fridge/freezer, spreading rapidly throughout the building mainly due to sub-standard cladding. 71 people died as a consequence.

H

Hansard – edited outcome from debates from the House of Commons Parliamentary debates.

Healthcare Commission – took over in 2004 they were 'overwhelmed' by complaints with no follow up. This body was in turn abolished in 2009 with the bulk of the monitoring role going to CQC who have no powers to investigate individual complaints.

Health Secretary – a member of the Cabinet in Parliament serving as Head of the Department for Health and Social Care and has the overall responsibility for the National Health Service.

Health Trust Europe – offer solutions for managing financial spending with a view for improving healthcare in the community.

Healthwatch – a network covering England set up in 2013 to examine how the NHS seek improvements based on feedback from the public to later share with those I power to make suitable changes.

Hemangioblastoma – benign vascular tumour.

Herald of Free Enterprise – was an eight-deck ferry that sank minutes after departing Belgium killing 193 passengers.

High Court – deals with civil cases and appeals against decisions.

HMCTS – Her Majesty's Court and Tribunals Service – created on 1 April 2011 merging Her Majesty's Courts Service and Tribunals Service.

Home Secretary – important role in the Cabinet Office managing internal affairs and immigration.

Hillsborough disaster – a preventable crush disaster at Hillsborough Stadium causing 96 fatalities. It took campaigners 30 years to achieve justice for their families.

HMP Liverpool – HM Prison Liverpool, unsafe care was delivered to the inmates (2017) via Liverpool Community Heath NHS Trust (LCH).

Home Office – a Ministerial Department dealing with immigration, social security, law and order, visas and fire and rescue services in the United Kingdom.

HSC - Health Select Committee – (The Health and Social Care Select Committee) is a department of the House of Commons. It is a legislative committee who monitor the work of the Ombudsman in relation to NHS complaints handling.

HSJ - Health Service Journal containing news and jobs for health care leaders.

Human Rights Act – The UK passed this act to incorporate the rights of the European Convention of Human Rights into UK law and includes the right to democracy.

HSIB - Healthcare Safety Investigation Branch - new name given to IPSIS (Independent Patient Safety Service) – investigates patient concerns in the NHS. (About 30 cases per year)

Human Rights Act (article 6) – the right to a fair trial heard by a fair and impartial judge. Fundamental to law and democracy.

I

ICE – Independent Case Examiner. Works for the Department of Work and Pensions dealing with complaints about benefits, work and financial support.

ICT – Information and Communication Technology – electronic means for storing, transmitting and receiving information, which includes books, instructions, email and distance learning.

Independent and impartial – short phrase coined by the Ombudsman serving to be seen as being independent and acting in the public interest, when in reality they support those in power.

Independent Review Panels 1999 – external monitoring of complaints.

Investigating Clinical Incidents in the NHS – report instigated by PASC (2015) to establish an expert panel to investigate clinical incidents with the same robust measures of the aviation industry.

Inclosure Acts – common land that used for generations was removed from people who had used in for a number of purposes for generations, such as harvesting, cultivation and pasturing animals. These Acts ensured that land was held by wealthy landowners whilst peasantry were driven to seek other work mainly by moving to overcrowded towns and cities.

IPCC – Independent Police Complaints Commission – responsible for overseeing the system than handles complaints about police forces in England and Wales.

IPSIS - Independent Patient Safety Investigation Service – mentions Ombudsman accountability to Parliament but not accountability towards the public. Now named HSIB (Healthcare Safety Investigation Branch).

J

Joint Intelligence Committee – gathers intelligence from agencies and presents it to Government Ministers to assist with policymaking.

Judicial Review – a legal process where a Judge reviews the legality of a decision or action carried out by a public body.

Judgement by Default – a judgment which is binding towards either party which has failed to take legal action.

Justice – definition: just behaviour or treatment '*a concern for justice, peace and genuine respect for people' Oxford English Dictionary.*

L

Labyrinth of Bureaucracy – report by the Patients Association following a public survey to determine weaknesses in complaint handling.

Law Commission Review – a wide ranging review of Public Ombudsmen regarding independence and accountability to improve public access and flexibility.

LCH – Liverpool Community Heath NHS Trust – now defunct, but whilst active instigated controversial end of life care.

Legal 500 – guide for clients seeking the best law firms specialising in Judicial Review and Public Law.

Letter before Claim – a letter that must be written to an opponent, before becoming Defendant to try and resolve the situation prior to taking action to start a claim.

Limitation Act 1980 – gives timescale limits in which legal action can be taken.

LINks– Local Involvement Network https://www.ombudsman.org.uk/news-and-blog/news/devastated-families-left-without-answers-avoidable-death-and-harm-incidents - replaced Public and Patient Forums but lacked specifics as to how it was to work, this was replaced by Healthwatch which is also unclear with regard to its aims for the public.

LIP – Litigant in Person, someone who represents themselves in court action.

Lockerbie Disaster – UK terror attack on a Pam Am aircraft, killing 270 which includes 11 on the ground when aircraft sections fell into a residential street.

M

Madopar – for the treatment of Parkinson's disease, working on the central nervous system.

Macrae and Vincent Report (2014) – instigated by PASC 'Learning from Failure: The need for independent safety investigation in healthcare.

Maladministration – inefficient or failure to take action, relating to a public body.

Manifesto – published statement of intentions, usually a Government document.

Mental Capacity Act – guidelines for help for those who lack the capacity to make decisions.

Mid Staffs Review/Inquiry (2013) – a 'scandal' where hospital patients died unnecessarily and prompted a public inquiry.

Minister for the Constitution – supports the Minister for the Cabinet Office with regard to policy which includes policymaking, democracy and transparency.

MIPO – Misconduct in Public Office – action or actions (or lack of action) deliberately carried out by a public officer holder derogatory to a member of the public.

MOJ – Ministry of Justice – a Government Department overarching the UK justice system working to protect and advance the principles of justice.

Money Saving Expert – an organisation dealing with saving money and also produces reports relating to money matters. They report was produced recommending the overhaul of Ombudsmen, which was backed by many MPs https://www.moneysavingexpert.com/news/2019/01/mps-call-for-overhaul-of-the-ombudsmen-system/

MONITOR - was a public body founded in 2004 to ensure the financial effectiveness of healthcare. It was merged with part of the NHS improvement scheme in 2016.

Monopolistic powers – making it impossible to challenge the activities of the Ombudsman/PHSO there is no route for a complainant to challenge or change unfair outcomes.

MOPAC – Mayor's Office for Policing and Crime, gives information relating to crime priorities.

More Complaints Please! (2014) – report issued by PASC focussing on the culture of complaint handling.

MPS – Metropolitan Police Service, responsible for law enforcement in the Metropolitan Police District covering 2 boroughs.

MRI – Magnetic resonance imaging, forms anatomy images and physiological images.

Multiple System Atrophy – a terminal disease of the brain, affecting three parts of the brain which deteriorates, leaving the sufferer with very little movement and a lot of pain.

N

NAO – National Audit Office - scrutinises public spending for Parliament.

National Autistic Society – a charity providing information and advice for autistic people.

New Society – was a weekly magazine running from 1962 to 1988 launched by an independent publisher who also launched New Scientist magazine. New Society was about social science.

NHS – National Health Service for the UK, funded by the public.

NHS Commercial Alliance – National Health Service Commercial Alliance, part of a hub to improve services to member Trusts.

NHS Constitution (National Health Service) – sets out rights and responsibilities for patients, staff and the public.

NHS Litigation Authority – manages negligence claims brought about by patients or their relatives against NHS England.

NHSE – National Health Service England.

NHS CPC – National Health Service/Crescent Purchasing Consortium, offer 'best value' purchasing advice and is open to some public sector bodies.

NHS Resolution – National Health Service Resolution, deal with compensation claims, appeals and disputes between primary care contractors and concerns regarding Doctors, Dentists and Pharmacists

NHS SBS – National Health Service/Shared Business Service, working to replace outdated paper processes.

NICE - National Institute for Health and Care Excellence – provide national guidelines for aspects of healthcare including drugs and management of care after an operation. Also offer management guidelines of healthcare conditions.

NIPSO – Northern Ireland Public \service Ombudsman - investigates complaints and maladministration relating to public services.

NMC – Nursing and Midwifery Council, hold a fee-paying register of nurses and midwives, and are a regulator for the nursing and midwifery professionals.

O

Off the Hook – case file report written by Della Reynolds explaining maladministration committed by the PHSO and supporting public bodies leads to lack of justice for citizens.

Ombudsman – head of a Government service to investigate complaints from citizens, apparently Independent of the Government but accountable to Parliament. An ombudsman, ombudsperson, ombud, or public advocate are in place to represent the interests of the public by investigating and addressing complaints of maladministration or a violation of rights.

Ombudsman's Toolbox – part of the PHSO's new three strategy plan to improve their new committed service to complainants.
https://www.ombudsman.org.uk/open-meeting-2018

Own Initiative Powers – gives the Ombudsman the authority to investigate without having received a complaint, whereupon the onus/initiative is granted to carry out their own research.

OCR – Oxford, Cambridge and Royal Society of Arts Examinations, an exam board that sets examinations and awards.

OFQUAL – The Office of Qualifications and Examinations Regulation, regulates examinations, tests and qualifications. Is non-Ministerial and reports to Parliament.

OFSTED – Office for Standards in Education, Children's Services and Skills, inspects schools, including some private, childcare, adoption and some teaching. Is non-ministerial and reports to Parliament.

OIA - Office of the Independent Adjudicator for Higher Education, a limited company and registered charity, dealing with complaints from higher education students.

P

Parliamentary Commissioner – designed by Parliament, but not instigated. Referred to as a 'swiz' by Quinton Hogg.

Parliamentary Commissioner Bill – related to the powers of the Ombudsman although injustice and maladministration remain undefined. The Parliamentary Commissioner should hold Parliamentarians to account.

Parliamentary Health Service Ombudsman (PHSO) – in place to represent the interests of citizens who have suffered medical error and/or negligence plus any other maladministration from public bodies.

Patients Association – small charity that works with the PHSO and Government bodies relating to patient safety. The sometimes advise members of the public.

PCO -Protective Costs Order - an order to limit litigation costs, with the purpose of enabling a claim to be brought which otherwise would not, due to high legal costs.

PCS Union – Public and Commercial Services Union - a trade union whose members work mainly for the Government and public bodies.

Pensions Act 1995 – set up following the death of Robert Maxwell, following his embezzlement of large sums of pension fund money. This Act also affected state pensions in that it started to bring about equal pension age for both men and women.

Pensions Act 2011 – making state pension age 66 for both men and women.

Permanent Secretary to the Home Office – the post holder keeps abreast of current issues and keeps the Minister informed and gives advice.

phsothefacts – pressure group concerned with patient safety and justice for victims, working specifically to bring about reform of the PHSO.

Podus Boot – medical device for heel and foot injuries, relieving pressure and preventing pressure sores.

Police and Criminal Evidence Act 1984 – a legislative framework for police powers to
combat crime, instigated by an Act of Parliament.

Pop-Up – a temporary event taking place in an unexpected location.

Prescription Pricing Authority – calculated payments for drugs and apparatus supplied by pharmacists, appliance contractors and general practitioners under the NHS. Abolished in 2006 and transferred to the NHS Business Services Authority.

Principles of Good Administration/Complaint Handling – a guide issued by the Ombudsman as a means of monitoring its own service.

PSD – Professional Standards Department - deals with complaints against police officers and staff.

PSoW – Public Services Ombudsman for Wales - represent the interests of citizens who have suffered medical error and/or negligence, plus other maladministration from public bodies.

PTSD – (Post Traumatic Stress Disorder) a type of anxiety and recognised mental condition caused by extreme stress either being involved with or witness to a traumatic event(s).

Powers of Compliance – a power to ensure an organisation complies with external rules and internal controls and meet its regulatory objectives.

Pulse – a magazine and website for General Practitioners containing news, points of view, jobs and education.

Public Administration Select Committee (PASC) forerunner to PACAC are a Committee that hold annual scrutiny sessions of Government Departments including the PHSO.

Public and Patient Forums – set up in 2002 for all NHS Trusts to monitor, inspect and enable representation of the public The forums were abolished in 2008 and were replaced by LINks..

Public Accounts Commission – study public audits.

Public confidence – a human need to feel safe and that those in authority share values such as justice ensuring it is enforced.

Public Interest – describes the need for the welfare and well-being of the general public.

Public Law – a factor that governs the relationship between the public and the Government.

Q

QA process – a review process aiming to ensure excellence for a product or service.

QC – Queens Counsel, appointed by the reigning monarch, consisting of barristers or solicitors who are expert in a certain aspect of the law.

Quality Committee – a National Health Service Department to ensure that mechanisms are identified, managed and put into place (escalated) in matters relating to safety, clinical effectiveness and patient experience.

R

RAFT – Review and Feedback Team - a department of the PHSO where they review a decision made by their colleagues.

Representative Group – part of a larger group where a small number speak on behalf of the whole group.

Restore public confidence – a short phrase which is used to describe what is required when a scandal breaks out into the public domain, when those in power instigate a public enquiry, not to be confused with 'putting things rights' but employment of words with promises that 'lessons will be learnt'.

Rotigotine – for the treatment of Parkinson's disease to help with dopamine function.

S

SAR- Subject Access Request - a request to ask an organisation to submit personal information they hold about the person making the request.

Service Model – a term used to describe a plan as to how grievances or dissatisfactions are to be resolved.

SET – Special Enquiry Team - part of the MET (Metropolitan Police Service) in pace to deal with a specific enquiry rather than a general enquiry.

Sheep dip approach – phrase to describe how some classroom training for staff later leads to expectations of them implementing the new skills directly into their workplace.

Skelton, Peter and Elizabeth, complained about the inept police handling of Robert Trigg (murderer).

Skripal Incident - Sergei Skripal and his daughter Yulia Skripal and Det Sgt Nick Bailey were poisoned with a nerve agent in their home, the highest dose found o the outside door handle. Sergei was a double agent (intelligence)

SPSO – Scottish Public Services Ombudsman – handles complaints relating to public services in Scotland.

Subjugation of women – societal means to keep women as inferior to men limiting their opportunities in life.

Suffragette – a member of the early 20th Century militant movement calling for the right to vote for women.

Systemic Corruption – inbuilt weaknesses which ensures no justice.

T

The People's Ombudsman - a report released by the Patients Association containing case studies, detailing the distressing stories experienced by service-users of the PHSO.

The Shared Society – article by Theresa May – regarding injustices that undermine society with provisos to tackle the situation.

Think Tanks – refers to a number of experts who give ideas and possible solutions relating to specific situations, usually political or relating to economics.

Time for a People's Ombudsman – How it Failed Us - report issued by PASC (2014), criticising the performance of the PHSO.

Tort – a common law civil wrong which causes harm or loss to the claimant.

Trust Pilot – a website that records and publishes consumer reviews of goods and services, including public services.

Twitter – a worldwide social media tool – where short messages or microblogs can be posted known as 'tweets.'

U

UKAJI – The UK Administrative Justice Institute – a community/network of administrative justice researchers who work to improve the quality of administrative justice from different walks in life including policy makers, politicians, ombudsmen and judges.

W

WASPI (Women Against State Pension Inequality) – an organisation campaigning against the unexpected and sudden delay in state pension age (of 66 years) leaving many women destitute.

Wednesbury unreasonableness – a term to describe that an authority could not reasonably have made a decision other than the one they have made.

Which? Campaign – collected 96,000 signatures presented to the Government with a view to improving public sector complaint handling.

Whistle-Blower – a person who raises concerns, specifically, within the Health Service, for patient safety.

Whyatt Report – written in the 1960s following the Crichel Down Affair laying out needed policies and procedures to safeguard citizens from injustice relating to inappropriate use of administrative discretion.

Printed in Great Britain
by Amazon

42815686R00343